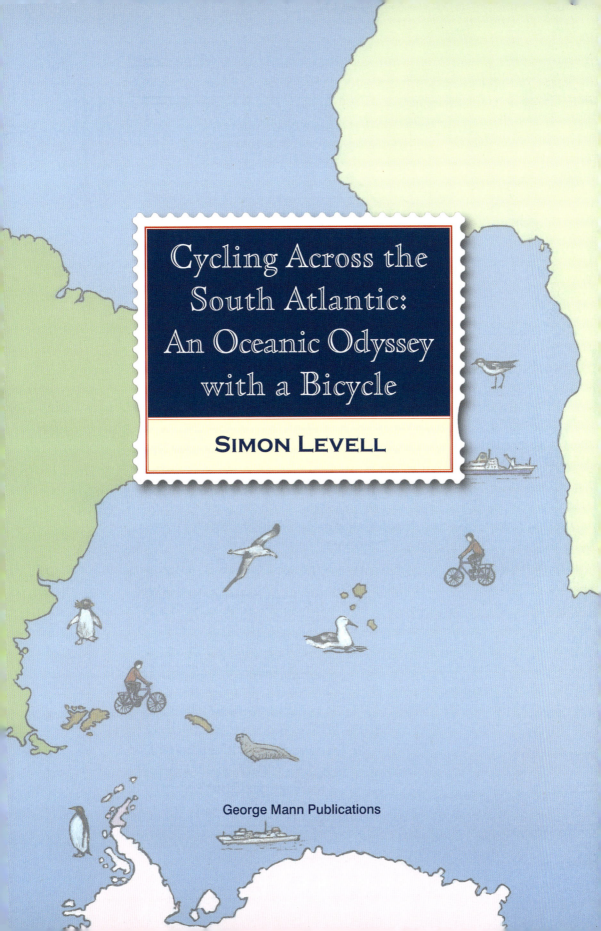

Published by
George Mann Publications
Easton, Winchester,
Hampshire SO21 1ES
georgemann@gmp.co.uk
01962 779944

Copyright © Simon Levell 2016
Cover illustration by Fiona Mead 2016

All rights reserved.
No part of this publication may
be reproduced, stored in a retrieval
system, or transmitted in any form or
by any means, electronic, mechanical,
photocopying, recording or otherwise,
without the prior permission
of the copyright holders.

A CIP catalogue record for this book
is available from the British Library

ISBN 9781907640155

George Mann Publications

To travel hopefully
is a better thing
than to arrive

Robert Louis Stevenson

To Janice & Mike

happy memories
of 2004-2007

Simon Lovell

Acknowledgements

When I initially elected to cycle across the South Atlantic, I never envisaged what an amazing adventure it would become. More significantly I had no idea that it would, in the fullness of time, lead to me deciding to write a book about my oceanic odyssey. I also didn't realise what a considerable task it would prove to be. Nevertheless, whilst I may lay claim to the authorship of this book, it would have been considerably more challenging without the assistance and encouragement of several people along the way:

I must therefore express my thanks to those friends and family members who have helped in any way, particularly in terms of technical support with preparing my original maps and photographs ready for printing. Special thanks are also due to my cover artist whose skills have provided an excellent front cover for my book. I am also most appreciative of all who have given me confidence to complete my endeavour: I should therefore like to pay tribute to my parents, who first encouraged my interest in collecting the postage stamps of faraway places which inspired a fascination for the islands of the South Atlantic and – ultimately – led to the opportunity to visit and cycle on these remote outposts of the United Kingdom.

I should additionally like to thank all those who have helped with the challenging transport logistics of my various expeditions to the South Atlantic region and beyond, spread over a period of around ten years: These include the helpful and attentive staff at Curnow Shipping and subsequently Andrew Weir Shipping; Peregrine and Audley Travel; the Royal Air Force; Falkland Islands Government Air Service; the ship's company and expedition leaders of Research Vessel *Vavilov*; and last – but certainly not least – the officers and crew of Royal Mail Ship *St Helena* who have, over a number of years, become an extended 'ocean family'.

However, the story of my oceanic cycling adventure would never have been possible without all the wonderful people I met during my travels – the people who live or work (or have journeyed with me) across the South Atlantic, all of whom I am greatly indebted to for their hearty welcome, acts of kindness, practical assistance, resourcefulness and genuine friendship. Throughout the pages of the book which follows I mention many of them by name, and by so doing I wish to thank each and every one of them most sincerely for their part in providing me with some of the most remarkable, meaningful and memorable experiences of my life. To all those I met and who at various times have lived and worked on Ascension, St Helena, Tristan da Cunha, the Falkland Islands, South Georgia and British Antarctic Territory – a heartfelt "thank you": This book is dedicated to you and is my token of gratitude for allowing me to share with you your island homes and the unparalleled splendours of the South Atlantic.

Simon Levell
Flore, Northamptonshire, England
March 2016

The Oceanic Odyssey with a Bicycle

1. Postage Stamps, a Remote Posting and a Royal Mail Ship 1
   How I Came to Cycle Across the South Atlantic

2. Lunar Ascents and Life on Mars 23
   An Expedition to Ascension on Two Wheels

3. A Week of Highs and Lows 53
   Cycling Round St Helena

4. Potato Patch Pedal Power 85
   Exploring Tristan da Cunha by Bicycle

5. Two Wheels, Wildlife, Wild Winds and Woolly Jumpers (1) 117
   Flying Around the Falkland Islands with a Bike (Week One)

6. Two Wheels, Wildlife, Wild Winds and Woolly Jumpers (2) 153
   Flying Around the Falkland Islands with a Bike (Week Two)

7. Tyre Tracks in the Wake of Shackleton 183
   An Unexpected Cycle on South Georgia

8. Icy Antarctic Waters and a Penguin Post Office 215
   British Antarctic Territory and a Bicycle

9. Reflections on an Oceanic Odyssey 243
   A Cyclist Returns Home from the South Atlantic

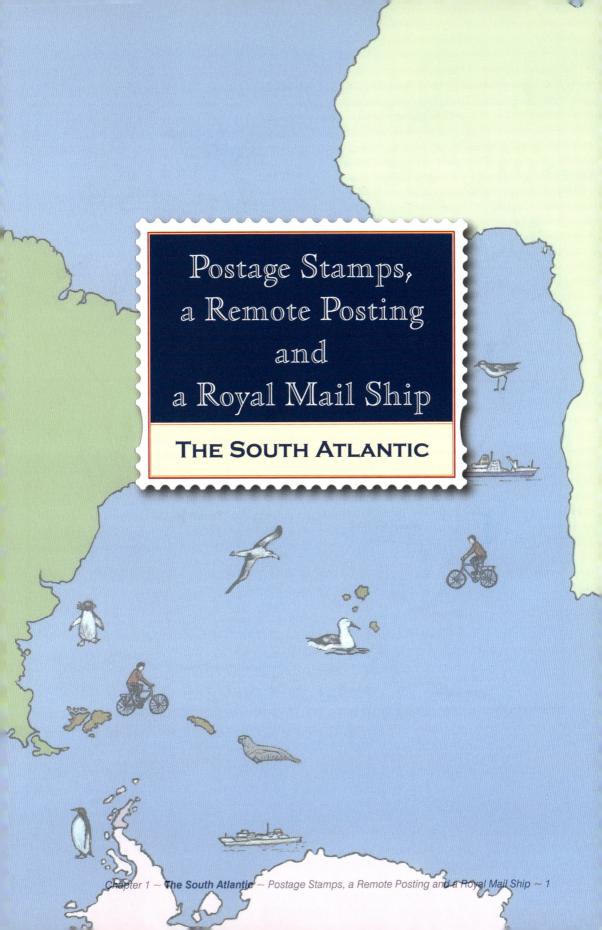

Chapter 1 ~ *The South Atlantic* ~ Postage Stamps, a Remote Posting and a Royal Mail Ship ~ 1

U.K. OVERSEAS TERRITORIES - SOUTH ATLANTIC

Chapter 1
How I Came to Cycle Across the South Atlantic

Simon, Tristan da Cunha "Remotest Island" signpost & Royal Mail Ship St Helena

There aren't many bus services on the moon, nor to my knowledge on Mars come to that…not that I've ever tried to visit either of them. Then again, I never consciously intended to cycle across the South Atlantic Ocean either: Whilst attempting to visit the first two – admittedly far-flung – destinations was perhaps on reflection somewhat ambitious, as far as the last named destination is concerned – and my preferred mode of transport thereon – it sort of, well, just 'happened'….

…Maybe at this point, lest anyone be starting to suspect that I have completely taken leave of my faculties, a degree of explanation would be in order by way of introduction: I have long been a keen cyclist, never in a competitive time-trial, road-racing sense, but rather as someone who from an early age recognised the immense possibilities offered by a bicycle to – literally – exercise one of my other great passions – exploring the great outdoors.

To my mind, the bicycle occupies a special, arguably unique, position in the transport mode hierarchy: Cycling has the same non-polluting, environmental 'green' credentials as walking, offering a similar intimacy with one's surroundings in terms of experiencing the elements at their best…and worst… whilst being able to explore 'off the beaten track' and feel part of the landscape in a way that just isn't possible in an enclosed motorised vehicle. Yet the bicycle offers considerable speed and distance advantages over walking and – whilst no match in those terms for a motorcycle, car or bus – nevertheless offers the chance to cover a great deal of ground and is certainly more flexible than its faster road-based competitors. This is especially so when loaded onto a train, ship or even plane to complete a long-haul journey to a distant cycle touring destination of choice.

My cycling explorations have, over the years, covered many parts of the British Isles, including tackling the 1,000 mile 'end-to-end' challenge ride from Land's End to John O'Groats and – albeit over several visits – a complete circuit of Ireland's coastline. I have cycled the length of the English Pennines and traversed the Lowlands and Highlands of Scotland, not forgetting more gentle terrain closer to my home in the Midlands. However for me it is islands that have always held the greatest appeal, the greatest feeling of being somewhere different, somewhere special, a civilisation in miniature, but above all somewhere absolutely ideal for discovering on a bicycle.

My cycling exploits have taken me to almost more islands than I care to remember, and yet I still remember them all, such is their individuality and allure…the islands of the Hebrides, Orkney and Shetland; the islands of the Clyde; the offshore islands of Ireland and Wales; the Isles of Scilly; the Isle of Wight; the Isle of Man…and the islands of the South Atlantic….Yes, the South Atlantic…which is where *this* story really begins – well almost, but actually it began a lot closer to home! Whilst visiting some of the more difficult-to-reach islands surrounding the British Isles often seemed adventurous at the time, the prospect of expanding my horizons to explore some of the United Kingdom's most remote, inaccessible and unusual Overseas Territories offered a whole new dimension. I am what might politely be termed – to put it mildly – an 'island enthusiast', or – to put it more bluntly as a local friend once described me – an 'island nut'!

The local friend in question was a certain Bill Sandham who, along with his wife Norma and two young sons, had taken up a remote posting of around three years in the mid-1970s on what is generally officially recognised (by none other than the Guinness Book of Records) as the World's remotest inhabited island – Tristan da Cunha in the South Atlantic. The incredibly isolated, almost mythical, territory that is Tristan has held an enduring fascination for me ever since childhood when at about the same time Bill Sandham and his family must have been on *their* remote posting I started some remote posting of my own – posting letters that is! I began to collect the postage stamps of Tristan da Cunha and correspond with the island's post office.

The philatelic interest had in its turn originally been catalysed one day after Christmas in 1976 when – about to return with my family by train from London – I spotted a stamp magazine on a newsagent's shelf at Euston Station. On the cover was a picture of an idyllic thatched cottage with a flower-filled garden together with some beautiful stamps showing landscape scenes by a Swedish artist named Roland Svensson. These were the first stamps of Tristan da Cunha I ever saw, and consequently the first in my collection. On the way home from London on the train I read the story behind the stamps – entitled "An Artist's View of Tristan" – and from that early beginning was sparked an interest in Tristan – and the wider South Atlantic – that grew and to this day is still fired with enthusiasm.

Meanwhile, at around the same time, I also recall having a large wall chart called "World of Stamps" which, whilst otherwise an ordinary World map, was surrounded by colour reproductions of over 200 stamps from across the globe, grouped together in blocks by continents and oceans. My attention was always drawn to the little block of stamps at the base of the map, almost forgotten in one corner, with the heading "Atlantic Ocean Islands" where one example was reproduced from each of half-a-dozen British Overseas Territories with such captivating names as Ascension, St Helena, Tristan da Cunha, the Falkland Islands and South Georgia, with British Antarctic Territory in the even smaller "Antarctica" block alongside. Finding these places subsequently on the map and realising their remoteness only served to further fuel my curiosity.

Something approaching 25 years must have passed, during which time I often dreamed of one day travelling to Tristan, until one day in 1999 I had cause to attend a local Women's Institute meeting in my home village. In case anyone is by now completely convinced as to my state of mind (notwithstanding the unfinished business of those infrequent buses on Mars and the moon to explain) I will elaborate: Bill Sandham was due to give a talk illustrated with slides to the local WI about his experience of life – as shared with Norma and the family – when he served on Tristan as a Government Treasurer (and for a short period as Interim Administrator) over 20 years earlier, and of course I just *had* to go!

On the appointed evening, after a few strange looks from the assembled female company and the regulation singing of "Jerusalem", around 30 ladies and one (slightly embarrassed) man sat down to listen to Bill's enthralling tales of life on the World's remotest inhabited island, suitably enhanced by a wonderful selection of colour slides. During the refreshments which followed, I mentioned to Bill about my long-standing interest in Tristan and the hope that one day I might be fortunate enough to go there. Bill smiled back at me and earnestly replied: "Simon, if ever you should get the chance to visit Tristan, my advice is *go!*"

I didn't have to wait all that long: One often hears about 'the law of unintended consequences', and in my case it certainly seemed to be true, for within a year I had noticed almost by accident a small advertisement in a magazine (the "Radio Times" as it happens) for a passenger-cargo liner by the name of Royal Mail Ship (RMS) *St Helena*. In the small print of the advertisement I saw the words "UK – Tenerife – Ascension – St Helena – Cape Town…and…TRISTAN DA CUNHA".

I wasted *no* time in ordering a brochure from the shipping agents – a small firm by the name of Curnow Shipping based in Cornwall – and on receiving it set about finding which voyages went to Tristan. I noted from the shipping schedule that the RMS *St Helena* – described as "the last ocean-going Royal Mail Ship in the World" – basically sailed four times per year on a mammoth out-and-back return voyage between the UK (Cardiff), Tenerife, Ascension Island, St Helena and Cape Town, South Africa, supplemented by a number of 'shuttle trips' between Cape Town, St Helena and Ascension whilst based in South Atlantic waters. However, just once a year, this pattern changed when the RMS was scheduled to make a single voyage out from Cape Town to Tristan da Cunha and back, anchoring at the island for just two nights / three days.

It was now July 2000, and the next RMS voyage to Tristan – voyage no. 49TDC – would be sailing from Cape Town in January 2001, yet still I couldn't make that decision. A further three months passed until – one day in October – I could procrastinate no longer. I picked up the telephone, called Curnow Shipping and made the enquiry that was to change everything and start a strong connection with – and deep affection for – the people and places of the

Simon onboard Royal Mail Ship at Tristan da Cunha & settlement of Edinburgh

Brick Front, home of Lars & Trina Repetto – where I first stayed on Tristan

*Chapter 1 ~ **The South Atlantic** ~ Postage Stamps, a Remote Posting and a Royal Mail Ship ~ 7*

Tristan da Cunha Post Office – source of postage stamps & my 'remote posting' site

St Mary's Anglican Church, Tristan da Cunha – located in Edinburgh settlement

South Atlantic that has continued ever since: "Yes, the RMS will be sailing to Tristan this January, and yes, there is still some room…just…I can offer you a berth in a four-berth cabin (with porthole!) on C deck…it's pretty well the last one left on the ship…if you want to take it". Did I want to take it? Too right I did! It was now or never and I reserved that berth there and then, and the rest, to use an over worn phrase, is history….

…Well, not quite – there were still such matters as booking a return flight from London to Cape Town to connect with the ship, securing hotel accommodation during the short time in South Africa, thinking about what to take – clothing, cameras, currency – if this was to be the trip of a lifetime there was a lot of preparation needed and only three months in which to do it all. There was also the matter of seeking somewhere to stay on Tristan itself, as I reasoned it was an awfully long way to travel – a 12 hour flight then (after a couple of nights in Cape Town) a five day voyage – if I was only to spend much of the time once there gazing across at the subject of my quest from the deck of a ship! Fortunately, and by way of a kind gesture for which I will always be grateful, Bill and Norma Sandham offered to try and contact two Tristan islanders with whom they had formed a firm friendship back in the 1970s named Lars and Trina Repetto: This consequently meant I was able to stay on the island with Lars and Trina at their home in Tristan's Edinburgh settlement – a traditional cottage named Brick Front – during the whole time the RMS was at anchor offshore.

That time ashore was very precious, and I used it to the full: I was thankful for being personally shown around many parts of the island as well as opportunities to explore myself, including visiting the Tristan da Cunha Post Office from where I had been receiving postage stamps for many years, plus as many places of interest as possible – such as St Mary's Anglican Church – many of which had at one time or another been depicted on those same postage stamps. Above all though I experienced amazing Tristan hospitality from Lars, Trina and their family, and the wider island community more generally – it may only have been two nights and three days, but it was a wonderful privilege I shall never forget. I remember sailing away from Tristan on the third day hoping one day to return, stay for longer and explore more extensively than had been possible during that initial visit – but in 2001 that was still the future, and making a trip to Tristan is hardly an everyday undertaking, nor for that matter even a yearly one.

Sailing away from Tristan heading south-west after initial visit to island in 2001

St Helena – view overlooking Jamestown & RMS at anchor offshore

Two more years passed, and the yearning to return to the South Atlantic showed no signs of waning, although even I reckoned a return visit to Tristan might perhaps be a little too soon at that stage, despite having been totally captivated by the place. The journey to the South Atlantic in early 2001 had in fact been a wonderful adventure on three fronts, and certainly gives credence to the old adage that "travel broadens the mind" – the fulfilment of my 'discovery' of Tristan goes without saying, however my first visit to South Africa was also very enlightening, as was the completion of a long sea voyage (over 3,000 nautical miles) onboard the RMS *St Helena*. I may have fallen in love with Tristan, and been encouraged by South Africa, but the experience of the RMS was addictive – almost intoxicating – in the best possible sense: The genuine friendliness and yet total professionalism of the predominantly British and St Helenian officers and crew, the unique routine onboard ship, the excellent food and – last but certainly not least – the endearing, invariably hilarious and memorable organised activities.

I quickly realised this was clearly no large, impersonal cruise ship, where one is a number amongst maybe thousands, but rather more like an extended family comprising around 50 ship's company and perhaps 100 passengers. An extended family where everyone is on first-name terms and one becomes immersed for days on end in an isolated – almost surreal – yet totally stimulating world. A world surrounded by marine wildlife and the vast emptiness of the South Atlantic which simultaneously offers the diversion of gazing out at a stack of shipping containers on the foredeck loaded with essential supplies – or some other cargo – bound for the remote islands which the ship was primarily built to serve…not forgetting the all-important Royal Mail of course!

There have been several excellent books written over the years about the RMS *St Helena*, and here is not the time or place to attempt to add to them, but suffice it to say that first experience of the RMS and its St Helenian crew during my landmark voyage to Tristan inspired me to visit *their* island, the ship's namesake island and its principal reason for existence – St Helena itself. So it was that 'the law of unintended consequences' struck again – or maybe it was just an inevitability – when I found myself telephoning the shipping agent (Andrew Weir Shipping of London) early in 2003 to enquire about availability of berths on the RMS for a voyage leaving Cape Town in April of that year – voyage no. 57C – bound for St Helena and thereafter Ascension Island.

It so happened that a berth was free in cabin C48 – the very same one in which I had sailed to Tristan two years previously – and so for the second time

Wellington House, Jamestown – my first lodgings on St Helena

Simon standing in the historic setting of Grand Parade, Jamestown

St Helena Post Office in Main Street, Jamestown – an inevitable 'port of call'

Sailing away from St Helena heading north-west after initial visit in 2003

*Chapter 1 ~ **The South Atlantic** ~ Postage Stamps, a Remote Posting and a Royal Mail Ship ~ 13*

reservations were made, flights booked and a room at the (same) hotel secured in Cape Town. Fortunately, my preparations were less fraught second time round as I knew what to take – and what not to take – but what I perhaps wasn't as well prepared for was the incredible amount of sightseeing I was going to have to 'cram in' whilst on St Helena: Lack of time precluded me from staying very long, given the logistics of travel which still involved 12 hours flying to South Africa and then five days and 1,700 nautical miles at sea, not to mention the return trip – of which more later.

The ship's schedule only allowed me two nights / three days – the same duration as my visit to Tristan – to try and absorb and experience all that St Helena had to offer, which could have presented a problem. However, I was fortunate for the assistance offered by the RMS chief purser – Geoff Shallcross – a genial and knowledgeable 'man of the sea' who rescued the situation. Geoff had previously served for many years on the former Union-Castle ships plying the Southampton to Cape Town run, and knew the South Atlantic and its people intimately. Consequently, he helpfully arranged a taxi and driver / guide – local islander Hensil Peters – to escort me round many of the principal sights of St Helena in the limited time available to me.

In fact I spent so much time touring with Hensil that I didn't see a great deal of my lodgings – the excellent Wellington House in Main Street, Jamestown – ably and professionally run by Ivy, its friendly proprietor, whose cooking was exemplary and complemented by her effusive welcome and hospitality! I did however manage to explore Jamestown fairly extensively, which as the island's only town includes many historic buildings in and around the square known as Grand Parade, and paid a visit to the St Helena Post Office – the latter a grand-looking building located in Main Street. The visit to St Helena passed all too quickly and, as I embarked once more on the RMS on the third day, I had similar feelings to those experienced when leaving Tristan, hoping some day to return for longer and explore 'under my own steam'.

There followed 'the law of unintended consequences' for the third time – actually, that isn't true at all, for I knew exactly where I would be bound for on leaving St Helena from the time I booked a berth on the ship: I had deliberately chosen to sail on voyage no. 57C as – rather than another five days sailing back to Cape Town – this voyage offered the bonus of just two more days at sea (a 'mere' 700 nautical miles!) and the chance to visit a third South Atlantic island – namely Ascension Island, or Ascension as it is more generally known.

The ship's schedule allowed for a three night / four day stay on the island before connecting with a Royal Air Force flight – an experience in its own right – for an eight hour journey home to the UK via RAF Brize Norton. This would see me leaving Ascension on Maundy Thursday and arriving home on Good Friday, and there was something almost poetic about the Biblical irony that somehow appealed to me and seemed right. Holy Week that year had started with the Bishop of St Helena providing palm crosses to passengers on the ship on Palm Sunday, and the thought of returning from such remote parts just in time for Easter had a certain ring to it.

Such celestial thoughts are a reminder that an explanation is long overdue concerning my initial reference to there not being many bus services on either Mars or the moon: I categorically know there aren't, as I discovered when I paid a visit for a few memorable days during that Holy Week in 2003, and resorted to cycling instead.

Nothing quite prepares you for your first sight of Ascension, whether you arrive by sea or by air, and the effect is even more startling when at last you set foot on the out-of-this-world island and begin to explore. Yes – it may be a time-worn cliché that has been quoted many times before – but Ascension really does resemble a fusion of all that most of us imagine the surface of the moon and texture of Mars to be like, albeit an image that has been informed by decades of space exploration.

As the RMS *St Helena* made its approach to Ascension in the early light of a mid-April dawn, I was immediately struck by the island's alien, almost threatening appearance. As the ship moved gradually closer and the rising sun began to give increasing colour definition to its gaunt features, I quickly concurred with that oft-quoted description likening this isolated island outpost in the mid South Atlantic to both the Red Planet and Earth's lunar 'satellite'. Viewed from the sea, my initial impression was that the entire island seemed to consist of a series of volcanic peaks dumped at random, mostly conical in shape and of varying size and colour, although the predominant shades were rust-red, grey and almost black.

    By contrast, towards the heart of the island lay the misty heights of what – with the aid of a map – I realised must be the aptly-named Green Mountain, its verdant hues contrasting with the more barren slopes closer to the coast. As the RMS continued to move nearer, and the sun increased in intensity, I spotted amongst the bare wilderness first the buildings associated with

Wideawake Airfield (Ascension's airport) and then those of Georgetown, the island's main settlement.

Arguably more significant though were the multitude of masts, aerials, satellite 'dishes', oversized white 'golf balls' and other communications paraphernalia present on several hilltops and coastal promontories, with a handful of wind turbines thrown into the mix for good measure. In short, the whole effect was somewhat eerie. This was a timely reminder to me that Ascension was clearly no tourist 'honey pot' – despite its sun-drenched sandy beaches – but essentially a 'working island' in that, with a few exceptions, nobody resides there permanently, but stays on short or longer term contracts.

Most of the population (amounting to approximately 1,000) are employed in one of the various communications or military establishments which are spread throughout the island. Many working on the island are St Helenian, and in many ways Ascension could be termed 'the crossroads of the South Atlantic', its strategic mid-ocean location being at the intersection point of the RMS sea route between Cape Town, St Helena and the UK, and the air route operated by the Royal Air Force between its UK base at RAF Brize Norton and the Falkland Islands. Or – more fancifully – if there was a vast railway right across the South Atlantic, then Ascension would be its Crewe Station!

The terrifying prospect of 'hell with the fire put out' lay before me – to use another, less prosaic, description of Ascension – and it was only then it dawned on me that, unlike both Tristan da Cunha and St Helena where I had been guided round the sights by local people, exploration of this particular South Atlantic outpost would be a very different proposition. Or – to at last put that opening remark in this introductory chapter in its full context – *there aren't many bus services on the moon, nor on Mars.* If I was to discover the best of Ascension, then I was on my own, and – as might be expected given my cycling credentials – that meant availing myself of a bicycle.

Actually, for the record, I could have taken advantage of a hire car, or even booked on an island minibus tour, the latter generally only run for the benefit of passengers coming ashore from the RMS during some of its periodic visits to the island. After all, to be technically accurate, I did say there weren't *many* bus services! Knowing the 'circumstances' on Ascension when I initially planned the trip, I had wisely taken the advance precaution of arranging to hire a bicycle from my booked accommodation, the Obsidian Hotel, so knew obtaining a suitable machine would not present a problem...or so I thought...of which more a little later.

Ascension viewed from the sea in early dawn light showing its many volcanic hills

Simon on deck of RMS arriving at Ascension – Georgetown is in background

*Chapter 1 ~ **The South Atlantic** ~ Postage Stamps, a Remote Posting and a Royal Mail Ship ~ 17*

First though I had to get ashore: The ship had anchored something like a mile offshore from Georgetown in Clarence Bay, and – after the local police had come onboard to carry out immigration formalities and stamp passports – I was issued with a lifejacket, descended the ship's gangway and, by way of an intermediate pontoon bobbing alarmingly in the swell, jumped into a waiting launch. As the launch sped towards the shore, I observed that the ship's onboard crane had – literally – swung into action and was busy unloading containers onto waiting cargo lighters ready to ferry supplies ashore. Five minutes later, the launch reached the pierhead steps – a seemingly undistinguished gateway to a territory by any standard – and I stepped onto Ascension for the first time.

I emphasise first time because over the ensuing years, as I progressively explored the territories of the South Atlantic, I found myself passing through Ascension on a number of occasions; after all, as an oceanic 'Crewe Station' it was inevitable, be it joining or leaving the RMS *en route* between St Helena, Cape Town or the UK, or travelling on an RAF flight between Ascension and the UK or Falklands. As a result I have become increasingly familiar with this mysterious yet engaging island over the years and have been able to enjoy its unique character through time, albeit for the most part during comparatively short visits dictated by the 'in transit' waiting time between ship and plane.

Nevertheless, it is always first impressions that are remembered, and this was *my* first visit to Ascension. I had seen the island from the sea, now it was time to experience it close-up, having first booked into the appropriately-named Obsidian Hotel (after a type of volcanic rock), in actual fact a re-branding of what had formerly served as the rather grandly-titled Government Guesthouse. On reaching my room I noted a mosquito net hanging over the bed, not the most auspicious or reassuring of starts, although I should not have been that surprised given that Ascension only lies around 8 degrees south of the Equator and is therefore firmly in the tropics!

There was also at this point no sign of the bicycle I had pre-booked to convey me round the island, which did not augur well, but with the tropical heat increasing rapidly and not that conducive to cycling anyway, I chose instead to 'get my bearings' so spent the rest of the day exploring the immediate locality on foot. This began with a perambulation of Georgetown which – apart from a number of significant buildings dating from the military developments on the island from the early 19th century onwards – seemed to be characterised largely by low, chalet-like and fairly modern buildings rather reminiscent of

Ascension Island Post Office, Georgetown – complete with red pillar box

Simon standing outside the pretty white St Mary's Church in Georgetown

*Chapter 1 ~ **The South Atlantic** ~ Postage Stamps, a Remote Posting and a Royal Mail Ship ~ 19*

a holiday camp, located somewhat randomly in a wasteland of dusty roads, volcanic ash and almost no vegetation.

On closer inspection, I discovered the various public buildings that assured Georgetown's status as Ascension's 'capital' – the Ascension Island Post Office complete with red pillar box, the general stores / supermarket, the police station, the Administrator's office and a coffee shop. Further exploration revealed St Mary's Church (a pretty white building with miniature steeple), former Exiles Club (of military pedigree), Saints Club (a bar favoured by St Helenians – or 'Saints' – based on Ascension), other visitor accommodation, the Government building, small hospital and finally various offices associated with the communications and other installations on the island.

My bicycle did not in fact materialise until my second day ashore, after I had spent a – mercifully – good night's sleep enveloped in my mosquito net at the Obsidian, which kept the irritating but otherwise harmless insects at bay. Whilst basically a mountain bike and arguably suited to the terrain I hoped to explore, it was delivered with a punctured front tyre – clearly there wasn't much turnover of clients as far as Ascension's bike hire market was concerned! Fortunately a member of the Obsidian Hotel staff offered to mend it and I was soon in a position to at last start my two-wheeled discovery of Ascension.

Over the three days before flying back to the UK, I managed to travel by pedal power to several corners of Ascension, including the steep road up Green Mountain and locations closer to Georgetown such as the viewpoint of Cross Hill: Thus – in the absence of any bus tours – I managed a 'self guided' tour of my own to a number of the island highlights, albeit that the same old story of time constraints precluded me from seeing quite as much as I would ideally have hoped, or spending sufficient time at certain locations. However – in contrast to St Helena barely a week previously and Tristan da Cunha two years before that – I could at last say that I had actually cycled 'in the ocean', or rather – for the sake of accuracy – on an island set in the ocean: Thus it was that those few days in April 2003 truly marked the point at which I began cycling across the South Atlantic.

Despite several visits to Ascension whilst 'in transit' over the years that followed, I was never on the island long enough – typically no more than one night / two days – such that any further chance to comprehensively cover the island by bicycle just wasn't feasible. During those somewhat fleeting visits on the way to somewhere else, I did on several occasions choose to join one of the aforementioned minibus tours, which covered quite a good selection

Where I began cycling across the South Atlantic – Ascension (Green Mountain)

View west from Cross Hill over Georgetown during 2003 initial visit to Ascension

Chapter 1 ~ **The South Atlantic** ~ *Postage Stamps, a Remote Posting and a Royal Mail Ship* ~ 21

of Ascension's 'hot spots' in a matter of a few hours. These were invariably organised by the chief purser from the RMS, who would come ashore from the ship then both drive the minibus and provide interesting – and often amusing – commentary *en route*. I recall two such tours, one where Geoff Shallcross was tour guide, and the other where his 'opposite number' in the chief purser role – Colin Dellar – did the honours. Colin, also an experienced maritime man, had like Geoff formerly served on the Union-Castle ships which – until the mid-1970s – regularly sailed between Southampton and Cape Town.

By way of brief digression at this point, the St Helena shipping service (and that to Ascension) really came into being as a result of the demise of the Union-Castle liners, whereupon Colin and Geoff both transferred to a ship requisitioned from Canada (the *Northland Prince*) that was converted for its new role, re-named RMS *St Helena*, and which served its namesake island between 1978 and 1990. In 1990, that vessel was replaced by the purpose-built RMS, on which Colin and Geoff continued as chief pursers, and what they *didn't* know about the South Atlantic could probably be written on the back of a postage stamp!

Anyway, the minibuses used on these island tours were invariably supplied by local islanders Cedric and Sylvia Henry, who also provided similar tours themselves. Over successive visits to Ascension, I was also fortunate enough to be escorted by them round the island on bespoke itineraries, and as a result I came to know them well as friends, often visiting them and on occasion staying with them at their home – South West Lodge – situated on the edge of Georgetown.

So much for all these bus tours then, but what about the unfinished business of wanting to return to Ascension to comprehensively and methodically tackle it on a bike? The opportunity did not arise again until several years later, when I flew for more than eight hours south from RAF Brize Norton with the intention of visiting Ascension in its own right and spending a solid 'week' – well a five day one at any rate – seriously exploring the island by bike, before joining the RMS *St Helena* to sail for 12 days north back to the UK port of Portland in Dorset, on voyage no. 164.

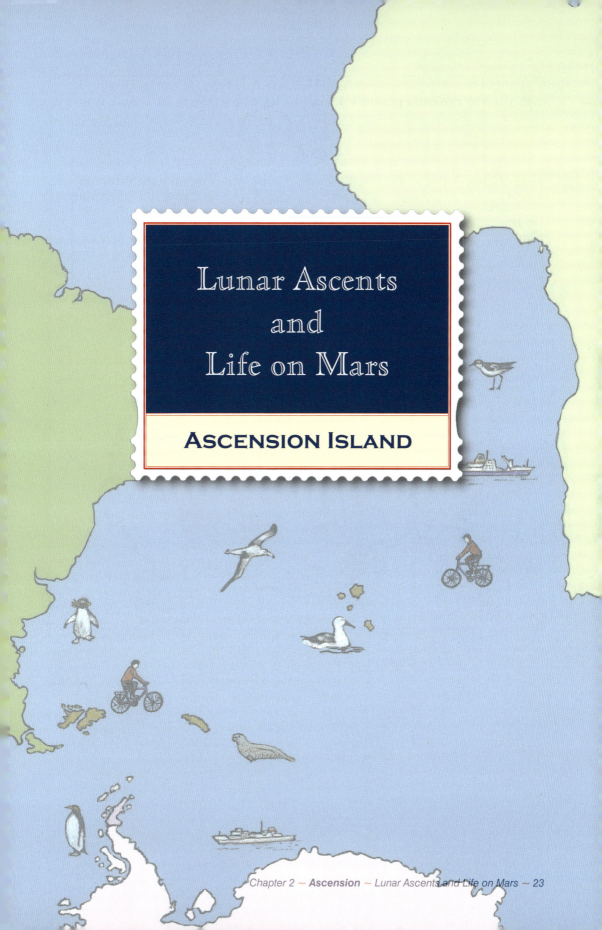

Chapter 2 ~ *Ascension* ~ Lunar Ascents and Life on Mars ~ 23

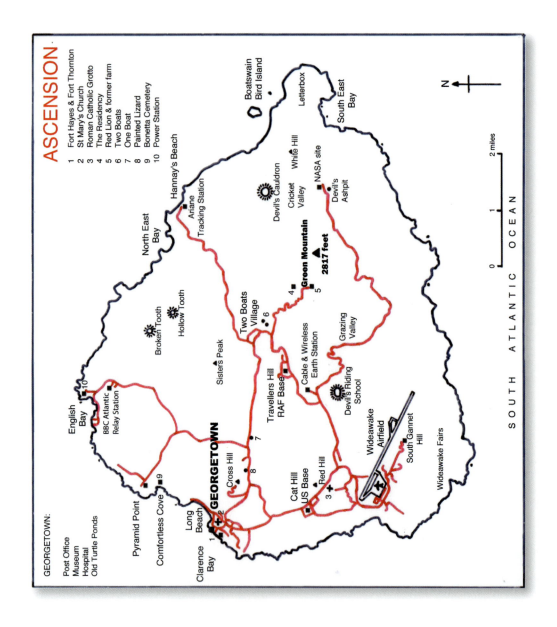

24 ~ Chapter 2 ~ **Ascension** ~ Lunar Ascents and Life on Mars

Chapter 2
An Expedition to Ascension on Two Wheels

Simon on bicycle & "Ascension Island Quincentenary" sign, Georgetown

Arriving at Ascension by air offers a different perspective to arriving by sea, but the sense of anticipation and excitement is the same when – after flying for hours across hundreds of miles of deep blue ocean far below – in the distance there suddenly appears, in the thin light of dawn, a dark grey mass seemingly no larger than a pebble and so insignificant as to be dismissed as an isolated patch of low raincloud. This was certainly my experience, and as the plane descended, banked round and made its final approach, that 'low patch of dark cloud' resolved itself into something much more definite, more distinct, as through dispersing early morning mist the shadowy and forbidding volcanic peaks of Ascension revealed themselves, set like serried ranks of enormous, oversized colliery slag heaps somehow transported to a desert island.

The plane landed at Wideawake Airfield, returned up the runway and came to rest near the modest terminal building, and I was once again struck by the barren volcanic landscape of the island, almost devoid of vegetation this close to sea level. I was also struck (or maybe that should read "almost struck down!") by the tropical heat as I left the aircraft and walked across with the other passengers (mostly forces personnel bound for the Falklands) to clear immigration, have my passport stamped and reclaim my luggage. I was back on Ascension at last, and after being conveyed by courtesy bus the few short miles into Georgetown, I presented myself once more at the Obsidian Hotel and set about unpacking.

I was keen to make the most of the day, but first there were a few 'essential tourist tasks' to complete, including buying a selection of postcards and an obligatory visit to the post office to buy Ascension stamps for said postcards, as well as other souvenir items. I also visited a newly-opened café situated opposite the Ascension Island Government building for a tasty lunch of battered fish, which was fortuitous since the coffee shop I remembered from previous visits did not appear to be operational: A consequence of visiting a place at intervals over time is that one notices the small – as well as the big – changes, and Ascension was obviously no exception to that rule!

Early that afternoon, I walked the short distance out of Georgetown to South West Lodge, home to my friends Cedric and Sylvia Henry – both St Helenians in common with many on Ascension – although some years previously they had chosen to settle there and had become the first officially resident islanders, or true Ascensionites if you prefer! On arrival, I was greeted by Sylvia who informed me that Cedric – usually known as Cedi – was not at home, but that I would find him at the Saints Club. She also reassured me that he had arranged for a bicycle to be loaned to me for use whilst on Ascension.

On my first visit to the island back in 2003 it will be recalled I had obtained a bike via the Obsidian Hotel, but on enquiries to that source prior to this particular visit it had transpired that the Obsidian's (admittedly low-key) cycle hire 'business' had ceased. Further enquiries via these channels regarding borrowing a machine from the military had also come to nothing, so it was a great relief that Cedi had been able to provide me with the crucial set of two wheels, and I expressed my appreciation when I met up with him at the Saints Club a short while later for a drink. A little while afterwards, I was back at the Obsidian, and the mountain bike was waiting for me as promised.

RAF flight at Ascension's Wideawake Airfield after arrival from the UK

Obsidian Hotel, Georgetown – my base for the week whilst on Ascension in 2011

Chapter 2 ~ **Ascension** ~ Lunar Ascents and Life on Mars ~ 27

My 'week' on Ascension was to last precisely five days, and it was already some time after lunch on day one, a Thursday as it happens; if I was to comprehensively cover the island by bike in the manner envisaged I needed to be organised and I needed to have some sort of plan. For the uninitiated, and to help put this statement in context, in size terms Ascension covers a land area of 34 square miles – making it about 50% bigger than the Channel Island of Guernsey – and is roughly trapezoidal in shape. However – as will have been gathered by now – that is where any kind of visual similarity ends.

Viewed on a map, Ascension might also be deemed, with a little imagination, to resemble a giant turtle, with Georgetown on the west coast as its head and the elevated land leading eastwards up to Green Mountain as its shell (or carapace to be zoologically correct) with the flatter lands extending north and south down to the sea masquerading as flippers!...I, however, wasn't going to be riding a turtle, I was hoping to ride a bike, and for that I needed roads which – fortunately – are for the most part very well-surfaced and maintained on Ascension; this is a legacy of the various military and communications sites that have been established, and added to, at intervals over many years, and which are spread across the island. Furthermore, there is a need to regularly reach – and guarantee constant access to – such sites, often over what, in the absence of a tarmac link, would be impossibly hostile terrain.

In terms of the roads themselves, in very broad terms there are basically two key routes out of Georgetown into the island interior – the Old Mountain Road which leads directly to Two Boats Village thence onto Green Mountain itself, and the New Mountain Road which takes a more circuitous route towards Two Boats Village by way of the US Air Force and Royal Air Force bases at Cat Hill and Travellers Hill respectively. From these two main 'spines', roads lead off to communications sites at various island extremities: Going anti-clockwise these head south to Wideawake Airfield, east to the (even more) intriguingly-named Devil's Ashpit, north-east to North East Bay (less original!) and north / north-west to English Bay / Comfortless Cove (also intriguing).

So far so good I thought, all seemed fairly straightforward...or was it? Well, for a start, it was now afternoon and I noted the routes to Green Mountain, the Devil's Ashpit and North East Bay were all quite lengthy, not to mention extremely hilly, so I decided they were best left for full-day excursions on days two, three and four, leaving day five to 'fill in' any gaps around and close to Georgetown. So that just left the roads to English Bay and Comfortless Cove for what was left of day one, which – fortuitously – were of moderate length and somewhat flatter than the alternatives.

I was soon on my way, having first obtained a few nourishment supplies from Georgetown's supermarket to sustain me on my travels – a golden rule for any cyclist going into unknown territory is to conserve energy levels, and I knew the territory I was going into wouldn't offer me another chance! My route out of town initially started along the road towards the US Base and airfield (along which I had been transported from the air terminal that morning) but I soon turned left onto a short length of road to join the Old Mountain Road above Georgetown: One particular limitation of Ascension's road system I quickly had to get used to was the fact that the Old Mountain Road was one-way only downhill for about the last mile into Georgetown, so one basically couldn't ever *leave* town by that route (unless walking and pushing the bike uphill and I would be doing plenty of that in the days ahead!)…So this short 'bypass' road was most welcome.

Once onto the Old Mountain Road, I soon came across two of Ascension's most quirky features right beside the road: The first of these was the 'Painted Lizard' – a small stone sculpture allegedly of, well, a lizard I suppose, but literally overwhelmed with paint of many colours which had seemingly been tipped over it by the pot load. The second, a little further along the road, was One Boat – a single, upended wooden boat set into the ground with a bus stop sign next to it.
   I had early on come to learn that often all is not what it seems on Ascension: I already knew the story behind the 'painted lizard' – traditionally, anyone leaving the island and never intending to return is supposed to empty the contents of a paint tin over it – hence its appearance. As for the bus stop sign at One Boat, this had puzzled me back in 2003, for it is nothing of the sort. I'll try not to remind anyone again about the lack of bus services, but actually I was told it has its origins in a prank by armed services personnel who were keen to have some fun at the expense of some newly-arrived recruits! Still, the boat itself – which pre-dates the sign – served as a good shelter from the sun.

At the nearby junction by the island's filling station I turned north off the Old Mountain Road and past what has been dubbed 'probably the worst golf course in the World' – and given its lack of 'greens' I could see why!

One of Ascension's quirky features – the 'Painted Lizard' near Cross Hill

Another quirky feature – upended wooden boat named One Boat & false bus stop

This road then continued, gently undulating through a strange and barren landscape utterly dominated by what I can only describe as a dense forest of masts, aerials, satellite dishes and other – presumably communications-based – apparatus of almost every shape and size imaginable. In this part of the island, almost totally devoid of vegetation, where the overwhelming colour is red and the entire landscape is literally littered with volcanic debris, it is easy to see how that likening to the surface of Mars has become ingrained. This is seen to greatest effect in the twin, rust-red, smooth outlines of Sisters Peak, forming a backdrop to the whole desolate scene.

Meanwhile the presence of several craters, or cinder cones, also reinforces the moonscape comparison, and it is perhaps no accident that Ascension was selected by the US National Aeronautics and Space Administration (NASA) for testing lunar exploration modules in the preparations for the Apollo missions to the moon. That said, I don't believe there are any camels on the moon: A little further along the road I pulled my brakes up sharply and skidded to a halt. The reason for my sudden stop was an authentic-looking road sign – a red warning triangle bearing the black image of a camel – perhaps those responsible for it (presumably military pranksters again) felt that this landscape reminded them rather more of a sand-blown desert!

The road along which I was travelling then dipped down towards the north coast, and the orchestra of aerials – whose whining, wind-induced music had been serenading me – reached its crescendo as four massive pylons and an interconnecting web of wires heralded my arrival at the BBC Atlantic Relay Station. This facility was built to relay radio signals carrying the BBC World Service from the UK to Africa and South America. It is, in effect, the modern-day equivalent of the web of submarine telegraph cables that were first laid over a century before and which – centred on Ascension – eventually connected the UK, Europe, West and South Africa and South America, and so yet another example of the island's previously-mentioned pivotal function as 'the crossroads of the South Atlantic'.

The road then fell more steeply, and I was soon freewheeling, past the island's power station and water desalination plant, to its terminus at English Bay, where I found a beautiful sandy beach – however the music here was provided courtesy of the ocean rollers crashing onto the shore. This seemed like a good place to pause for refreshment before proceeding to the next 'port of call'.

Dense forest of strange masts & aerials alongside road leading to English Bay

Cycling past Mars-like & rust-red Sisters Peak through Ascension's moonscape

32 ~ Chapter 2 ~ **Ascension** ~ Lunar Ascents and Life on Mars

Suitably rested, I pedalled away from English Bay along the road from whence I had earlier come, only this time I had to battle against the wind as I threaded my way back through 'aerial city', which shouldn't really have surprised me given the easy run on the outward trip when I had pretty well been blown there! Fortunately, a change of direction eased things somewhat as I took a right turn onto a desolate, straight stretch of road towards the north-west. This ended after about a mile at a place called Pyramid Point where stands a strange-looking white tracking station.

From here, I took a rough track through loose lava dust, my wheels struggling to make any form of traction, which brought me to a small, secluded beach by the name of Comfortless Cove. This apparent serenity hides a sad past though, for just behind the pretty little cove a short path leads through the shattered lava to the Bonetta Cemetery, where lie the graves of a number of yellow fever victims. This poignant little graveyard takes its name from HMS *Bonetta*, a naval ship engaged in suppressing the West African slave trade in the 1830s. Many of the crew members onboard contracted yellow fever and were subsequently quarantined on the beach here. Many became victims, and so the beach – previously simply called Comfort Cove – became known as Comfortless Cove for reasons which should need no further explanation.

The next leg of my first day's cycle exploration saw me returning back to the English Bay Road, then to the Old Mountain Road at One Boat, before taking advantage of a rapid freewheel downhill into Georgetown, safe in the knowledge this stretch was a one-way road so I – hopefully – wasn't going to meet anybody coming uphill out of town. Well, it would have been an uninterrupted descent, but ever curious to explore, I opted on the spur of the moment to make a detour onto the red-brown dusty slopes of Cross Hill – the 'peak' which rises menacingly over 800 feet behind Georgetown.

As soon as I left the tarmac road, I was quickly reduced to pushing the bike since it was no match for the voracious volcanic scree which seemed intent on swallowing the wheels at every turn. I was, however, rewarded with a fine view at a point where two cannons stand sentinel on an old battery, and from where I was able to enjoy a panoramic vista across Georgetown and nearby Long Beach, with the glistening ocean extending away for ever it seemed in almost every direction.

There was one more detour though, as I continued down to the base of Cross Hill and then cycled just behind and along the length of Long Beach, where wind-blown sand covered the road and an unusual (but this time 'official') sign declared that vehicles were banned between the hours of 21.00 and 06.00 during turtle nesting season! Fortunately, being the wrong time of year (as well as the wrong time of day) this rule did not apply. It was however more unfortunate that I was not able to witness again one of the highlights of my initial visit to Ascension in April 2003:

On this very beach I had been privileged to observe the truly magnificent sight of three separate female giant green turtles – one I recall was 'making tracks' up the beach to lay her eggs, another was observed actually laying her eggs in a depression she had dug in the sand with her flippers, while the third was returning to the sea after egg laying. Meanwhile – perhaps best of all – had been the sight of dozens of newly-hatched baby turtles scurrying across the sand to the sea. The life-cycle of these giant green turtles is remarkable when one considers that they spend most of their lives in the waters off South America's Brazilian coast before returning some 1,400 miles across the South Atlantic to lay their eggs on the beaches of Ascension, or "Turtle Island" as I like to think of it as!

The light was fading though, and whilst the day's cycling hadn't been *too* demanding, I was tired from the flight the night before, so pedalled slowly back into Georgetown for a filling meal at the Obsidian. The day's turtle connections weren't *quite* over though, for that evening I walked down to the "Turtle Nest": Located in the colonnaded old Exiles Club building, this was the name given to the grocery-and-hardware shop run by Cedric and Sylvia – Ascension's very own 'late shop'. Needless to say, they were keen to know how I had survived my first day in the saddle, not to mention how the bike itself had performed!

Friday morning on day two called for a filling breakfast, not forgetting additional sustenance bought from the nearby supermarket, since maintaining energy levels would be critical given the strenuous day I had planned: I had decreed that this would be the day I made an excursion by bicycle and finally on foot to the highest point on Ascension – the summit of Green Mountain. I cycled out of Georgetown the same way as the previous afternoon (on account of the Old Mountain Road being one-way into town), but instead of taking the link across to that road, continued on past the ranks of low, grey buildings forming the US Base at Cat Hill, where the 'Stars and Stripes' fluttering away at the entrance and the distinctive vehicle types within served to reinforce the fact in case one was in any doubt.

A little further on I reached my first stop of the day, an altogether more peaceful location: Lying in the shadow of Red Hill is the Roman Catholic Grotto, effectively serving as the RC Church on Ascension, an unusual design open to the elements on at least two sides. I then continued along the New Mountain Road towards the interior of the island, punctuated by a short diversion up onto Command Hill which affords an excellent panoramic view of Wideawake Airfield, itself overlooked by yet more 'golf balls' and satellite dishes on South Gannet Hill and other volcanic protrusions.

Just after passing a group of four wind turbines the road began to climb in earnest, and as it did so I felt the sweat pouring off my brow and my heartbeat quicken. The tropical humidity was building, as was the heat of the sun, such that it was important to seek out what little shade there was under the sparse, scrubby vegetation, rest every so often and gulp down mineral water. As the road continued to climb, past the complex of buildings forming the RAF Base at Travellers Hill, I noted the gradual 'greening' of the environment, such that the RAF Base – owing to its more elevated position and relatively botanical-rich surroundings – appeared more attractive than its US counterpart given the latter's barren and arid setting.

I continued on, still climbing, and at length reached Two Boats Village, right in the centre of the island. Two Boats School is located here, the only school serving Ascension and catering for the entire age range. At this point I abandoned the bike briefly and went for a short uphill walk, through scrubby vegetation, to where two upended wooden boats set in the ground faced each other across a cast iron water pipe – the Two Boats after which the community is named. In similar vein to the One Boat much further downhill, seen the previous day, these boats provided shade from the sun, and were originally placed in the early part of the 19th century as resting places for sailors when collecting much-needed fresh water from high on Green Mountain. As time went by, improvements were made, and a permanent fixed water supply was constructed by means of the cast iron pipe, enabling water to run by gravity feed all the way from Green Mountain down to Georgetown.

All this thought of water was making me thirsty too, so I sought out the oasis that is Two Boats Club, to my mind the best 'watering hole' on Ascension: This tree-shaded bar enjoys stunning views of Sisters Peak and the western half of the island from its terrace area, and I was glad to use it as a lunch stop before resuming my cycling assault on Green Mountain.

When I say "resuming my *cycling* assault" I am being rather economical with the truth, because beyond Two Boats the road started to steepen quite alarmingly. At an altitude of something a little over 1,000 feet, where the volcanic lava finally gave way to greener vegetation, I passed a sign and information point announcing that I was now entering Green Mountain National Park. The road now ascended much more steeply, typically as steep as 1 in 3, via a seemingly endless series of tortuous hairpin bends, some so extreme that the only way to get up them was on the outside of the bend.

Most of the time I was forced to push what was supposed to be a 'mountain' bike, so fearsome was the climb that even the lowest gear was rendered useless. As can be imagined, stops were frequent – almost every other bend in fact – but the ever-improving views made them worth it as I continued to consume my rapidly dwindling supply of water. At one such stop, I noticed a little signpost pointing along a rough path with the word "Convalescence" on it, which I found somewhat apt given that I felt increasingly in need of some sort of convalescence myself on account of the physical purgatory I was putting myself through.

The road ascended yet further, and straightened out slightly, meanwhile the vegetation closed in and before long the whole ambience had changed from alpine forest to sub-tropical jungle. A little further on, I took a turning onto a driveway to my left, which led downhill slightly, in order to view the Residency, home of Ascension's Administrator. The property has a commanding view across the island, and as expected – being the official residence of the representative of HM Government on the island – has a Union Flag flying outside. The Residency in fact started life as the Mountain Hospital, a convalescent home for sailors, and I later discovered that footpath sign bearing the word "Convalescence" denoted one of a series of graded walks around Green Mountain formerly used by recovering patients as they regained their strength.

I could have done with regaining *my* strength as, returning to the mountain road, the energy-sapping climb continued. Near the top of this section I came across some 'high level' roadworks where a landslip had taken away much of the road (which was now being painstakingly reinstated) thus barring onward passage by motor vehicles, but fortunately leaving a narrow section just wide enough for pedestrians and *push* bikes. I pushed on, now through a virtual 'tunnel' of banana palms, until suddenly – and quite without warning – the surfaced road came to an abrupt end at a fine

The Two Boats provided shelter for sailors collecting water from Green Mountain

This wooden shelter acts as an information point for Green Mountain

*Chapter 2 ~ **Ascension** ~ Lunar Ascents and Life on Mars ~ 37*

Cycling up Green Mountain – a stop at one of many steep hairpin bends

End of cycle part of ascent up Green Mountain at the Red Lion – note vegetation

looking building adorned with a clock tower and known as Red Lion. At well over 2,000 feet up, I chose to abandon the bike here (it had after all weighed me down over the preceding 1,000 foot climb!) and continue my exploration on foot.

Pausing for a moment to admire the fantastic panorama over south, west and north Ascension, I then passed through a stone archway into an attractive garden, flanked by various buildings which were part of the former, but now abandoned, mountain farm. In one corner of this green oasis, offering a cool retreat from the unremitting heat down below from whence I had come, I observed the entrance to a long foot tunnel which cuts under a flank of the mountain to emerge in Breakneck Valley. I had previously explored this tunnel in 2003, and noted the aforementioned cast iron pipe (as seen at Two Boats) passing through it, supplied by water from catchments constructed to channel rainfall into it.

From Red Lion – originally a hostel for farm workers but being progressively restored as a visitor centre – I walked up what was now a winding rough track which took me through a short lava tunnel up to a point where I could look down over the water catchment area above Breakneck Valley. This was the wettest part of the island, right in the path of the moist south-easterly trade winds, and so the obvious choice for locating this pioneering water supply system. Another brief detour on foot took me along a contour path (once serving as a military lookout post) through yet more short lava tunnels.

It was, however, time to make my final assault on Green Mountain summit, so I took the path upwards between ferns along a narrow ridge offering spectacular coastal views, followed by an even narrower path through thick, almost impenetrable sub-jungle, although progress was eased in that a boardwalk had helpfully been provided, quite an improvement on the steep, slippery and muddy path I remembered from my first visit where one had to haul oneself up with the aid of ropes! At length, I completed my 'ascension of Ascension' and arrived at the summit of Green Mountain, 2,817 feet above sea level.

Yet this was quite the strangest mountain summit I had ever encountered – instead of a cairn or 'trig' point, I was confronted by a little circular dew pond with lilies floating on it, surrounded by dense bamboo canes, amongst the many alien forms of vegetation planted on the island by sailors over the years. I recalled that the only other feature – a small post-mounted 'letterbox' – had historically contained a visitors' book to sign, and a handstamp to record one's feat, but on this particular visit a notice on the letterbox advised both of these could now be found at Red Lion – presumably for their safekeeping given the dampness of the location. Returning to Red Lion from the summit I found the items there as promised, so I was able to record the event.

After the 'foot' part of the descent the 'cycle' part quickly followed – literally! The hours spent toiling up from sea level to over 2,000 feet were rewarded first with a nerve-wracking, twisting freewheel down through the hairpin bends section (also known as The Ramps) where control of the bike and constant brake application were vital if I was to avoid leaving the road – and mountain – altogether. This took a mere 15 minutes, and brought me to Two Boats Village where I stopped (of course!) for a drink enjoying the fine view from Two Boats Club.

The second half of the descent was quite different, by way of the Old Mountain Road – which is reasonably straight by contrast – and was characterised by a high speed freewheel taking me down the remaining 1,000 feet into Georgetown in a further 15 minutes. I certainly enjoyed my dinner at the Obsidian that evening, and had plenty to report to Cedi and Sylvia when I met them again a bit later on.

~~~

It was Saturday morning – day three – and I was already nearly at the midpoint of my 'week' of cycling on Ascension. Whilst I already knew where I intended to cycle on this particular day, I had made some plans for the morning before I left Georgetown, based primarily around a visit to the Ascension Island Museum. I was becoming used to the unusual (at least from my perspective) opening hours of various shops and bars on the island, and museum opening hours were no exception – if I was to fit in a visit, Saturday morning it had to be.

The museum is actually located on three, closely related sites, and I chose to begin in the gallery: Within a fairly anonymous-looking building are to be found several rooms of photographs (and much other material) which tell the story of Ascension, beginning with its discovery in 1501 by Portuguese seafarer Joao da Nova, who named it Concepcion, although it wasn't until two years later, on Ascension Day in 1503, that the island was officially claimed and named by fellow countryman Alphonse d'Albuquerque.

The history of the island is fascinating, and includes the era when its prime function was a mid-ocean 'service station' in the days of sail (that 'South Atlantic crossroads' analogy is nothing new!) as well as the various phases of military occupation, starting in 1815 when the captured French Emperor, Napoleon Bonaparte, was exiled on St Helena resulting in a small British naval garrison being established on Ascension in case the French should attempt to launch a rescue mission. Other parts of the museum tell the story of the island's role as a telegraph cable 'hub' and the later development of all manner of communications-based functions, the space exploration programme and not forgetting the establishment (by the US Government in conjunction with Britain) of Wideawake Airfield in 1942 and its intensive use during the 1982 Falklands Conflict. I found a room recounting the postal history of Ascension particularly interesting.

As well as the gallery, I also visited the small coach house, housing a few old vehicles, and the imposing Fort Hayes which – with its 'twin' Fort Thornton – was built to guard the seaward approaches to Georgetown. Whilst on the ramparts I noticed a green-and-white ship had anchored out in Clarence Bay, a supply vessel on its long journey south to the Falklands, and a timely reminder of Ascension's enduring role down the centuries.

I was though by now itching to get back in the saddle, as I had a long ride ahead of me – in fact the furthest point out from Georgetown it is possible to go by road, towards the far east of the island. I began as I had the day before – out past the US Base and along the New Mountain Road in the direction of Travellers Hill. However, just before the road began to climb towards the latter, I took instead a road signposted to the Devil's Ashpit – with a name like that this promised to be no ordinary road, and I was not to be disappointed! The first staging post along the way came quite quickly – the large white antenna 'dish' of the Cable & Wireless Earth Station could hardly be missed.

Easier to miss – in the sense it was hidden from the road and required a scramble on foot across loose volcanic clinker – was the appropriately-named Devil's Riding School. This amazing volcanic feature actually resembles an oval 'racecourse', or perhaps a Roman amphitheatre in that the perimeter slopes upwards rather like tiered seating. I suppose I could have tried cycling a circuit of it, but I knew by now it was probably easier to swim through treacle than risk the bike becoming devoured by the unforgiving lava 'soup', or the tyres punctured on the razor-sharp debris that was scattered everywhere.

Returning to the tarmac – and the bike – the road suddenly steepened and began to twist and turn in a series of long, wide hairpin bends as it rapidly gained height. I was glad of the refreshment I had brought with me, yet again mostly liquid-based, as there would be no opportunity to obtain an antidote to dehydration on this road: Sure enough, the intense heat and humidity was starting to take its toll again, and stops were frequent. This road was on a bigger scale than the narrow, tortuous one up Green Mountain I had tackled the day before, as witnessed by a huge cutting engineered clean through the rock at one point: Known as the NASA Road, it was built in the 1960s with the purpose of accessing the site of a space tracking station.

Once through the cutting, the barren moonscape was left behind, at least temporarily, as I progressed through an easier, flattish section called Grazing Valley where greenery was more evident. Not for long though, since the ascent then resumed fairly relentlessly past cactus-rich scrubland, and at a gradient which was annoyingly too steep to easily cycle up but too gradual for it to be worth pushing the bike – that's my excuse anyway, it was probably more a combination of the south-easterly wind and my exhaustion! As if that wasn't bad enough it was also getting even hotter, with a disorientating mist rolling in off the ocean making things difficult.

After what seemed like an age, having passed along the entire southern flank of Green Mountain and well beyond, I at last reached the geological phenomenon that is the Devil's Ashpit – a deep 'canyon' disappearing into the ground, its almost vertical sides a vivid combination of red, orange and black volcanic rock, and well worth the effort to discover. A short distance further on the road spluttered to a halt at the site of the former NASA tracking station which once followed the Apollo spacecraft on those pioneering lunar expeditions of times past. The desolate-looking control building had found a new use as an outdoor activities centre, whilst nearby I found the foundations which once housed the antennae aerials that tracked man's missions to the moon: I found it both moving and at the same time somewhat melancholy.

Perhaps more cheerfully, I was now 1,750 feet up, and the views from this exposed spot were spectacular, taking in White Hill (which it is!) and the coastline around South East Bay far below, whilst beyond lay Ascension's eastern extremity, the Letterbox peninsula: The latter takes its name from the days of sailing ships when – as a mid-ocean 'postbox' – Ascension was

Arrival by cycle at the geological phenomenon known as Devil's Ashpit

Bright yellow-orange land crab crossing road as seen on descent from NASA site

used by sailors on voyages out from Europe who would leave messages for home which they hoped would be collected by crews of ships sailing the other way. Considerably more alarming in terms of its name, as viewed across Cricket Valley to the north, was the Devil's Cauldron – a near vertical-sided volcanic protrusion which has a concave interior rather akin to a cooking pot – enough said!...

...Stirring stuff, maybe, but it was time to begin the journey back, and perhaps not surprisingly I hoped there would be no more devilish distractions along the way; I was, however, to be proved wrong. As I started to descend the road away from the Devil's Ashpit, and began coasting down through the area dominated by scrubland and cactus, I was confronted by the little devils – first one, then two, then several more, as with a clatter of claws they 'beat a tattoo' across the tarmac in front of me. I am referring to possibly Ascension's oldest residents – the large, bright yellow-orange land crabs which tend to venture out at dusk or after a period of rain.

These amazing creatures get everywhere, and whilst they return to the sea to breed, I can recall seeing them in a similar habitat on the road from North East Bay and even high up on Green Mountain! They are also quite unpredictable, and their sudden surging across the road made it important to stay alert so as to avoid them – on occasion necessitating some pretty sharp braking and swerving manoeuvres. Oh...and aggressive too...one or two decided to rattle out from the scrub, stop suddenly right in my path, then engage me in a hostile stand-off, their beady eyes locked onto me or else waiving their claws in a fearsome show of defiance!

My crustacean crisis soon passed though as – for the second day running – I enjoyed a long-distance, gravity-fuelled descent where my ears certainly felt the rapid change in air pressure. In a matter of no time, I was heading back past the Cable & Wireless Earth Station towards the US Base, although I chose not to proceed directly back to Georgetown but instead made a detour to the south, right past the buildings and runway of Wideawake Airfield until the road petered out in more of that wheel-swallowing black volcanic ash.

From here, I continued on foot to explore the fringes of the windswept southern coastal plain of Ascension, otherwise known as Wideawake Fairs. At certain times of year this is an excellent area to view breeding seabirds – particularly sooty terns, or 'wideawakes' as they are locally known. I finally cycled back into Georgetown via the US Base, but could not resist calling in on the way for a drink at the Volcano Club, where the ambience is that of a 1950s American diner and even if payment is made in pounds sterling the change is invariably in US dollars...well, cents at any rate!

It had been a long day, and as sunset approached I pedalled slowly back into town, where the only signs of life seemed to be a few feral donkeys (examples of *imported* Ascension wildlife) walking down the main street! The day ended most pleasantly down at the Exiles Club building, where – in the covered walkway outside their "Turtle Nest" shop – Cedi and Sylvia had set-up a buffet supper, to which they had kindly invited me as well as a number of local people. The evening passed agreeably in convivial company whilst we were serenaded by the sounds of an impromptu live music session, Ascension-style, sitting under the stars and enjoying the warm, tropical night air.

Sunday, my fourth day on Ascension, started with a leisurely breakfast followed by a short stroll around town, during which I happened to meet the Anglican priest on Ascension – Father Chris Brown – walking across the dusty ground to St Mary's Church from the nearby vicarage. I had planned to attend the morning service at St Mary's, and during a short chat – in which I introduced myself – he confirmed that there was indeed a service at 10.30am. Not long afterwards, the single bell hanging in the small white steeple could be heard chiming across a peaceful Georgetown – the first time I had heard it since Maundy Thursday on my initial visit back in 2003 – and a few minutes later I was welcomed by Father Chris and other members of the congregation.
    The interior of St Mary's Church is delightful, well-kept and reminiscent of a small English country church, and the service itself was well-attended and a reminder of Sundays back home. There were also several very singable hymns, which was to be expected given that Father Chris originally hailed from Wales! Afterwards, I spoke to Father Chris for a while, and he was most interested in my cycle exploration of the island, so much so that he graciously invited me over to the vicarage that evening.

Meanwhile, however, it was time for the day's cycle excursion – the last one exploring some of the more far-flung parts of the island: I rode out of Georgetown past the home of Cedi and Sylvia at South West Lodge, and then cut across on the 'bypass' link to the Old Mountain Road, proceeding past One Boat and up the ever-steepening gradient to Two Boats Village.

On the way, I was struck by how green Ascension looked from this aspect, a result – I had been told – of comparatively more rain in recent years. It was also spring, a relative concept in these latitudes, but certainly evidenced by many brightly-coloured flowers by the roadside as I climbed higher and out of the arid lower regions. After a brief snack lunch at Two Boats Club, I headed north-east on the road signposted to North East Bay (where else?), certainly a more mundane-sounding destination than the Devil's Ashpit the previous day.

I was already at around 1,000 feet above sea level, and heading for the coast, so the next few miles were downhill and consequently pure delight as I made a gradual descent on a scenic road, the last key route I had hitherto not cycled along during my visit. As the road fell away from the mountainous heart of the island, past Sisters Peak, it seemed as if I had exchanged the Devil's lair for the dentist's despair, as there were good views of two volcanic craters bearing the jaw-achingly appropriate names of Broken Tooth and Hollow Tooth! Equally impressive, though in a different way, was a view of the northern aspect of Green Mountain soaring upwards towards the sky. As the road continued to drop through scrubland with an avenue of trees to 'beautify' it I was relieved the midday heat was keeping the land crabs at bay as this was again their typical habitat!

At length, the road swooped down towards the ocean and, via a rough track, I arrived on the beach at North East Bay itself which – like several on Ascension – proclaimed that it was a turtle nesting beach, at least in season, although there were tell-tale signs of 'caterpillar tracks' and depressions in the sand to prove the point. I did muse upon the fact that this beach faced West Africa, not South America, but then again after an epic journey across the South Atlantic, those giant green turtles would think nothing of a few extra miles around Ascension's coastline for a quieter place to lay their eggs than Long Beach; as we all know, the best beaches always need a bit of extra effort to find!

After some refreshment at this idyllic spot, I proceeded a short distance to the end of the tarmac road at the Ariane Tracking Station, yet another example of Ascension's pivotal role in space exploration: This particular installation was built to track the rockets of the Ariane (European) space agency rocket launches.

From here, it was back to foot-slogging as I passed another beach (Hannay's) and scrambled over difficult volcanic scree to reach one of the most remote

Sign at North East Bay proclaiming it to be a turtle nesting beach

End of the road & cycling extremity for the day at the Ariane Tracking Station

*Chapter 2 ~ **Ascension** ~ Lunar Ascents and Life on Mars ~ 47*

and stunning vistas on Ascension: Before me was an amazing marble-effect mountain backdrop plunging down to the sea, variously coloured red, brown, black, grey and white. Meanwhile, just out from the shore stood the outlying Boatswain Bird Island, complete with a natural rock arch – a South Atlantic rival to Dorset's Durdle Door perhaps, and which is home to vast numbers of seabirds, some of which I observed circling around just above me.

Returning to the bike which I had left by the Ariane site, I started the long ride back to Georgetown, beginning with a steep climb out of North East Bay and on upwards towards Two Boats Village: Perhaps it was a point of honour after the rather pedestrian cycling to reach Green Mountain and the Devil's Ashpit, but it was with a sense of achievement that I reached Two Boats without ever pushing the bike once on the 1,000 foot climb!

After this, it was all plain sailing on generally downhill grades, past the RAF and US sites at Travellers Hill and Cat Hill, with a final flourish on the one-way incline past Cross Hill into Georgetown. Before dinner though I had arranged to visit Cedi and Sylvia for some tea, preceded by photographs of me – on the bicycle – by the nearby "Welcome to Georgetown" sign, and of them standing outside their South West Lodge home, as a record of my visit.

That evening, as arranged earlier, I spent an enjoyable hour or so at St Mary's vicarage as Father Chris Brown's guest, and in the course of conversation discovered we had a number of mutual friends spread across the South Atlantic islands, plus RMS *St Helena* crew members and folk in the UK. These included my friends Lars and Trina Repetto on Tristan da Cunha and several others on St Helena: Despite its vastness, the South Atlantic is paradoxically a very small place, and in any case Father Chris had served as a priest on both those islands before taking up the post on Ascension!

Monday, my fifth and final day on Ascension, began early on account of needing to pack luggage ready to be taken down to the pierhead warehouse prior to my impending departure. Shortly after breakfast, I left the Obsidian for the last time and walked across to the vicarage: I had discovered, following church on Sunday, that on Monday mornings there was often a local walking group, and I had been invited to join them. After all the strenuous cycling of the previous few days I welcomed a change and so had agreed to go along.

Father Chris took me to a location along the northern perimeter fence of Wideawake Airfield where we were met by Sylvia and two other friends for an enjoyable, leisurely walk through the barren volcanic landscape south of the Devil's Riding School and in the general direction of Mountain Red Hill for about a mile, before returning to our starting point. There was even the bonus (at around 10.00am) of watching at close quarters as the twice-weekly RAF flight from Ascension onwards to the Falklands took-off from the airfield. On returning to Georgetown I thanked Father Chris for his hospitality before bidding him farewell.

There was still *some* more cycling I wished to do however, so after lunch I spent the first half of the afternoon basically completing a slow cycle tour of virtually every road in or close to Georgetown. This took me, amongst other places, via the fire service building, along the beach at Clarence Bay, past the hospital and out to the oil tank installation beyond town. By now though I concluded it was probably time to stop pedalling. My route did however also include a stop at the old turtle ponds near Long Beach – dating from the first half of the 19th century these are a relic of the days when turtles were captured in considerable numbers, and stored here, later to be used as a food source by crews of passing ships and even as a delicacy in the form of turtle soup for the dining tables of the Admiralty... quite a sobering thought....

...Alas, it was also a sobering thought that my time on "Turtle Island" was coming to an end, for out in Clarence Bay anchorage the RMS *St Helena* had arrived and was working cargo. It would soon be time to leave. For the last time I jumped on the loaned bicycle that had served me so well, and pedalled the short distance out to South West Lodge where I returned it to Cedi, congratulating him for his excellent choice of machine. Saying "goodbye" is never easy in the South Atlantic, and there is always a tendency to make every last minute count, but time was racing on. So – after a pleasant half-hour spent chatting with Cedi and Sylvia in their garden – I thanked them for all their kindness whilst I had been on Ascension, then walked back into Georgetown and down to the pierhead to wait in the modest passenger terminal.

Within an hour, I had descended the pierhead steps, boarded a launch and climbed onboard the RMS *St Helena*, where I was welcomed by some of the ship's officers and crew – all of them familiar faces from previous voyages – before settling into my cabin, C49 on C deck. Later that afternoon, with three blasts on the ship's whistle, the RMS set sail on voyage no. 164 on a generally northerly course towards the UK.

Final cycle around Georgetown – a stop by old turtle ponds & RMS at anchorage

Ascension from RMS bound for the UK – Green Mountain & English Bay visible

50 ~ Chapter 2 ~ **Ascension** *~ Lunar Ascents and Life on Mars*

Over the next 12 days, I would meet up with St Helenian 'shipmates' Patrick and Hazel Fagan whom I met on a previous RMS voyage in 2005 and were great company. I would in turn experience the ceremony of 'crossing the line' at the Equator, sail off the coast of West Africa into the North Atlantic, spend a day in Tenerife whilst the ship took on fuel, sail past Madeira and – eventually – reach European waters, the Bay of Biscay and the English Channel before journey's end at Portland in Dorset.

The ceremony of 'crossing the line' is something of a maritime institution, marking the transition from one hemisphere to another, and traditionally involves members of the ship's company – in various colourful costumes – staging a hilarious theatrical farce out on deck based around a 'mock court' presided over by King Neptune (invariably the ship's captain) and his Queen: It is also a 'rite of passage' for those who have never previously crossed the Equator (I had been this way before and knew *exactly* what to expect!) and typically involves a number of pre-chosen victims being brought by a clerk before King Neptune and in turn charged with ridiculous 'offences' where they are *always* declared guilty. Justice is administered – courtesy of other members of the ship's crew variously dressed as policemen, a surgeon, a nurse and a barber – and involves being covered in slimy, odious concoctions of substances from the galley, before a final ritual plunge into the ship's swimming pool....I suppose had I been an unfortunate victim, my 'crime' would have been cycling across the South Atlantic without Neptune's consent, but in the circumstances I was not about to admit to anything!

For the most part though, the 12 day passage would – by contrast – offer the experience of a leisurely and relaxing ocean voyage of over 3,700 nautical miles with plenty of time to participate in the various activities onboard – be they films with a South Atlantic theme (including one about the building of the RMS *St Helena* at an Aberdeen shipyard), games out on deck, or the homespun, inimitable evening entertainment so synonymous with the RMS. Of course there would also be opportunities to just watch the ocean, its wildlife and the occasional passing ship, or spend time talking to the ship's officers, crew members and other passengers – many of them St Helenians travelling to visit relatives in the UK.

All that, though, was still in the future as I stood on deck and watched Ascension recede into the distance: First the buildings of Georgetown, then the BBC Atlantic Relay Station at English Bay, and finally those bare, red volcanic peaks and misty heights of Green Mountain gradually faded into a blue nothing, then they were gone.

As the sun set over a shimmering South Atlantic for the last time, I reflected on the week I had just spent on Ascension, and how being able to cycle across much of the island had greatly amplified the experience. Purely in terms of distance I later calculated that I had covered around 85 miles on two wheels and a further 15 miles on foot whilst there, although it seemed a lot further. However, it is not really *how far* I went that was important, but rather *where* I had explored and *what* I had learnt. I had uncovered much about the island's fascinating history and its rich, diverse heritage, not to mention its present-day engaging quirkiness, granted, but there was something else too: I had succeeded in reaching the moon without the aid of a space rocket and had discovered that many forms of life do indeed exist on Mars!

Ascension proved to be a worthy 'launching pad' for my subsequent cycling progress across the isolated territories of the South Atlantic: There was only one thing left to say…onwards and upwards!

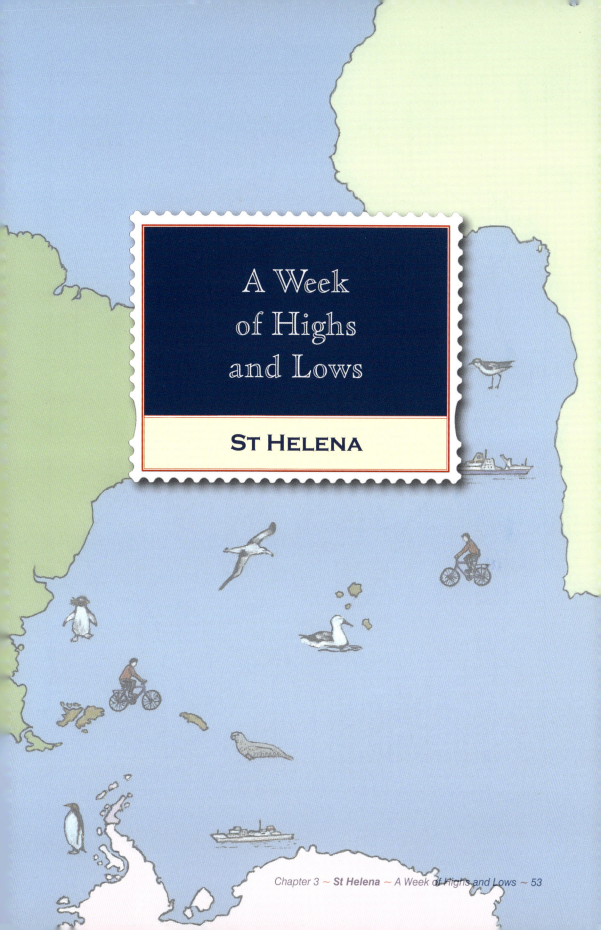

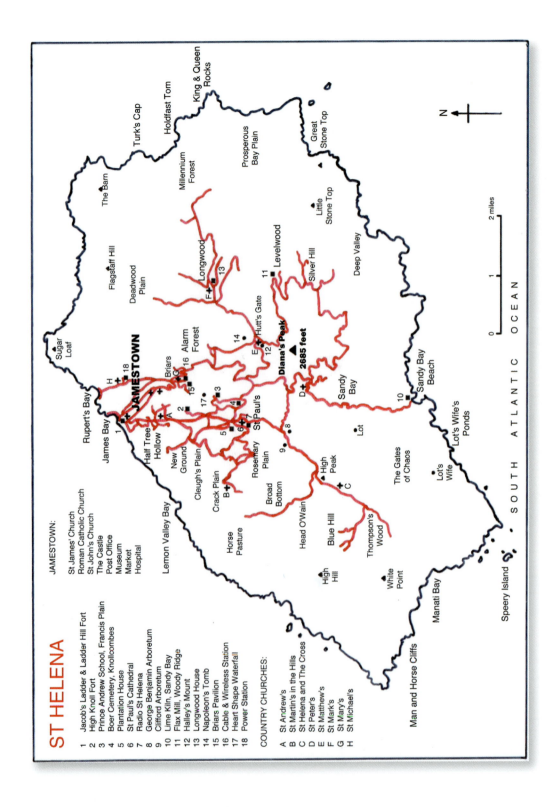

54 ~ Chapter 3 ~ **St Helena** ~ A Week of Highs and Lows

Chapter 3
Cycling Round St Helena

Simon on deck of RMS at St Helena – Jamestown is in the background

"So you're planning to cycle round St Helena – I hope you're fit!"…"You say you're going down to Sandy Bay ON A BICYCLE?!"…"Now you do know you're not supposed to cycle down Side Path, Ladder Hill Road and Half Tree Hollow, don't you?"…

…It was my first evening on St Helena having arrived on the Royal Mail Ship from Ascension Island a few hours previously: I was sitting in the bar-diner on Jamestown seafront known as Donny's Place enjoying a drink and gazing across towards the RMS anchored out in James Bay as a fiery-orange sun dipped below a shimmering South Atlantic horizon: A beautiful prospect undoubtedly, yet it was not so much what I was seeing that was having the profoundest impact on me at the time, but rather what I was hearing as I listened with increasing trepidation to the small gathering of St Helenians who had joined me and Bishop John Salt (who had graciously invited me to stay with him for the week) on our table at Donny's.

They were – without exception – showing a friendly interest in my plans for the week on St Helena, but in particular my intention to spend the days ahead exploring the island by bicycle. Whilst I welcomed the enthusiastic encouragement shown by the assembled company, their raised eyebrows and even more elevated intonation at the mere mention of "cycling" and "St Helena" in the same breath led me – rather rapidly – to the conclusion that what I was embarking upon was at best unusual, certainly quirky – but at worst downright mad, perhaps even foolhardy. St Helena, it seemed, was usually explored by car, charabanc – even on foot – but by bicycle?…whilst no-one said it was never done, well, that seemed to be rather, er-um, unprecedented.

It will be recalled that I mentioned cycling having been a passion for many years, and the fact I had previously cycled extensively throughout the British Isles, including several upland areas and offshore islands. During those explorations of the English Pennines, Scottish Highlands and Islands, and Ireland's coastline, I often covered between 50 and 70 miles a day. Surely, therefore, touring St Helena on two wheels appeared to offer the ideal opportunity to experience the island at a leisurely pace and yet still get to explore the more far-flung corners of this 47 square mile gem set in the South Atlantic Ocean.

However, in marked contrast to all my previous cycling exploits much closer to home – extensive though many of them were – the issue of cycling on St Helena presented some particularly unique challenges, the first of which was the rather fundamental matter of obtaining a bicycle: I had briefly investigated the possibility of hiring a bike on St Helena for the purpose of exploring during my only previous visit to the island the year before – a visit which had lasted little more than two days whilst *en route* between Cape Town and Ascension. However, enquiries on that occasion about cycle hire made to authoritative sources such as the St Helena Tourist Office in Jamestown prior to my visit served to confirm in my mind that – unlike Ascension – hiring a bike wasn't really an option: Given the reaction I experienced that evening in Donny's having arrived on St Helena a second time, I perhaps shouldn't have been all that surprised that bike hire hadn't caught on quite as much as more traditional forms of touring such as by charabanc!…

…Anyway, the consequence of the non-availability of bikes (and non-availability of scheduled charabanc tours the two days I was on the island) meant on that first occasion, as explained in the introductory chapter, Geoff Shallcross – chief purser on the RMS – had helpfully secured the services of Hensil Peters – St Helena taxi driver – to guide me round the island and ensure I saw as much as possible in what was, looking back, an impossibly short length of stay. Thanks to Hensil's extensive knowledge of the island – and taking advantage of localised weather conditions – I couldn't have asked for more, but the interest awakened by the experience was such that I left the island on the third morning vowing to return and do things a bit more leisurely second time around.

If 'a bit more leisurely second time around' was to involve cycling, there was no getting away from the fact – I would need to take my own bike with me. This certainly had its advantages so far as being comfortable and familiar with my machine was concerned – and confident of its capabilities. (For the record I have a Raleigh Amazon 21-speed mountain bike, which for touring the hillier parts of Britain is just ideal). As for *my* capabilities touring St Helena…well, that was still an unknown quantity.

The next challenge lay in how I was going to get the bike from my home in the English Midlands to an island 4,500 miles away in the South Atlantic; this needed quite a bit of planning. Whilst I was booked to fly via Royal Air Force Brize Norton to Ascension and join the RMS there for the two day 'shuttle' to St Helena in early July 2004, taking my bike with the RAF wasn't a particularly realistic option. I had, therefore, no alternative other than to travel down to Portland in Dorset two weeks earlier and load my bike into a container as unaccompanied baggage to be shipped aboard the RMS for the 12 day sail down to Ascension (where bike and owner would hopefully be reunited) thence on to St Helena.

Significantly, this was voyage no. 62, the last complete UK – Cape Town – UK out-and-back voyage before the RMS shipping schedule changed in September 2004, and was then thus also the last – relatively straightforward – opportunity for the foreseeable future to ensure my bike reached St Helena *and returned safely to the UK afterwards.* Needless to say, I also had to make another long day trip from my home down to Portland when the RMS returned to the UK early in the September, for purposes of 'bicycle repatriation' some six weeks after its rider had returned from the South Atlantic…I won't bore you with the paperwork involved!

Two weeks after saying "goodbye" to my bicycle at Portland, I was onboard the RMS sailing south-east from Ascension on the two day passage to St Helena, and desperately hoping my bike was in one of the containers stacked on the ship's foredeck. Approaching by sea from the north, my first glimpse

About to load Simon's bicycle on the RMS at Portland, UK as cargo for St Helena

View from RMS on arrival at James Bay anchorage with St Helena flag hoisted

58 ~ Chapter 3 ~ **St Helena** ~ *A Week of Highs and Lows*

of St Helena was simply a grey-blue outline on the far horizon, rather like a great whale rising out of the ocean and therefore not all that different to any island when seen from afar: It could in fact have been Lundy Island in the Bristol Channel (where the church coincidentally is dedicated to St Helena!) However, as the ship moved closer, the colour changed to a deep red-brown shade and the island appeared to increasingly resemble Ayers Rock (or Uluru) – the huge monolith that sits at Australia's heart.

On yet closer examination, I observed that most of the coastline consisted of soaring, impregnable cliffs of chocolate-brown volcanic rock bare of all vegetation, whilst further inland the impression was of lush, green valleys and hills rising to what I guessed was Diana's Peak, the highest point. Indeed, one description often applied to St Helena is "an emerald cast in bronze". Less poetically, one could describe the near-vertical perimeter as that of a giant Yorkshire pudding hiding the succulent meat and green vegetables heaped up in layers within.

Whatever its appearance, to many people, the island is synonymous with arguably its most famous 'resident' – one Napoleon Bonaparte – who was exiled there between 1815 and 1821, and viewing this mid-ocean natural 'fortress' from the sea it was not hard to see why it was chosen by the British to imprison the former French Emperor. Apart from three locations on the north coast (Rupert's, James and Lemon Valleys) and one on the south side (Sandy Bay Valley) – all of which had fortifications built and strengthened over the years across their entry points to the sea – there are no real beaches, and thus the island was inherently suited to defend against attack.

Portuguese admiral Joao da Nova first came upon the island whilst sailing home from India (a year after discovering Ascension); the day was 21st May 1502, the anniversary of St Helena, mother of Emperor Constantine, and he named it in her honour. The Portuguese quickly recognised the potential the island offered: Being located between the Cape of Good Hope and Cape Verde, it became a calling point to supply their ships returning from the east, and its fertile interior served as an oceanic larder where fruit trees grew, vegetables were planted and livestock was left to graze. I would learn more about the history of St Helena as the week progressed, but in the meantime my attention was focussed on the here-and-now as the RMS dropped anchor in James Bay opposite the island's capital – Jamestown – set in the steep-sided ravine of James Valley.

In similar vein to arriving at Ascension by sea, the (now familiar) 'South Atlantic formalities' then began in earnest as immigration officials came onboard and my passport was stamped. A short ride by launch to the wharf steps followed, and – after briefly stepping ashore next to the busy cargo-handling area (and anxiously wondering if my bike was in one of the containers being brought off the ship) – an even shorter bus ride conveyed me to the customs shed. I finally emerged on the other side, where I was met by Bishop John, and we walked the short distance along the seafront to the aforementioned Donny's Place for *that* welcome drink, where the conversation in relation to cycling had not seemed *quite* so welcome, and for me initially had set more than a few alarm bells ringing.

Transporting my bike to and from St Helena was challenge enough, but the physical – not to mention further logistical – challenges were only just beginning: That first evening at Donny's was a valuable learning experience, since I realised that cycling on the island would not be quite as straightforward as I had first envisaged, although I didn't appreciate the full impact of the wise words offered me at the time. Enquiries as to my fitness, or my awareness of the topography of St Helena's roads (going up when they weren't going down!), were not too worrying; I considered myself to be an experienced cyclist and not afraid of a few hills – in any case, I had briefly visited before, so knew it wasn't exactly flat.

Perhaps the biggest blow to my confidence was that restrictions on cycling on the two main routes in and out of Jamestown, plus the whole length of Half Tree Hollow, would considerably limit my ability to get about the island on two wheels not to mention severely constrain my itinerary. After all, isn't the best bit about cycling being able to freewheel downhill?…and yet arguably the three best, straightest (on an island full of twisty roads) and uninterrupted downhill runs on St Helena were officially 'off limits'. The prognosis was not good; I resigned myself to the fact that my style would be well and truly cramped as another drink was thrust in my direction.

Still, I wasn't going to be cycling anywhere until reunited with my bike, which didn't in fact take place until the following afternoon (how many containers were there on the ship I wondered?) In the meantime, I chose to spend several hours touring in more traditional style aboard Colin Corker's wonderful 1929 Chevrolet charabanc, and deservedly something of an institution on St Helena! It will be recalled I missed out on this St Helena 'essential' during my first visit the year before, and so it proved a good re-introduction to the island:

The assembly point for the tour was on the steps outside the Consulate Hotel – an evocative colonial-style verandahed building in the heart of Jamestown's

Main Street. Taking around a dozen passengers, the ancient green open-topped charabanc climbed slowly out of Jamestown up Side Path (…one of those "NO CYCLING" roads…), clinging to the steep eastern flank of James Valley, and came to the first stop high above the Briars Pavilion: This is one of three Napoleonic-related sites on the island and where the captured former French Emperor spent some time early on in his exile. Heading into the green heart of the island, the charabanc continued to climb before the road levelled off and Longwood village was reached:

Longwood House – with a little sentry box at the entrance and a blue-white-and-red *tricolour* flag flying proudly in the well-tended garden – is 'a little bit of France on St Helena', and I enjoyed an informative guided tour of the series of rooms where Napoleon spent the majority of his exile, featuring such items of note as a billiard table, Napoleon's 'campaign cot' and his bedroom, plus numerous pictures and documents. After a delicious hot meal (served at the nearby golf club pavilion by Tracey Corker, Colin's daughter) the Napoleonic 'pilgrimage' continued, as the charabanc reached the site of Napoleon's Tomb – a simple, un-inscribed slab enclosed by railings, set in a beautiful garden deep in the Sane Valley – and likewise flying the French *tricolour*.

It was, however, time for more island history, as Colin drove the charabanc through more lush, green countryside to reach Plantation House, a fine old Georgian building dating from 1792, originally built for the East India Company Governors of St Helena, and since 1834 official residence of the island's Governors under the Crown. (Another important – and lengthy – period of St Helena's history lasting nearly two centuries concerns the English East India Company, which was granted a charter in the mid-1600s to colonise and fortify the island on behalf of the Crown, and to establish it as a maritime supply station, thus marking its beginnings as a British possession). On the lawn outside Plantation House there was an opportunity to view another St Helena institution – Jonathan the giant tortoise – believed to be 'around' 200 years old and the island's oldest resident by quite a margin, along with a few 'younger' tortoises, relatively speaking!

The final leg of the charabanc tour included a brief stop by Ladder Hill Fort, perched high on the west side of James Valley and with a stunning aerial view over Jamestown. The final descent into town was via Ladder Hill Road, heading inland down the western side of the valley, although I could have chosen the 'direct' route and instead walked down the 699 steps of Jacob's Ladder – originally built as an inclined plane used to haul military supplies up to the adjoining fort.

A St Helena institution – a stop outside Longwood House on island charabanc tour

Bishopsholme, St Paul's area – cycling base for my week touring St Helena in 2004

The charabanc tour was most enjoyable…but where was my bicycle? Once back in Jamestown, I walked along to the customs shed on the quayside where the contents of various containers unloaded from the RMS had been deposited randomly around the floor creating a scene resembling a jumble sale; there – surrounded by washing machines, fridges and other domestic paraphernalia that had accompanied it on the long journey from England – I was relieved to discover my bike, safe and well!

The next problem was how to get the bike to Bishopsholme, residence of Bishop John and my home for the week, set high in St Helena's green, hilly interior just above St Paul's Cathedral and almost 2,000 feet above sea level. It was only then that the enormity of what I planned to undertake fully dawned on me – simply getting back from Jamestown to my lodgings each evening would entail a climb matched, in British terms, only by the fearsome Bealach na Ba – or Applecross road – in North West Scotland which rises from sea level to over 2,000 feet and back down again in a few miles of terrifying hairpin bends and sheer drops. In other words, a normal everyday route on St Helena was the equivalent cycling challenge of Britain's highest and most testing road!

My heart sank even lower than the night before, but Bishop John – sensing my unease – fortunately offered to take the bike in the back of his car (a feat only accomplished after removing a wheel) up the never-ending incline, via Ladder Hill Road and Half Tree Hollow, back to Bishopsholme. Yes – the views were spectacular – but it was the red-and-white "NO CYCLING" signs placed at intervals along the route that were preoccupying me and at which I scowled in disdain as we drove onwards and upwards – well, mostly upwards at any rate, as meanwhile my enthusiasm was spiralling downwards!

It was now Tuesday, and I had been on St Helena a day already, so felt it high time I got started on some cycling: I thought I would ease into it gently, so restricted myself to a short local ride in the St Paul's area: Beginning with an easy downhill coast from Bishopsholme, I came to Red Gate (a location marking the lower entrance to Plantation House and *fortunately* outside the "NO CYCLING" zone) followed by a steady climb up to High Knoll Fort.

However, before returning slowly back uphill to St Paul's via Plantation House (with a glimpse of both house and garden from the White Gate entrance), I took time to enjoy the excellent island-wide views available from High Knoll. The fort here was originally built towards the end of the 18th century to help defend the island, but was rebuilt around 100 years later. The oval-shaped perimeter walls enclosing the fort provide arguably the best 360 degree panoramic view of St Helena, and give the visitor a good appreciation of its geography and – more importantly from a cyclist's perspective – its topography.

At this point, it is worth briefly describing the road network on St Helena: Although more complex than that on Ascension, many of the roads away from Jamestown are quite narrow and tortuous, as well as very 'up-and-down', albeit reasonably well-surfaced. The Side Path route out of town climbs steeply inland, past a turning back down into Rupert's Valley, then via Briars village and the Alarm Forest district to a junction of several roads known as Hutt's Gate: Here one has the choice of proceeding north-east to Longwood, south-east to Levelwood and around Diana's Peak, or west across the heart of the island towards St Paul's.
    The other main route out of town, Ladder Hill Road, climbs out of James Valley, then the road proceeds inland through Half Tree Hollow to St Paul's (with several local routes heading off west along the way). It subsequently climbs up to the central ridges, offering routes south to Sandy Bay, south-west to Blue Hill and north-west to an area rejoicing in the name of Horse Pasture: This is an over-simplification, but represents the basic 'web' of roads that I would be using.

It was while standing on the ramparts at High Knoll Fort that suddenly – for a pleasant change – a more positive realisation came over me as I looked south towards Bishopsholme and the undulating green profile of the peaks and ridges at the island's heart: The realisation was that perhaps being based almost 2,000 feet up in the centre of the island *wasn't* as bad from a cycling perspective as I had first thought. Taking a more reasoned and considered view of things, it gave me ready access to the network of high level roads extending to the far corners of the island, avoiding the need to start each day with the cycling equivalent of walking half way up Ben Nevis had I been staying down in Jamestown, which I could reach easily enough if I wanted to: Lifts into town were reasonably plentiful, and a bus service had been introduced since my previous visit, so no real problems there.
    No, looking at the matter pragmatically, I had brought my bike with me to seek out the harder-to-reach parts of the island beyond the limits of bus routes and charabanc tours, and living up in the clouds – literally sometimes – I would have a head start every day! Buoyed up with a 'glass half full' rather than 'glass half empty' perspective on things, it was with renewed enthusiasm that I joined with Geoff Shallcross and others from the RMS

Diana's Peak (horizon) & Francis Plain (foreground) viewed from High Knoll Fort

Looking up the 699 steps of Jacob's Ladder towards Ladder Hill Fort

for drinks at the Consulate Hotel in Jamestown that evening. I must have been feeling better as I made the trip from Bishopsholme on foot, including walking down *and up* all 699 steps of Jacob's Ladder!

I was up before sunrise on the Wednesday morning, not in order to get 40 miles cycling in before lunch (some hope!) but owing to the fact that Bishop John had a meeting with Captain Martin Smith, master of the RMS, before the ship set sail on the 'shuttle' to Ascension and thus providing me with a lift into Jamestown where I planned to do one further organised tourist activity before getting down to the serious cycling – the Historical Town Walk. After a filling cooked breakfast at Ann's Place – a delightful venue overlooking the Castle Gardens – which was eaten to the screeching accompaniment of mynah birds, I assembled at the Cenotaph with several other passengers who had arrived on the RMS and we were duly met by island tour guide Basil George who showed us round many of the buildings and features in and around Grand Parade:

The tour began by passing under the Town Gate, which bears the East India Company coat of arms on the seaward side, with a wirebird and two arum lilies – emblems of St Helena – on the town side. Several buildings were visited, or observed, around Grand Parade, including The Castle – home to the St Helena Government (and dating from 1867), police station, court house, library and St James' Church – the latter recognised as the oldest Anglican church in the southern hemisphere.

There was even a visit to the base of Jacob's Ladder, where Basil demonstrated how Saints used to slide down the 602 foot drop draped sideways over the railings either side of the 699 steps, albeit his demonstration – wisely – only involved the last dozen steps! The walk finished with coffee at Wellington House, where I had stayed during my first visit to St Helena – it was good to meet up with Ivy, its genial host, once again.

The heart of Jamestown is in fact full of fine old buildings, many of them from the Georgian era, and it has a timeless, unhurried quality that exudes history at every turn. My curiosity having been awakened by much of that history over the first couple of days on the island, I made the first of two visits to the excellent museum where I spent some time studying the various displays and artefacts describing variously the history, geology, flora, fauna, ships, life and people of the island: St Helenians are very diverse in terms of their origins, representing a mixture of many nationalities and influences, and each period of the island's history has brought people from different corners of the globe.

What unites the population though (of between 4,000 and 5,000) is a great commitment to their island plus an openness and friendliness to visitors that is both infectious and refreshing. Whilst at the museum, I met islander (and one-time school headteacher) Edith Timm – she too was most interested in my cycling plans, though still perplexed, as others had been, that I intended to include Sandy Bay in my itinerary....

...Back at Bishopsholme that afternoon I could contain myself no longer, I just had to 'take the bull by the horns' – or rather 'the bike by the handlebars' – and start exploring. I only had a few hours of daylight left, so reasoned the easiest out-and-back trip to an island extremity, mileage-wise, would be – you've guessed it – SANDY BAY...big mistake! Things certainly started out fairly straightforwardly – a steady, if somewhat energy-sapping climb the final few hundred feet up from St Paul's to Bates Branch and the island's high level central 'spine' at Sandy Bay Ridge, where I passed Colin Corker and his charabanc full of most of those who had been on the Town Walk in the morning.

From here, I was able to appreciate the wonderful views down the valley – past the huge pillar of rock known as Lot (and another behind called Lot's Wife) – to the beach over 2,000 feet below. The next hour or so was pure pleasure, a snaking, downhill gradient all the way, where the only effort required was making sure my brake blocks didn't catch fire owing to almost constant application. Still, there was little opportunity to gather any serious speed on account of countless hairpin bends and blind corners, and in any event the descent was frequently punctuated (as opposed to punctured – none of those I am glad to say!) by stops to visit the half-hidden St Peter's Church, isolated Baptist Chapel and other diversions – or simply to take in the ever-changing vista unfolding before me.

Feeling quite proud, I eventually reached Sandy Bay Beach, a wild, bare and atmospheric place hemmed in by barren volcanic hills and with remains of various fortifications and cannons offering visual reminders of St Helena's past as a fortress island throughout much of its occupied history; there was also an interesting old lime kiln. Having got thus far, I couldn't resist the temptation to continue on foot over the steep scree slopes to reach the geological phenomenon known as Lot's Wife's Ponds, which are wave-filled natural basins formed behind a wall of rock. This in itself was quite an undertaking, as well as time consuming, and it was only after gazing south from above the ponds across the empty vastness of the South Atlantic – musing that the next bit of inhabited land in that direction was Tristan da Cunha over 1,300 miles away – that it occurred to me this was no place to be as light began to fade.

Fortunately that was still some way off, but I swiftly returned to Sandy Bay Beach, from where I started cycling back up the hill…well, for the first few hundred yards anyway, for the gradient soon steepened and – still going nowhere fast despite having got through all 21 of my 21 gears – I was left with no choice but to get off and push…and push…and push. Sandy Bay Beach to the central ridge is a climb of well over 2,000 feet and it was now the wrong side of five o'clock during the St Helenian winter – albeit blessed by fine weather – but in another hour it would be almost dark.

Despite valiant efforts, progress slowed as the road climbed ever higher, and the weight of the bike seemed to double in just half-an-hour which only added to my increasing exhaustion. More frequent stops for breath only prolonged the pain whilst simultaneously accelerating the onset of dusk. I continued thus in a state of body-and-mind numbing delirium until at length I reached a bend near Solomon's shop, just up from Colin's Bar, when the awful truth dawned that I wasn't going to make it back up to the central ridge still hundreds of feet above me – let alone Bishopsholme – before dark. Some drastic action was required. Seeing a bus parked outside a nearby house, and reasoning (wrongly) that the occupier of the house might be its driver, I trudged wearily up to the door and explained my predicament to those within. Whilst not the bus driver, to my utter relief the man of the house – a friendly Saint also called Colin if I remember rightly (but not of the nearby bar) – kindly agreed to drive me and bike to the top of the hill in his car, which still seemed a long way despite me not having to expend any energy!

By the time we reached the top, it was near enough dark, such is the speed that night falls in these latitudes – about 16 degrees south of the Equator. I thanked him profusely and freewheeled the last mile back to Bishopsholme, taking great care to ensure I didn't fall off the edge of the road, bike lights being pretty well useless in the middle of the inky blackness that is a South Atlantic night, so far from any light pollution. It was a salutary lesson. That evening, by coincidence, Bishop John had invited Edith Timm (whom I had met at the museum) round for dinner, and she remarked "So you cycled all the way to Sandy Bay AND BACK?"; I didn't have the heart to admit I hadn't *quite* done it all under my own steam!

A pause cycling down to Sandy Bay – view of Baptist Chapel, Lot & Lot's Wife

Cleugh's Plain – pleasant cycling country between Rosemary Plain & New Ground

*Chapter 3 ~ **St Helena** ~ A Week of Highs and Lows ~ 69*

Thursday's explorations called for a bit of lateral thinking, but by now I was getting used to 'going with the flow' so was not unduly concerned. I was anxious to get a decent day's cycling in – it was after all my third full day on the island, and I hadn't brought my bike all the way from England to let it gather dust! However, I was also interested in joining Colin Corker's tour of the day, in particular the two visits *en route* to Prince Andrew School and Radio St Helena.

In common with all the charabanc tours, this one commenced in Jamestown, but there was little point going all the way there only to come most of the way back, so instead I spent the first half of the morning exploring a different corner of the island – the north-western part. This is a particularly attractive region of St Helena, characterised by pretty, well-wooded lanes, rolling green fields and lush valleys – more like Devon really, and as a result very pleasant cycling country. The hills, whilst often steep, were rarely long, and interspersed with moderately flat sections, an altogether more intimate landscape than barren Sandy Bay the day before.

My route took me initially from Bishopsholme around a number of small rural communities all within the wider St Paul's parish. These included Farm Lodge at Rosemary Plain – site of a coffee plantation – and Crack Plain, which brought me to the beautifully situated St Martin's in the Hills Church, set high above verdant Lemon Valley – a deep ravine plunging down to the sea at Lemon Valley Bay. From here, I continued via New Ground, Sapper Way and Red Gate down onto Francis Plain, site of Prince Andrew School – and a rare flat piece of land on St Helena, hence ideal as a sports field. I had calculated Colin Corker's tour would arrive here at around 10.30am...and I wasn't wrong, for he arrived right on cue, although in a minibus rather than the charabanc on this occasion.

I 'parked' my bike and was soon enjoying a comprehensive (no pun intended!) tour of St Helena's only secondary school, ably conducted by two of its pupils. I then joined the minibus for the continuation of Colin's tour, via the Boer Cemetery at Knollcombes to White Gate, then up onto the central ridges and west to the fantastic scenery around the Blue Hill and Thompson's Wood areas – almost as far as it is possible to get from Jamestown. Returning along the ridges, a picnic lunch near the conical High Peak followed, then a descent to the St Helena Radio Station for the second conducted visit of the day – again very informative.

By now though, I was itching to get back on my bike, so I left the minibus tour here – in any case the remainder of its itinerary took in parts of the island I had cycled round in the morning. Instead, I walked the mile or so down to Francis Plain to 'reclaim' my bike from outside Prince Andrew School, and then set about tackling one of the highest roads on the island – that from beautifully-named Lemon Tree Gut up to Stitch's Ridge on the upper slopes of Diana's Peak. The real purpose of this ride was to get my bike as close to the island's highest point as possible and walk on from there to the top.

I eventually reached a wooden sign bearing the legend "Cabbage Tree Road" where I abandoned the bike for the second time that day and headed up a steep but well-maintained path between high 'walls' of New Zealand flax which brought me at length, via the intermediate summit of Cuckhold's Point, to the summit of Diana's Peak, 2,685 feet up and the 'roof' of St Helena. There were incredible views in all directions, but cloud was rolling in rapidly from the south – and the previous day's events 'escaping' from Sandy Bay were etched on my mind: So after photographs, signing the visitors' book and obtaining a souvenir handstamp (both to be found in a 'letterbox' at the summit along the same lines as Green Mountain on Ascension) I retraced my steps, returned to my bike and cycled via Bates Branch back down to Bishopsholme before sundown.

That evening, I joined the last of Colin Corker's charabanc tours – a 'pub crawl' under the stars of the southern hemisphere – this included visits to Pub Paradise in Longwood and two further venues in the large, dispersed community of Half Tree Hollow, with excellent food provided by Tracey Corker at all three. At the last pub I met another Colin – my Sandy Bay 'rescuer' from the night before – and we both had a chuckle about the whole thing, although I am glad there was no-one else around at the time to hear!

It was Friday morning, and my week cycling round St Helena had already reached its half way point; so much still to see and yet too little time left! It was obviously time for a change of strategy, after the varied and unpredictable experiences of the previous few days in (and often out of) the saddle. Today, I decreed, was to be the day I spent exclusively cycling, and nothing was going to distract me, not even the weather.

At this point, it is perhaps worth noting that despite being the St Helenian winter (July) the weather was, by and large, exemplary for cycling, and every day featured much sunshine – but not the intense heat that would have made travel by bike an ordeal had I attempted it in, say, January. That said, whilst the temperature was fairly typical for the time of year, many Saints impressed upon me how fortunate I was not to experience long periods of rain and low cloud which would have detracted considerably from my enjoyment of the week and clarity of the views.

I had decided to make first for the far south-west of the island, so pedalled steadily up from my base at St Paul's to the central ridges then west on the road towards Blue Hill. It was a lovely day, and I was in no hurry, so stops were frequent – these included the George Benjamin Arboretum, home to many of St Helena's endemic plants, the nearby Clifford Arboretum (planted to mark the Queen's Silver Jubilee in 1977), then the isolated St Helena and The Cross Church which serves the remote community of Blue Hill. This road was pure delight – a high ridge which rose and fell only moderately, so maximum effort could be put into enjoying the ever-changing views of the island's north and south coasts simultaneously, whilst exerting minimum physical effort in order to do so. A particular highlight was the amazing volcanic amphitheatre called The Gates of Chaos.

Of course, all good things come to an end, and this road was no exception, for upon reaching Thompson's Wood it rapidly descended several hundred feet, the exhilaration of the five minute freewheel being tempered by the nagging feeling of dread that I would have to come back up every single foot of the way – and probably *on* foot to boot! The road degenerated into a potholed track, then pretty much disappeared altogether, so I left my trusty steed in the long grass and continued on foot up onto White Point, a beautiful walk through scenery reminiscent of the Scottish Lowlands, and a known habitat of St Helena's rare endemic bird – the wirebird – though alas there were no sightings. This route culminated in a viewpoint taking in the entire western part of the island. My determination to reach this lonely extremity of the island was principally to view the jagged outline of Speery Island – an impressive rock resembling the head of a spear off St Helena's southern coast, home to countless seabirds and only visible from this remote corner of the island.

'Drunk' on so much fine scenery, and with noon fast approaching, it was time to get on my way again: There followed a foot-slogging uphill return with bike to attain the ridge, only to drop down yet again in order to visit Blue Hill village, set against the green backdrop of aptly-named High Hill. The day was turning into one of highs and lows: After yet another detour downhill, naturally necessitating another energy-draining ascent, I was beginning to

A 'bike break' in remote Blue Hill village – High Hill is in the background

Flax-lined road near Silver Hill & Levelwood – Little & Great Stone Top visible

Chapter 3 ~ **St Helena** ~ A Week of Highs and Lows ~ 73

experience the feeling of faintness any serious cyclist will recognise when the 'batteries' are running low, and so food supplies quickly assumed importance on the agenda.

I returned slowly towards the centre of the island, then branched off onto Sandy Bay Ridge, but with the memory of two days before still etched on my mind, I only descended as far as was necessary into Sandy Bay Valley itself in order to visit the idyllically situated Thorpe's grocery shop, where I bought sufficient ingredients for a picnic lunch of substance. After all, to turn a common expression on its head, what goes down must come back up, and I was taking no chances!

My 'batteries' thus recharged, I then set off into a warm and sunny afternoon towards the south-east of the island along a wonderful flax-flanked switchback road which zigzagged seemingly for ever around the 'back' of Diana's Peak, towering far above me to the left. There were occasional views to the south-east down beautiful ravines such as Deep Valley and a derelict old flax mill at Rock Rose added interest.

After an hour or so, I turned a corner and entered a different landscape altogether – the scattered buildings of Silver Hill and Levelwood lay spread out below me, strung along two parallel promontories like beads on a pair of necklaces, while beyond lay the angular twin peaks of Great Stone Top and Little Stone Top, the former having more than a passing resemblance to the Rock of Gibraltar. The exertions of the afternoon had been quite dehydrating, so I was relieved the local Solomon's shop was open for refreshment, even if the adjacent Silver Hill Bar wasn't!

With thirst quenched, I climbed out of Levelwood and past another abandoned flax mill at Woody Ridge, relic of a one-time successful industry on St Helena, which used to supply twine for British Post Office mail bags, until replacement by synthetic fibres in 1966 sadly brought about its demise. (Ironically, the flax industry had itself been developed in the wake of a downturn in St Helena's economic fortunes following the opening of the Suez Canal in 1869, which reduced the number of ships calling as there was suddenly a much shorter way to reach the Indian Ocean than via the Cape of Good Hope).

In turn I came to the Black Gate entrance to Diana's Peak National Park. The sun was still up, and the sky blue and unthreatening, so for the second time in as many days I made an assault on foot to the top of the mountain, this time approaching from the opposite side via Mount Actaeon. On this attempt, the visibility was superior to the day before, and I had an uninterrupted view right across the island. I stayed as long as I dared, before returning to the bike and cycling on, via Hutt's Gate junction and the appropriately-named "W-Road" (a zigzagging and useful short-ish cut across the centre of the island) to return to St Paul's before sundown: All in all, a very satisfying and successful day, including 'circumcycling' (!) Diana's Peak. Later that evening I joined Bishop John, 'shipmates' and several islanders down in Jamestown for a meal at Donny's, an altogether more relaxed occasion than when I had last been there, wondering quite what I had let myself in for!

I was up promptly on Saturday morning, keen to make the best of the weather and with the aim of accomplishing another full day 'in the saddle'. This time, I was heading for the east and north-east of the island, and left St Paul's in an easterly direction, taking the "W-Road", and detouring through the lush, semi-tropical woodland of the Alarm Forest area to Gordon's Post junction, before tackling a manageable climb up the Sane Valley to Hutt's Gate.

The two main points of interest here are Halley's Mount (where the famous astronomer Edmund Halley once established an observatory to study the transit of Mercury and the southern stars) and nearby St Matthew's Church. A pleasant mile or so of easy cycling brought me to Longwood Gate, but not before stopping to talk to a friendly Saint I had first met two days before near Diana's Peak – another golden rule of touring St Helena is to allow oneself 'talking time', and quite right too!

On reaching Longwood, I wisely took the precaution of buying some lunch from the shop next to St Mark's Church – I didn't want to get caught out a second time on the food-into-energy front – before cycling on past 'French territory' (Napoleon's 'prison' at Longwood House) towards the golf course and Piccolo Hill. It was then that I saw them – the cyclists that is – or to be more precise two local schoolboys out on their bikes and enjoying the Saturday sunshine.

In fact, I saw more bikes lying around that day than any other, and furthermore, it was about the only time I saw bikes *and people actually riding them* the whole week I was on the island: So Longwood was the 'cycling capital' of St Helena, and it wasn't hard to see why; despite being well over a thousand feet up, Longwood and its hinterland represents the largest continuous area of level – or near level – land in the entire island with a network of roads to suit, but as soon as one tries to get anywhere else on the island, it's back to plummeting ravines or soaring inclines.

Musing on the absurdity of it all, it occurred to me that Levelwood might have been a more appropriate name for Longwood, and perhaps Levelwood (which isn't flat) better named Longwood (on account of its endless switchback roads through well-wooded country!) I then made my way even further east to one of the strangest landscapes to be found on the island – and even flatter than Longwood village (though still in its parish) which is saying something by St Helenian standards. As the road petered out into a rutted track beyond the turning to the fairly recently-planted Millennium Forest, I continued on foot into an area of semi-desert, ochre-brown and orange, studded with prickly cactus and punctuated by strangely-named – and even stranger looking – rocky outcrops such as King & Queen Rocks and Holdfast Tom:

I was standing on Prosperous Bay Plain, St Helena's answer to Arizona, or maybe Australia, and – as the flattest bit of land this side of Ascension – the site selected to become an airport for the island. A strange, eerie silence hung over the place – this was truly the South Atlantic outback and I half expected to see galloping horsemen appear on the horizon as if in some Western film set!...In fact I saw no-one.

Returning to my bike, I pedalled back through Longwood, then north onto Deadwood Plain (site of a former Boer prisoner of war camp) as far as reasonably practicable before again resorting to 'shanks pony' mode for an ascent of Flagstaff Hill – a St Helenian Matterhorn, rising directly alongside The Barn – the latter an absurdly contrasting imitation of Table Mountain in Cape Town! One of the delights of St Helena is the tremendous diversity of scenery packed into an island not much bigger than the Channel Island of Jersey – where else could one see scenes reminiscent of the USA, Switzerland and South Africa in the space of a few hours? Fortunately the Matterhorn analogy did not extend to icy slopes and snowy wastes, for the summit of Flagstaff Hill was agreeably warm and offered one of the best panoramas I had yet seen on St Helena, including glimpses of Turk's Cap and Sugar Loaf – prominent topographical features on the eastern and northern coasts respectively – as well as the glistening ocean far below.

I enjoyed lunch surrounded by all this vista of loveliness, and the experience was made all the more satisfying, as I returned across Deadwood Plain, by a brief sighting – I think – of one of the island's rare endemic birds, the elusive wirebird: St Helena's 'national bird' is basically a small, long-legged, grey-brown and white plover, which tends to dart about in short, jerky movements before suddenly taking to the air and disappearing. Consequently, trying to photograph it was a dead

Flagstaff Hill & The Barn viewed from east of Deadwood Plain (wirebird habitat)

Simon's bicycle at Town Gate in Jamestown – note wirebird & arum lilies emblems

Chapter 3 ~ *St Helena* ~ A Week of Highs and Lows ~ 77

loss, so knowing when I was beaten, decided to stick to cycling and leave ornithology to the experts!

Back on more familiar ground, I cycled away from Longwood, past Hutt's Gate and then began a gradual descent lasting several miles through Alarm Forest in the general direction of Jamestown. Just before a particularly tight hairpin bend called Button Up Corner, I passed the first of those dreaded "NO CYCLING" signs and came to an abrupt halt – not so much on account of the sign but because, outside a house right on the bend, a man who had until a few moments before been cleaning his car suddenly stood up and with a beaming smile and booming voice shouted "AH – THE MAN WITH THE BICYCLE!"...It was Stedson George, the island's astronomer and one of those who had been sitting with me and the Bishop at Donny's that first evening. "How is it going then?" he enquired, adding mischievously for the second time "You know you can't cycle down Side Path etc. etc." I smiled and said "Well, I'm not walking *all* the way into Jamestown if I can help it, sign or no sign" to which he replied with a twinkle in his eye "If you didn't see the sign, neither did I!"

Needing no further encouragement, I remounted my bike and for the first time – rather unwisely – started coasting downhill in a 'restricted zone', but not for very long: It soon became obvious why the "NO CYCLING" signs were there after the first couple of hairpins – self-preservation! Not only was the hill steep, it was also long, and – most significantly – pretty well straight as the proverbial arrow for most of the descent into Jamestown. There had been no need for such restrictions on roads such as that down into Sandy Bay where the tightness and frequency of the bends regulated speed anyway, irrespective of the effects of gravity, but Side Path and its ilk were different, offering the cyclist potentially terrifying speeds verging on terminal velocity, followed by almost inevitable 'take off' into oblivion over the edge of the low stone wall bordering the road as it descended the cliff face of James Valley. Veering a bit close to the wall for comfort, and with my brakes screeching, I chose instead to ride 'side saddle' as if on a horse, interspersed with rather ungainly trotting at regular intervals. That way control was maintained, speeds were kept in check, and yet I didn't lose out on the free ride entirely!

I didn't go directly into Jamestown though, as there were still a couple of detours I wished to make – the first took me past St Mary's Church into Briars village in order to gain a close-up view of the Briars Pavilion, where Napoleon spent his first two months on St Helena as Longwood House was not initially ready to accommodate him; it is generally believed this period was the happiest of his almost six year incarceration on the island. In complete contrast, a more modern addition was the nearby Cable & Wireless complex – headquarters for telephone and satellite communications on St Helena – and a reminder of similar sights I had seen on Ascension.

The second detour was a longer one down another steep incline into Rupert's Valley and on to Rupert's Bay, St Helena's 'industrial powerhouse', and home to its generating station, fuel tank 'farm', fish factory (the island exports modest amounts of tuna) and the incongruously-sited St Michael's Church. The bare, fjord-like valley reminded me of the Shetland Islands, yet another example of a landscape familiar to me from elsewhere in the World but represented in miniature on St Helena. The only realistic way out of Rupert's Valley with a bike was back up the same road, so it was a case of foot-slogging-bike-pushing for the umpteenth time before finally *carefully* descending Side Path into Lower Jamestown.

It seemed strange to be cycling round the familiar streets of St Helena's capital for the first time, having confined my explorations by bike to practically everywhere else up until now, but I was about to be reminded of precisely *why* I had chosen *not* to venture there on two wheels unless absolutely unavoidable: Time was now of the essence, and I had to return to Bishopsholme before nightfall, but this time – unlike the day I collected my bike off the ship – there was no Bishop or Bishop's car to assist (and if I was honest, rather in the spirit of a climber tackling Mount Everest, I wanted to do the monumental climb up to St Paul's just once *because it was there*). So, lubricated with lemonade from Thorpe's grocery shop, I climbed steadily up through Upper Jamestown, past the Roman Catholic Church, St John's Church and the island's hospital onto Ladder Hill Road, which is almost the mirror image of Side Path – a long, steep hill scaling the opposite side of the valley and clinging to vertiginous volcanic slopes.

I never really understood why the "NO CYCLING" rule applied in the uphill direction, but the signs seemed fairly pointless in this instance since, despite my numerous gears, I had resorted to pushing before reaching the fort at the top of Ladder Hill. In any case, on this side of James Valley, I was on that side of the road furthest from the sheer drop, so there was little chance of being knocked over the edge (although falling rocks could potentially present problems as mini-landslides are not uncommon). Furthermore, the interminable stretch up through Half Tree Hollow which followed was so relentless an incline that I was glad of stops every few hundred yards, such as

St Andrew's Church from where I watched the sun dip towards the horizon. As darkness fell, I made it back to Bishopsholme, exhausted after a full day's tour of much of the island, with a marathon climb of almost 2,000 feet from sea level right at the end.

Sunday, the day of rest, arrived – and with it a rest from cycling too – well, almost: There was still one corner of the island left unexplored, and with my cycling 'on the wane', it seemed somehow appropriate to be off to an area rejoicing in the name of Head O'Wain – home to an isolated Baptist Chapel, health clinic and handful of houses. This I reached by cycling up through the damp morning gloom, and west towards Blue Hill, before turning right (near the site of a second former Boer prisoner of war camp at Broad Bottom) down a narrow twisting road; this led north along another ridge onto a hill called The Saddle, thence on to Horse Pasture, set above the island's north coast, where a beautiful sunrise was experienced.

I returned to Bishopsholme for breakfast, and a little later the rest of the day swung into action: I attended morning service at the delightfully sited St Helena and The Cross Church – conducted by Bishop John – before continuing on to Crack Plain for a most convivial Sunday lunch at the home of Edith Timm, together with other 'shipmates' she had invited. This was in turn followed by evensong at St Paul's Cathedral. (At this point it is worthy of mention that St Paul's Cathedral, unlike its London namesake, is like a large English country church inside and out, but it *does* have a bishop's throne and is what qualifies St Helena as a diocese).

The day concluded very pleasantly with an invitation to dinner at nearby Plantation House, courtesy of the St Helena Governor David Hollamby and his wife Helena, whom I had first met and come to know on my first visit to the South Atlantic aboard the RMS in 2001. David Hollamby cheerfully met me at his front door that evening and exclaimed "My goodness, how do you manage to keep such a trim figure?" – "I guess it must be down to all the cycling" was the first response to spring to mind, and after the week I'd had attempting to cycle up virtually every hill on St Helena, I probably wasn't all that wide of the mark! A most enjoyable evening followed, including a bespoke tour of the historical property enthusiastically conducted by Helena.

All too soon, Monday morning came and with it my week on St Helena came to an end. The RMS, having returned the night before from Ascension, was not due to sail until the late afternoon however, so the day still offered

Outside the clinic & phone box at Head O'Wain – an early morning bike ride

St Paul's Cathedral – like an English country church & site of Sunday evensong

Arrival at Plantation House, the Governor's residence, for Sunday evening dinner

Final day of cycling – when I discovered St Helena's only roundabout at Scotland

possibilities, including the chance of a final spin on the bike. For my final – seventh – day cycling round the island, I elected to do a fairly modest 'figure-of-eight' route centred on St Paul's; this took me past New Ground, Cleugh's Plain and the Agriculture Department at strangely-named Scotland (which as far as I could see it perversely *doesn't* resemble and where I discovered St Helena's only roundabout!) back to White Gate, followed by a second loop via Francis Plain and Knollcombes, including a detour on foot to explore the geological wonder that is the Heart Shape Waterfall (which more reassuringly it *does* resemble!)

With this final flourish, I had ended up covering just about every road of note on the island during my week of 'two wheel touring'. It was with reluctance that I returned to Bishopsholme for the last time, where I parted company with my bike and left it in the safe keeping of Bishop John until the RMS called six weeks later, whereupon it would be loaded on the ship for the two week voyage north back to England.

For me though it was almost time to leave, and the afternoon was spent exploring in and around Jamestown *on foot for a change.* This included the post office – a building full of period character – for philatelic items; and the old covered market – assembled from prefabricated iron components originally shipped from Britain – for a St Helena tuna lunch. I could alternatively have chosen another St Helenian speciality for my lunch – spicy fishcakes – one of several local dishes to have been influenced by the tastes of the Orient. I also engaged in some souvenir hunting at a number of traditional old shops, where I felt I had walked into a 'time warp' as the goods were stacked on high wooden shelving behind a large counter! I also took a short but interesting walk over Munden's Hill to Sampson's Battery – an old gun site guarding the approaches to James Bay.

However, it was not long before the inevitable drift of both Saints and visitors down towards the quayside signalled that embarkation was about to commence. I said my goodbyes to everybody – well, quite a lot of people at any rate – and was soon descending the wharf steps and crashing through the spray in a launch towards the waiting ship. As the RMS set sail on the continuation of voyage no. 62S towards Cape Town, and with the lowering sun illuminating the stunning coastline so it shone like gold, I was able to recognise many of the places I had reached during my week on the island. After a semi-circumnavigation taking in the west and south coasts, including such highlights as Man and Horse Cliffs, Manati Bay and Speery Island, we sailed off into the night.

My last view of St Helena came as I sat with chief purser Geoff Shallcross on the sundeck of the RMS, enjoying a glass of South African beer and watching as the reddening rays of the setting sun framed the profile of the island in silhouette. "Well Simon – that was St Helena" he murmured as we set course for the five day stretch to Cape Town and the island became a memory. The experience had been remarkable, and whilst I may not have covered the sorts of distances I could have managed in a week of cycle touring in Britain – given that I seemed to have got through all 21 gears on my bike at least 21 times daily – I nevertheless clocked-up around a hundred miles with the bike alone, without counting numerous additional explorations on foot. They were, though, about the toughest hundred miles I have *ever* cycled! It had been a week of highs and lows both literally and metaphorically, yet what the experience may have lacked in pure distance terms was more than compensated for by a unique view of an incredible island – St Helena.

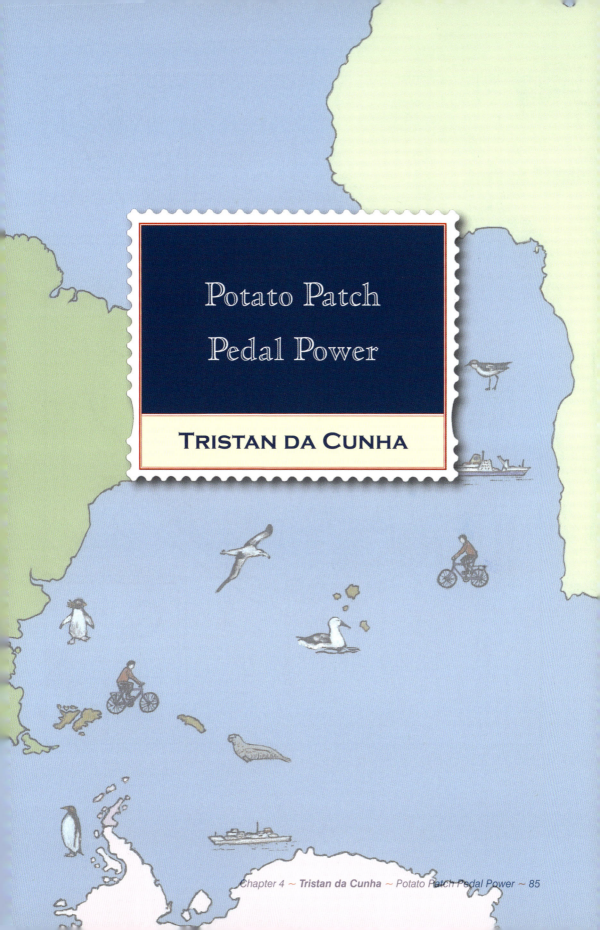

Chapter 4 ~ **Tristan da Cunha** ~ *Potato Patch Pedal Power* ~ 85

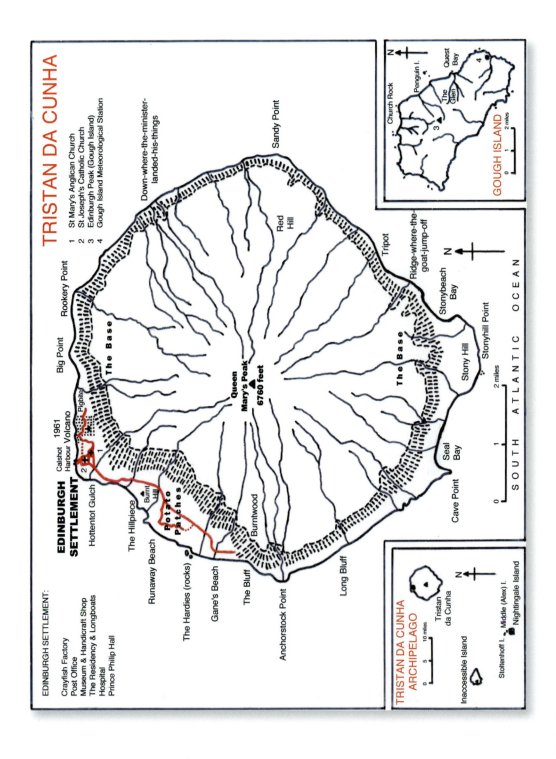

86 ~ Chapter 4 ~ **Tristan da Cunha** ~ Potato Patch Pedal Power

Chapter 4
Exploring Tristan da Cunha by Bicycle

Simon with bike next to "Remotest Island" sign & fingerpost on Tristan da Cunha

"Cycling on Tristan da Cunha? – There's only one road!" was said to me several times when I announced my plans to people. Other amused onlookers quipped "You could always ride out from the settlement to the potato patches and back a few times!" In late October 2005 when – for the second time – I presented my bicycle at Portland in Dorset, ready to be loaded onto the Royal Mail Ship *St Helena*, even the port agent expressed his surprise that I intended transporting my machine half way round the World and back just to ride a mere handful of miles on Tristan!...

...Perhaps that last sentiment holds the key to what inspired me, as a cyclist, rather in the same way that polar explorers are inspired by the South Pole. Or maybe, since I had previously cycled on both Ascension and St Helena, there was still the obvious challenge of cycling on Tristan.

Three months later in early February 2006 – and somewhere on the South Atlantic – it was with some trepidation that I descended into the ship's cargo hold to pump-up my bike tyres the evening before the RMS 2006 quincentenary voyage reached the island: When Captain Rodney Young – master of the RMS on this particular voyage – suggested that I checked over my bike, I didn't need to be told twice given that it had been conveyed continually around the Atlantic Ocean for several months since leaving the UK on voyage no. 79. In any case, I wanted to reassure myself it was 'fit for purpose', so only finding a couple of rather deflated tyres came as something of a relief!

When the RMS *St Helena* sailed from Cape Town at the end of January 2006 on what was otherwise more mundanely known as voyage no. 82, it was also the beginning of a special voyage to Tristan da Cunha to mark the 500th anniversary of its discovery, as part of which the ship was scheduled to remain anchored off the island for a whole week. The island that is today called Tristan da Cunha was discovered in 1506 by the Portuguese explorer Tristao da Cunha, and – although he did not land there – did name it after himself.

The 2006 voyage to Tristan began in South Africa at Cape Town's Duncan Dock – the unashamedly 'workaday' part of the city's port, yet just a short distance from the exciting Victoria & Alfred Waterfront, the latter full of sparkling marinas, smart yachts, bars, restaurants, shops and other tourist attractions, which only the previous day I had visited during an open-top bus tour of the city. By contrast, Duncan Dock is characterised by high steel fences, grimy old warehouses and transit sheds, huge cranes and large ships variously being loaded with – or relieved of – containers stacked by the hundreds on the dockside. Almost dwarfed by all this, moored alongside in E Berth, was the blue hull, white superstructure and jaunty yellow funnel of the RMS *St Helena*. Perhaps not the most prepossessing or promising of gateways to a keenly-anticipated voyage loaded with expectation, and destined for the remotest inhabited island in the World: However, as two previous departures from this very spot had taught me, one should never judge a book by its cover, or – in this case – a ship by its surroundings.

Having been brought by bus from the Townhouse Hotel in the commercial heart of Cape Town, where I had spent the night following a 12 hour flight from London Heathrow, I assembled with other passengers in a transit shed on the quayside for passport and security checks, and waited to embark. Before too long I was walking up the gangway onto the ship, and straightaway that 'home from home' feeling came flooding back as I was welcomed onboard by various ship's officers and crew, most of them familiar faces from earlier voyages. Once settled into my cabin – C49 on C deck – I proceeded to the open deck just in time to see the last of the containers bound for Tristan being craned into the forward cargo hold.

It was late afternoon when – assisted by two tug boats and guided by the port pilot – the RMS manoeuvred carefully away from the quayside of Duncan Dock and set sail out into Table Bay. As the ship left the port, there were dramatic views of central Cape Town and the breathtaking, iconic backdrop of Table Mountain rising steeply to its summit almost 3,500 feet above the city: The perfect excuse for a frenzy of photography where I was not alone in capturing the moment.

The departure from Cape Town was dramatic and memorable, but of course this was not 'just another' large cruise ship with a packed itinerary of tourist 'hot spots' to tick-off, or for that matter an anonymous container vessel *en route* to some other continent loaded with merchandise: This was "the last ocean-going Royal Mail Ship in the World" bound for one of the most isolated territories in the World, and therefore it was where we were going – rather than where we had just left – that was already dominating most of the conversation out on deck that afternoon. Meanwhile, old friendships were renewed whilst new ones were only just beginning. As Table Mountain and South Africa's Cape Peninsula faded into the distance, reddened by the setting sun, the RMS set a west-south-westerly course out across the South Atlantic and steamed away into the night.

The outward voyage which lay ahead, of over 1,500 nautical miles, would last six nights / seven days, a day longer than when I first visited Tristan in 2001, although travelling at a slightly more sedate 'rate of knots' (to conserve fuel) meant the trip was less rough than five years before: When sailing towards St Helena from Cape Town, on a generally north-westerly course, the south-east trade winds and direction of the swell quite often means a smooth passage. By contrast, the journey out from Cape Town to Tristan da Cunha is predominantly against the prevailing south-westerly winds and swell which can often make for quite an uncomfortable experience; it is therefore essential to acquire one's 'sea legs' at an early stage!

With the best part of a week at sea, it was also essential to get into some sort of routine, but fortunately I knew from past voyages that boredom or idleness weren't really options – the unique 'RMS experience' would see to that! Over the course of the next few days, I variously took part in a team quiz, enjoyed games either out on deck or as part of the after-dinner entertainment which included an RMS favourite – 'frog' racing – which needless to say did not involve actual live amphibians, but which I *was* rather good at! I found time to read at length about Tristan and the South Atlantic. I was also fortunate enough to have guided tours of the ship's bridge *and* engine room. Meanwhile, I listened to slide-illustrated talks – and watched film documentaries – about both Tristan and the amazing wildlife of the South Atlantic. Oh...and of course...I wrote several postcards and posted them onboard with Tristan da Cunha stamps; I was, after all, travelling on a Royal Mail Ship!

However, the real highlight came four days after leaving Cape Town, when the first sightings were made of some impressive seabirds – petrels, shearwaters and most graceful and beautiful of them all – albatrosses. Seeing these amazing birds, so closely associated with the South Atlantic, was a privilege, and for the first time on the voyage there was a palpable sense that Tristan was getting tantalisingly close. There are basically three varieties of albatross to be seen flying over the vast, empty ocean around Tristan – the Tristan (or wandering) albatross, the yellow-nosed albatross and the sooty albatross, and although not much of an expert in matters of ornithology (as my experience with the St Helena wirebird demonstrated only too well!) I nevertheless became increasingly proficient at telling the difference between the various types, admittedly assisted by those onboard who knew about such things.

On both the outward and return sectors of the voyage, several hours were spent simply gazing out from the deck as one, or two, or sometimes several, of these magnificent creatures followed the ship at close quarters – often for miles at a time – continually soaring, diving, or simply gliding, their huge wingspan and effortless flight almost mesmerising: Yet the albatross is an endangered species, and for too long they have sadly become victims of long-line fishing nets, a sobering thought that left one wondering as to how much longer, without more stringent protection, it would be possible to witness such wonderful sights.

I was awake very early on the morning of Sunday 5th February, as this was the day the RMS was scheduled to arrive at Tristan da Cunha: Shortly after 5.00am, whilst it was still dark, I went up on deck as – similarly to five years previously – I was keen to witness the island appear on the ocean's western horizon. As it gradually became lighter, the weather started to worsen with squally showers and a strong wind blowing, accompanied by a low cloud base: There was unfortunately not going to be a first sighting from afar, followed by a gradual approach, as had been my experience in 2001.

Instead, just after 6.00am, Tristan suddenly loomed out of the grey cloud

View of Table Mountain leaving Cape Town docks on the RMS bound for Tristan

RMS – with Tristan flag raised – arriving at anchorage off the island in 2006

and mist on the starboard side of the ship, appearing as a huge mountain rising straight out of the sea. Had the weather been clear, I would have been able to appreciate just how apt a description this is, for although – like both Ascension and St Helena – Tristan da Cunha is a volcanic island situated on the flanks of the Mid-Atlantic Ridge, its appearance – on first impression – is that of a single, almost perfectly conical peak rising steeply to a central summit crater, and resting on a large base with near-vertical sides rising out of the ocean. A good analogy would be that of a massive 'big top' circus tent.

In physical terms, the island covers around 38 square miles, and is approximately circular, with sheer cliffs rising up to 2,000 feet from sea level over about two-thirds of its circumference (known as The Base), above which it slopes up concentrically to almost 7,000 feet at Queen Mary's Peak (or simply just The Peak). Sloping down from the central peak are a series of river valleys – called gulches – which radiate out across the mountainside like the spokes of a bicycle wheel before cascading down the steep cliffs of The Base to the sea. At three locations around the edge of the island, where the massive cliffs are set back from the coast, flatter land shelves down to the sea – one such area is to be found around Stonyhill Point on the south 'side' of this round island and is used for the grazing of livestock. Another, much smaller, area is at Sandy Point on the east 'side' and the location of fruit trees and some woodland.

However, the largest and most significant of these 'land shelves' extends along the entire north-west quadrant of the island between the headlands at Big Point in the north and Anchorstock Point to the west. It is this last area of land – usually termed the settlement plain – that primarily enables life to be sustained and a human community to exist in what would otherwise be an incredibly challenging environment.

With reference to a map, I was able to identify that the ship was sailing just off the southern extremity of Tristan near Stonyhill Point and the sloping grassland plateau of Stony Hill. The vessel then turned north and commenced a close coastal passage around the eastern half of the island, taking in Stonybeach Bay, the steep cliffs around Tripot, the aforementioned area of trees at Sandy Point, and on towards Rookery Point. Place names on Tristan are delightful, and often refer to an isolated event in the island's past; two of my favourite place names along this section of coast are "Ridge-where-the-goat-jump-off" and "Down-where-the-minister-landed-his-things". As the coastal tour continued, the sun came out at intervals and illuminated the wonderful shades of green, grey and brown, whilst through gaps in the cloud it was occasionally possible to see the higher slopes of the mountain towards The Peak, including Red Hill and other localised craters, as well as the succession of gulches carving their way down the hillside.

As the RMS reached the north side of the island and rounded Big Point, I had my first glimpse of the settlement plain. Moving closer, the buildings of Tristan's only village gradually became more distinct – or the settlement of Edinburgh of the Seven Seas to give it its full name. Finally, with three blasts on the ship's whistle and with a clanking of chains, the RMS came to rest at the Falmouth Bay anchorage around 8.00am thereby signifying journey's end.

Radio contact had already been made with the island, and it was not long before things started to happen in quick succession: A launch came out from the shore with immigration officials as I finished a hasty breakfast, then having completed formalities – and gained another prized Tristan da Cunha stamp in my passport – I waited to board a boat to the island. However, this is where disembarkation procedures were to prove very different – and certainly more challenging – than those at either Ascension or St Helena: As the sea swells were a bit high, it was deemed too dangerous to use the ship's gangway, so instead it proved necessary to use a rope ladder to climb down the side of the ship, before jumping (when told to do so by a reassuring Tristanian boatman) and landing, hopefully still on both feet, in the waiting boat which was bobbing wildly up and down in the lively swell!

Actually, it was quite a novel experience and the *real* way of arriving at Tristan I had read about so many years before, and yet not required to do in 2001 when the sea conditions had been calmer. Once the boat was full, an exhilarating, bumpy journey lasting around five minutes followed, accompanied by showers of spray being thrown across everyone as it powered through the waves. Then – with a final thrust – the boat surged into the island's Calshot Harbour, turned sharply to the right and stopped by the harbour steps, where I set foot on Tristan just before noon.

Arriving at Tristan on that Sunday morning had indeed been a spectacular experience, yet still surpassed by the incredible welcome received from the islanders on arrival at Calshot Harbour and hospitality shown by them throughout the following week. I was met by my friend Lars Repetto who, along with his wife Trina, had kindly accommodated me in their home – called Brick Front – when I first visited Tristan in 2001. As five years previously, Trina and Lars were again to be my hosts, although this time I would be staying at their daughter Debbie's home. As I walked away from the harbour,

I observed that the islanders were certainly getting into the 'quincentenary spirit' as a large sign bearing the words "Welcome to Tristan da Cunha" had been augmented with "500th Anniversary (1506-2006)".

Lars then led me up the steep road from the harbour and into the village, continuing more gently uphill until we arrived at his home: Brick Front – in common with many on the island – is a typical Tristan house, essentially a white-painted, single-storey cottage built between two large 'bookend' gables fashioned from volcanic stone blocks, and set behind a pretty front garden. In former times it would have been thatched with flax. It could almost have been the idyllic thatched cottage pictured on one of those very first Tristan stamps I saw back in 1976 and which first inspired my interest in the island.

It wasn't just memories from 30 years before that were stirred though, as those from five years previously came flooding back too: As Lars and I walked up the garden path, Trina was at the half-open stable door of the house, waiting to greet me, along with their son Andre (their other son Paul was in England at the time). I was soon being invited in for a very welcome cup of tea and before long we were chatting and laughing, or simply 'catching up': It was as if I had never been away – five years had passed, yet here I was sitting in the front room of a Tristan house that seemed so familiar and feeling as much at home as if I had called in at a friend's house in my local village back in England. I even remembered the painting on the wall by Roland Svensson, the Swedish artist who also designed *those* Tristan stamps that started everything, and whom Lars and Trina knew personally. Moments like that are very special anywhere, but on Tristan they assume an even more intense sense of privilege.

In due course, Trina walked further up the hill with me to her daughter's house and my accommodation for the week – Rockhopper Cottage – beautifully situated above the village and, again in true Tristan fashion, built with its front looking out to sea and its back to the mountain. Appropriately, above the entrance was a picture of rockhopper penguins – wildlife closely associated with Tristan. Meanwhile, a tractor and trailer arrived with some of my luggage from the ship, though at this stage that did *not* include my bicycle! After settling into my new abode and an enjoyable picnic lunch sitting in the garden simply gazing out past the RMS *St Helena* at anchor across the blue vastness of the South Atlantic Ocean, I set off to explore my new surroundings.

The first day was largely spent renewing old friendships and reacquainting myself with Edinburgh settlement, and began with a walk back down through the village to Calshot Harbour, where I met islander Stanley Swain, the harbour master, who was overseeing the intense activity which was still ongoing as further passengers arrived ashore and the harbour crane swung to and fro landing more heavily-anticipated cargo. The harbour takes its name from the small English village of Calshot, on the shore of Southampton Water, which came to play a crucial role in arguably the most significant event of Tristan's inhabited history, an event and a history which would be increasingly revealed as my week's explorations unfolded.

In the meantime though, there were things to do and people to see: At the top of the road leading back up from the harbour, I just *had* to do the obligatory "I was there" thing, by which I mean being photographed standing by a sign proclaiming Tristan as the remotest inhabited island in the World. As if to reinforce the point, a sign incidentally accompanied by a fingerpost with several arrows pointing to the 'nearest neighbours' – none of these within 1,343 miles (St Helena) – and others, such as London (5,337 miles), much further away indeed.

My perambulations through the settlement brought me to Prince Philip Hall, the excellent community facility which lies right at the heart of the village and which incorporates the local pub named (appropriately for the South Atlantic) the Albatross Bar. A crowd had already gathered outside, and a pleasant half-hour or so was spent chatting with Lars' and Trina's son Andre, as well as several other islanders, some of whom I remembered (or they remembered me!) from my initial 2001 visit.

In the late afternoon, I made my way to St Joseph's Catholic Church, the newer of the island's two church buildings and featuring a beautiful stained-glass window in the entrance porch bearing an image of the island accompanied by a longboat and an angel. It being a Sunday, I attended a service here which was led by the chief islander Anne Green, during which there was recognition of the island's quincentenary.

Afterwards, I walked along to pay a visit to St Mary's Anglican Church, tucked away in a quiet corner of the village, featuring an attractive screen behind the altar and with a church bell that was retrieved from an old ship called the *Mabel Clark*. With views across the rooftops of the village to the ocean beyond, the church was an oasis of calm in already peaceful surroundings; some years later, on my third visit to Tristan, I would have the privilege of attending a service here too, when Lars Repetto – in his capacity as a lay reader – conducted proceedings.

Simon outside Rockhopper Cottage (home for week) reunited with bike from RMS

Simon on bike in front of "500th Anniversary (1506-2006)" sign at Calshot Harbour

96 ~ Chapter 4 ~ **Tristan da Cunha** ~ Potato Patch Pedal Power

As I continued to walk around the settlement, I met a number of islanders, and gradually immersed myself in the easy-going and friendly culture that prevails on Tristan where saying "hello" or some other cheery greeting becomes almost second-nature. On returning to Rockhopper Cottage later that afternoon, I was relieved to see my bicycle standing outside, having been unloaded from the RMS and still bedecked with baggage labels following its long journey from England which had begun when I loaded it into a container at Portland over three months before! Thus reunited with my bike, I could not resist going for a quick ride on my first day ashore, and so freewheeled directly down through the surfaced lanes of the settlement to the harbour in a matter of minutes to watch the activity there – yet again – before pedalling slowly back up through the village just in time for a welcome meal with my hosts Trina and Lars: My cycle-based exploration of Tristan was at last underway!

That evening, at Brick Front, Trina laid on a wonderful spread which included salad, cold meat and two Tristan specialities – fresh local potatoes and crayfish, followed by some delicious Tristan (milk) tart. The evening passed pleasantly in conversation, from which I eventually emerged into the dark of a still, peaceful night sky, and returned – tired but contented – to Rockhopper Cottage.

Monday – my first full day on Tristan – was heralded by a beautiful, still dawn. On cycling towards the harbour I noted that two ships – MV *Edinburgh* and MV *Kelso* – had now joined RMS *St Helena* at the anchorage: These were both South African fishing vessels engaged in the crayfish industry based in waters around the Tristan da Cunha group of islands, in addition to locally-caught crayfish processed in the fishing factory situated just above Tristan's harbour. After this initial 'warm up' ride I returned to Rockhopper Cottage for breakfast, following which my first priority was to try and locate the larger of my two bags brought ashore (and containing most of my clothes!) which had mysteriously not arrived at the house the day before. I initially reported the matter to local police officer Lorraine Repetto, and it was not long before someone approached me with the reassuring information that it had been delivered in error to the Mabel Clark (a guest house in another part of the village named after the same wrecked ship from which St Mary's Church bell had been salvaged). Sure enough, on reaching the said Mabel Clark, I was reunited with my belongings.

I mention this episode because it is an example of how close-knit a community Tristan is and how – with less than 300 inhabitants – information is swiftly relayed. A similar thing happened in 2001, when I lost my camera on the morning of departure from the island, but thanks to the helpfulness of the islanders it was located within an hour or so. This honesty and genuine friendliness of Tristanian society is both encouraging and refreshing, and has much to teach those of us living in the "outside world", as everywhere on Earth *apart* from Tristan is referred to by the islanders!

During the course of the morning and early afternoon I probably completed several – never identical – circuits of the village lanes as I variously sought out the administration building, library, post office, handicraft shop, school, playing field and finally the supermarket. It will be recalled when I first announced that I planned to cycle on Tristan, several people had remarked about there only being one road, by which they were referring to the 'main road' from Edinburgh settlement to the potato patches. However, this is not in fact true by any means, although it has to be admitted the road network is considerably more limited than that on either St Helena or Ascension.

Starting from the road climbing steeply from the harbour, past the fishing factory, an array of workshops, sheds and the island's radio / telephone masts, one is soon faced with a choice of two routes: To the right, a surfaced road leads past the supermarket, administration building, post office and small island hospital to the western edge of the village, before continuing for several miles as the 'main road' out towards the potato patches (where the road splits into two arms) and on towards the south-west of the settlement plain. Meanwhile, the road to the left proceeds past the Residency (official home of Tristan's Administrator), playing field, school and Prince Philip Hall, eventually exiting the east side of the village and heading towards the north-east of the settlement plain.

Within the settlement itself, there is a maze of winding lanes, tracks and paths connecting the hundred or so houses which are spread across the green, springy turf and which converge in a loose knot around Prince Philip Hall. In certain ways, Edinburgh settlement resembles a coastal community such as can be found in the Scottish Hebrides, although the fact most gardens have large amounts of New Zealand flax planted around them as a windbreak confirms that this is somewhere different.

Tristan's administration building is where the day-to-day business of governing the island takes place, and whilst there I briefly visited both the council chamber and library contained therein. By now though – as someone originally inspired by the postage stamps of this isolated British territory – I

Cycling up from Calshot Harbour – where islanders land locally-caught crayfish

'Dual carriageway' on Tristan – passing place on ride towards Hillpiece & Patches

*Chapter 4 ~ **Tristan da Cunha** ~ Potato Patch Pedal Power ~ 99*

thought it high time I paid a visit to Tristan da Cunha's post office, where I bought postcards and stamps and renewed acquaintance with some of the staff I had met back in 2001. My next 'port of call' was the handicraft shop for a few mementoes of my visit where – very appropriately – some island ladies were giving a demonstration of spinning wool on an old wooden spinning wheel: The production of hand-knitted woollens is a traditional island craft and, in addition to the export of crayfish and sale of postage stamps, a useful addition to the island's economy.

After some lunch at Brick Front with Lars, Trina and Andre, I attended yet more stimulating events which the island had laid on in recognition of the quincentenary celebrations: The first of these entailed a visit to St Mary's School (where Trina was once a teacher) for an excellent concert and play performed by the pupils, which featured several gems of island humour thrown in for good measure. This was immediately followed by an islanders versus fishing boat crew football match on the adjacent playing field – the latter team won! A visit to the island supermarket in turn followed that – for food supplies – as by now I had some 'self generated' entertainment in mind....

...Enjoyable as all these worthwhile diversions were, I had now been on Tristan a day already and hadn't yet ventured beyond the village confines, so was really keen to start some serious cycling. My route commenced from the edge of the settlement by a bus stop – yes, unlike Ascension, this was a *real* bus stop for a *real* bus service operating a few times each day between the village and potato patches for the benefit of islanders. I however had the benefit of my own transport, and began by following the main road, quite quickly crossing the deep and rocky Hottentot Gulch, plunging down from the mountain across the plain and towards the sea, although being summer it was fortunately pretty well dry.

I then followed the road through Tristan's *two* sections of dual carriageway ('split lane' passing places actually!), a ride characterised by a steady climb past the Hillpiece – an area of elevated land which is actually a long grassed-over volcanic eruption. Beyond the Hillpiece, there was an arrow-straight descent towards the potato patches which I planned to explore in more depth later in my visit. From here I continued over several gulches and through frequent gates, as the tarmac road progressively became a rough track and finally was no more than twin tyre marks in the grass. At length I reached the coast at a boulder-strewn beach washed by Atlantic rollers (called Gane's Beach) near the end of the settlement plain and close to the foot of Bluff Gulch.

I remember climbing 2,000 feet in 2001 up this very gulch to observe albatross chicks at the 'base' of the mountain. This walk had been incredibly steep, starting with soft red-brown volcanic rock underfoot, the slopes then becoming ever more precipitous with height through an area called Burntwood. The increasing amounts of vegetation – such as tree ferns – had proved invaluable as an aid to stability, not to mention ropes which had thoughtfully (well, essentially!) been provided to haul oneself up the near-vertical sections towards the top. That climb had been worthwhile though, not only for the tremendous views across the settlement plain and out to sea, but also in being able to view fluffy white albatross chicks amongst the green ferns at The Base – not that it was wise to get too close, as they are prone to spit over some distance by way of defence!

On a subsequent visit to Tristan some years later, I was fortunate enough to reach this spot again and see albatrosses variously in flight, engaged in a courtship display and egg incubating on the nest. For now though, there was no way that I was contemplating attempting on two wheels what I had achieved on two feet as I would have been carrying the bike the whole way…although little did I know what I would be doing later that week! At length I returned to the village the same way as I had come, past an array of sheep, cattle, donkeys and chickens grazing on different parts of the green settlement plain.

The day ended in true Tristanian style as a guest at an islander's 21st birthday party, to which the whole community and all the visitors were invited – that evening there were probably around 400 people crowded into Prince Philip Hall, the adjoining Albatross Bar and surrounding area outside, enjoying Tristan hospitality at its best with complimentary food, drink, music and dancing: I remarked to Lars and Trina that I had come to Tristan for a rest, but with so much going on I would have little chance of that, which greatly amused them both!

I awoke on Tuesday to the stillness of a Tristan dawn – however cloud was down over the mountain so some lower level exploration was the order of the day. I began by coasting down to the harbour to watch the boat activity there, where I met island policeman Conrad Glass and we talked for some time about a shared interest in cycling. It was also an opportunity for me to check with him regarding where it was acceptable to cycle. I was starting to fear that the potato patches and back might indeed be the limit outside the village, and I had already been to the former once and around the latter several times.

However, in speaking to Conrad, it transpired that just about *anywhere* on the settlement plain was permissible, whether on roads, paths, grassland, beaches or even volcanic lava; this would at least give me more scope. The settlement plain may only be around 5 miles long by 1½ miles wide at most, but there was still an awful lot to explore on that 'sloping shelf' twixt mountain and ocean.

Thus encouraged, I again pedalled along the main road out of the village as I had done the day before, over Hottentot Gulch and past the Hillpiece, until a fork in the road where I turned right instead of left; this route quickly brought me to the main area of patches, where I had arranged to meet Lars. The potato patches are almost a separate 'village' in their own right, but nobody lives there, at least not permanently – they are however an indispensible aspect of life on Tristan, playing an important part in its agriculture and essential to sustaining the island's community:

Extending for half-a-mile or more, the patches are a series of stone-walled allotments where islanders grow an assortment of vegetables as well as potatoes, the principal crop. Each family maintains plots at the patches, together with potato sheds, and needless to say a lot of time is spent there. As I reached the main area of patches, I spotted an old red tractor – registration no. TDC 27 – which I knew to belong to Lars, and I soon found him outside his camping hut where a convivial half-an-hour was spent chatting over a drink before he resumed harvesting his cabbages and potatoes.

Camping huts are also a feature of the patches, and many of them are to be found in amongst the allotments. The one I visited was furnished with beds, cooker, fridge, sink and other home comforts, and it was easy to see how they provide a welcome break from the village – or "for a bit of peace and quiet" as Lars eloquently put it…or, if preferred, a sort of Tristanian holiday camp where fresh food is always at hand should you require it! Meanwhile, I continued along the road which – after passing the island's second bus stop and countless more patches – became a grassy track and 'looped round' to rejoin the main road…although not before I met some RMS crew members on shore leave and nearly fell off on the damp grass as I wasn't paying enough attention to where I was going!

By the time I returned to Lars he was ready to go, so I cycled in convoy with him – and his two dogs running ahead of the tractor – back along the road towards the village as far as Burnt Hill and the Hillpiece: Here, I went into mountain biking mode and rode – or pushed – my bike up onto both adjoining

The distinctive landscape of Tristan's Potato Patches viewed from the Hillpiece

View towards Edinburgh settlement after cycling up the Hillpiece

hills in succession. Once on the Hillpiece, the reward was a terrific aerial view in one direction of the potato patches looking like multi-coloured chessboards far below, and Edinburgh settlement in the other direction – the only point on the 'plain' where both can be seen simultaneously. There followed a rapid descent of the Hillpiece and main road back to the village, where I paused at the little café by the island swimming pool for refreshment which included crayfish sandwich.

My next 'exploration' was rather less strenuous than the morning's excursion, as I made for the excellent museum, and spent time having an in-depth look at all the exhibits explaining – amongst other things – Tristan's history, wildlife and geology. Before I exhaust the supply of 'ex' words any further, a pause would be in order to examine a little more of the island's fascinating story: After discovery in 1506, Tristan was used occasionally as a base for sealing and whaling ships, and was briefly settled for a period and known as the "Islands of Refreshment" by one Jonathan Lambert and his companions from the USA.

However, the community that exists today traces its origins back to 1816, when a small garrison was sent to Tristan by the British as a further precautionary measure (as had been done on a larger scale at Ascension) to prevent the island being used to mount an operation to rescue Napoleon from St Helena. One of the soldiers of that garrison – a Corporal William Glass from Kelso, Scotland – elected to remain when the garrison was withdrawn, raised a family, and is regarded as the founder of the present community.

Over the years, others joined William Glass and his family, one of whom was Thomas Swain from Hastings, England, who claimed to have caught Admiral Lord Nelson when he fell fatally wounded aboard HMS *Victory* at the Battle of Trafalgar in 1805. In 1827 – courtesy of a passing ship's captain – five ladies were brought from St Helena, and the community started to grow. 1836 brought Dutchman Pieter Groen (later anglicised to Peter Green) to the island after being shipwrecked. 1837 and 1849 brought two more names to the island – American whalers Thomas Rogers and Andrew Hagan. Finally, in 1892, a ship from the Italian port of Camogli was wrecked off Tristan, whereupon two of the sailors – Andrea Repetto and Gaetano Lavarello – decided to stay. These seven surnames are the basis of the island families that exist today and the resourceful, hard-working community that call Tristan their home.

I was soon back on my bike and off again, though this time out on the road east from the village, cycling past – and over – the black lava flow from the 1961 volcanic eruption – an everyday, physical reminder of the island's more recent history which I intended to examine more fully another day. The metalled road rapidly degenerated into a rough track and then a 'sea' of fine lava dust which was not easy to cycle on.

I eventually reached a rocky beach at intriguingly-named Pigbite (yes, something to that effect is reputed to have taken place there!) before returning the same way, pausing to wash my wheels in the "watron" stream which flows past the edge of the village. An evening visit to Brick Front and the Albatross Bar with Andre ended an interesting day.

Although Tristan is incredibly isolated, it is not completely 'alone', and is actually one – albeit by far the largest – island in an archipelago known as the Tristan da Cunha Group which includes two other principal islands – both uninhabited – namely Inaccessible some 20 or so miles west-south-west, and Nightingale a similar distance south-south-west. Wednesday was dominated by a wonderful opportunity – courtesy of the fishing company – to travel aboard the MV *Kelso* to visit Nightingale Island. This also provided a day's interlude from cycling – albeit that several people joked that I hadn't taken my bike on the *Kelso* to Nightingale – now *that* would have been different!

It was a long day involving no less than four time-consuming boat-to-ship (or vice-versa) rope ladder transfers, but was rewarded by the chance to see albatrosses, fur seals, rockhopper penguins and Tristan thrushes at close quarters. Once anchored off Nightingale Island – which has two neighbouring subsidiary isles, Stoltenhoff Island and Middle (or Alex) Island – some of the islanders who had travelled on the *Kelso* went ashore in two island boats lowered over the side. These were loaded with timber which was to be used to repair some of the wooden huts that serve as shelters when islanders visit Nightingale and which had suffered storm damage.

Meanwhile, I was taken with others in a small inflatable boat to a sheltered landing place, and immediately upon jumping ashore we were confronted by numerous fur seals on the rocks. This made a perfect spot for a picnic lunch, watching and listening to the seals as we ate. We were then led slightly inland, walking up a steep path between 'walls' of tussock grass, onto the higher slopes of the island below its principal peak, where there were several sightings of a brown bird known as the Tristan thrush (or starchy).

There were also quite a number of rockhopper penguins – to my mind the

Nightingale Island – wooden huts & rockhopper penguins visible on rocks below

Approaching Inaccessible Island onboard fishing vessel MV Kelso

most comical looking of birds with their hooked beak, slanting and suspicious looking eyes, and yellow tufts (or crests) either side of their heads. I can remember the first rockhopper I ever saw – my first evening on Tristan in 2001 when Lars Repetto had taken me out to the patches and we had come across one lone bird wandering across the road – or "going for its evening stroll" as Lars amusingly put it!

All too soon it was time to re-board the inflatable and return to the *Kelso*, but the day was far from over as on the return to Tristan we sailed around Inaccessible Island, with excellent views of its dark, forbidding sheer cliffs (including a dramatic waterfall) and aptly-named Pyramid Rock, as well as the greener slopes on its western side which shone in the evening sunlight. Inaccessible Island is an important wildlife haven, and numerous seabirds – including albatrosses – followed us as they had done for most of the day. As sunset came, there was even the bonus of a magnificent rainbow across the eastern sky. By the time the *Kelso* reached Tristan it was nightfall.

Nevertheless, on returning to Tristan after dark, I still managed a brief cycle ride through the village between Rockhopper Cottage and Brick Front to take supper with Lars, Trina and Andre: With the wind gathering, a day at Nightingale became more a case of 'night-in-gale', but at least I remembered to switch on my bike lights – I didn't want to risk being apprehended by Conrad Glass!…

…Actually the 'gale' didn't arrive until Thursday…which also happened to be the longest and most challenging day's cycling of my entire visit, so I was glad the weather didn't "make up" (to use a Tristan expression) until that evening. I began my day's travels with a 'warm up' lap round the village: I started outside the Residency (sometimes known as the Administrator's Abode) just as the Union Flag was being raised.

    Nearby I noted a number of longboats which were stored on the wide grass verge beside the road: These traditional boats – made from wood and canvas – were formally used extensively by islanders over the years, particularly before more modern vessels became established, variously for local fishing trips as well as expeditions to Nightingale Island to collect penguin eggs and guano. The longboats can be rowed or propelled by sail, depending on sea and wind conditions.

I then headed across the school playing field towards the island's graveyard – which includes the grave of William Glass – before cycling across the "watron", which is intercepted further upstream to provide the island's water supply. This time though I tried *not* to get my feet *or* bicycle wheels wet – fortunately a thoughtfully-provided small bridge prevented an involuntary dip in the water. I re-entered the village via the road from the 1961 volcano, before cycling down the few remaining roads in the settlement I hadn't yet covered on two wheels:

I had discovered that Edinburgh, TDC, includes a beguiling maze of lanes and paths, and I still occasionally managed to get lost, but it all added to the fun! This meander through the village took me past the 'dong' that hangs behind Prince Philip Hall (a red gas canister which is hit repeatedly to announce incoming mail is ready for collection) as well as Camogli Hospital (named after the port in Italy from where the Repetto and Lavarello branches of the community originated), not forgetting stopping to watch the school sports day.

After a cup of tea with Trina, I set out on my longest excursion of all: I was now getting quite imaginative in terms of maximising the cycling potential of the settlement plain, and my aim was to complete a Tristan equivalent of Land's End to John O'Groats – in other words, the nearest thing to an 'end-to-end' on an island that is essentially circular! I firstly proceeded along the main road past the Hillpiece (where I met Lars returning from the patches), and in turn crossed cattle grids and then sheep pasture requiring me to lift my bike over several gates to avoid continually untying and re-tying their securing string. I cycled beyond the furthest point reached on earlier explorations this way and followed the 'road' until I could go no further. (On Tristan, 'road' describes anything from a tarmac surface to a narrow mountain footpath!) I dipped my feet (and bike wheels) in the sea on the black sand beach by The Bluff, where steep volcanic slopes plunge into the ocean at the south-west extremity of the settlement plain.

I then cycled back towards the village, taking a clifftop route around the patches, passing such coastline features as The Hardies rocks and Runaway Beach. Refreshed by fish'n'chips and a drink from Prince Philip Hall, I continued over the 1961 lava flow and finally took a dusty and very rocky 'road' to reach the beach just short of Big Point at the settlement plain's north-east limits. With 'foot-and-cycle-dipping' done, I returned along the coast to the village – a most fulfilling 12 mile 'round trip'....

...Yet one obvious challenge still remained – scaling the 1961 volcano by bike: This black-grey mound of lava several hundred feet high, and its associated

About to cycle 'end-to-end' on Tristan – bike on beach near The Bluff

Tristan's 'volcanic velodrome' – Simon cycling round crater rim of 1961 volcano

*Chapter 4 ~ **Tristan da Cunha** ~ Potato Patch Pedal Power ~ 109*

lava flow extending to the sea, is the legacy of the major event in Tristan's history which caused it to hit World headlines – and establish it in the conscience of people over a certain age – namely when the island's volcano erupted in October 1961. This event led to the entire island population being evacuated to Britain for nearly two years, but fortunately it was deemed safe to return in 1963, when the majority of islanders chose to resettle on Tristan. During the time they were in Britain, many Tristanians resided in Calshot, Hampshire, which in turn gave its name to the new harbour built subsequently to serve the island.

In exploring the volcano, I chose to approach via the far side from the village, a steep climb requiring me to carry my bike most of the way. I spent some time on – and circling around – the crater summit, enjoying stunning views over the village as well as savouring its surreal atmosphere – including the fact that in places the ground was quite hot to touch over 40 years later. Unbeknown to me, an Australian visitor by the name of Philip Moors – a botanical expert from Melbourne – had been watching my antics from a vantage point higher up the mountain and, amidst great amusement, photographed me cycling round Tristan's 'volcanic velodrome'. "Now I can show folks back home just how mad the Poms *really* are!" he chuckled. A difficult descent down loose scree followed, though once off the volcano I varied my route, returning to Rockhopper Cottage across grassland sloping up behind the village towards the mountain. I may have been exhausted, but the day wasn't over as there was still the official quincentenary reception to attend that evening at Prince Philip Hall, hosted by Administrator Mike Hentley and his wife Janice!

Friday dawned grey and wild-looking, with mist hanging over the mountain giving it a mysterious air. A keen wind was blowing as it had been for most of the night, accompanied by squally showers; it was clearly not a good day for doing much outdoors – or was it? The morning was spent avoiding the rain, although I did manage an interesting visit to the crayfish factory: Conveniently located directly above the harbour – from where crayfish caught by island fishing boats can easily be hoisted up – the factory on this site replaced the original one sited at Big Beach, east of the settlement, which was destroyed by the 1961 volcanic eruption, along with the islanders' best landing beaches both there and at nearby Little Beach. (Ironically, more recently a fire destroyed the second factory, such that a third now serves the fishing industry, on the site of the second, and which I can testify is an excellent, well-equipped facility).

Touring the factory in 2006 was most interesting, as it had been back in 2001, when Lars – who was working there at the time – kindly showed me round. Features included the conveyor chute where crayfish first arrive, crayfish holding tanks, and sections variously involved with sorting, removing the tails, weighing, preparation, packing and freezing. Additionally, the factory includes the generator supplying the settlement with electricity.

Emerging from the factory, I found that the rain was increasingly making its presence felt, and on cycling further downhill I observed that sea conditions had worsened considerably, with waves crashing against cliffs and surging into the harbour. At that moment, the RMS blew its whistle and set off through rough seas to find a more sheltered location. Meanwhile the rain intensified and turned to sleet, forcing me to seek refuge in the nearby museum: Unlike Ascension and St Helena which are located in the tropics, Tristan – at over 37 degrees south latitude and on the edge of the "Roaring Forties" – has a temperate and oceanic climate with rapid changes in weather which can lead to "four seasons in one day"...and this was one of those days!

When the rain eased somewhat, I decided to experience cycling in *real* Tristan weather, in contrast to the warmth and sunshine so far enjoyed: After putting on my waterproof, balaclava and gloves, I set off for a 'loop circuit' of the potato patches. Progress was very slow as I battled through a head wind and driving rain up the valley past the Hillpiece, the whole scene resembling a wild mountain pass in the Scottish Highlands. I continued on a circular route round the potato patches, where I attempted to photograph myself (using my camera's self-timer) next to the bus stop sign. Wet, bedraggled and miles from the village, I met Andre Repetto and another islander in a pick-up. Initially thinking the 'drowned rat' to be some unknown tourist, they had some fun at my expense by – almost – convincing me that I was about to miss the last boat back to the RMS before the ship sailed! "You're having me on!" I retorted when I realised my gullibility, laughing at myself as I cycled back towards the settlement.

My 'wild weather' cycling was still not quite over though, as I then decided to cycle up the east side of Hottentot Gulch on the grassy flanks of the mountain (I was riding a mountain bike after all!) until a vertical rock face – with a rope trailing down – convinced me I had reached the boundary of the settlement plain and thus advisable cycling limits. This was followed by a fantastic freewheel down. A quick cycle round the island's golf course (grazed by cattle) and along the cliffs above wave-lashed Hottentot Beach ended my two-wheeled trips for the day.

Simon cycling in wind & rain photographed at Potato Patches bus stop sign

Real mountain biking – view down over village from slopes east of Hottentot Gulch

112 ~ Chapter 4 ~ **Tristan da Cunha** ~ *Potato Patch Pedal Power*

It may have been the last evening on Tristan, yet the Tristanians had one last social event planned – this time an 18th birthday celebration, and another visit was made to Prince Philip Hall where there was much food, dancing and conversation, including with islanders who remembered me – or I them – from my first visit five years before.

Saturday morning came all too soon, bringing fine weather and signalling departure day from Tristan, and sure enough – during breakfast – I observed the Royal Mail Ship *St Helena* (to give its full name for a change) returning to its anchorage having sheltered in the lee of the island overnight. I meanwhile was about to become part of a 'reverse' postal service myself, as during the course of the morning I was given mail by Lars to take back to his old friends Bill and Norma Sandham in the UK, and also by Tracy Swain who knew Bill and Norma during their time on Tristan in the 1970s. Trina kindly gave me some traditional knitted white Tristan socks (with red and blue bands round the ankles) to take home. Meanwhile, visitors' luggage was being collected and taken to the harbour ready to load onto the RMS.

However, a fellow visitor from England reckoned there was still *one* island road I hadn't yet cycled on – and he was right! Predictably then, this proved to be my last 'purposeful' ride on Tristan – a short abandoned length of grassy track which was once the road to Big Beach and the first fishing factory, but which is now severed (and mostly covered) by the 1961 lava flow.

It was, alas, nearly time to leave – and to label my bicycle for its long journey back to Portland. I was soon cycling down to Calshot Harbour for the last time, where my 'trusty steed' was placed in a cargo net and craned onto a launch to take out to the ship. The long process of saying "goodbye" then began, Tristan-style, with numerous "thank yous" to everyone and especially to Lars, Trina and Andre. Tristan is never an easy place to leave, and the parting in 2006 was if anything harder than in 2001.

Finally, I walked down the harbour steps and into the waiting boat. A minute later I watched as the harbour – and those standing on it waving goodbye – grew smaller and more distant. Five minutes afterwards I was clambering up the rope ladder back onto the ship. Later in the afternoon, the anchor was raised, and with the customary three long whistle blasts, the RMS set sail, initially following the settlement plain to the south-west giving excellent views of Edinburgh, the Hillpiece and the potato patches. Beyond the easternmost limit of the island at Anchorstock Point there were views of the stunning cliffs of Long Bluff falling sheer into the sea, then south towards Cave Point and Seal Bay.

As the RMS sailed away, Tristan stood majestically in the ocean, rising 6,760 feet to its summit at Queen Mary's Peak, which was clearly visible against the blue afternoon sky. The voyage then proceeded past Inaccessible Island and Nightingale Island, before heading south-east for a 200 nautical mile overnight passage to Gough Island. Gradually, the three main islands of the Tristan da Cunha archipelago grew fainter then disappeared from view – Tristan, then Inaccessible, and finally Nightingale.

I was up on deck early on the Sunday morning, just in time to see a faint blue outline appear on the horizon – that of Gough Island, the outlying fourth main island also considered part of the Tristan group, at least administratively, despite being over 200 miles south-east of the archipelago. Lying at 40 degrees south latitude and definitely in the "Roaring Forties" the weather here can be very wild indeed, though this day was blessed with comparatively calm waters.

Gough is around two-thirds the size of Tristan, again with grey, sheer cliffs – and strange-looking rock stacks – around its perimeter, while streams cascade down from the green upper slopes, which are cloaked in lush, thick vegetation and rise over 3,000 feet to Edinburgh Peak, the island's highest point. On reaching the island, the RMS completed an anti-clockwise circumnavigation, offering stunning views of its coastline and interior. However – and conscious my bike was now safely stowed away in the ship's cargo hold – I very quickly concluded that a bicycle on Gough would – as on Inaccessible or Nightingale – be more of a hindrance than a help!

A particular highlight was a pause in Transvaal Bay on the south-east coast, above which is situated the only 'habitation' on Gough Island – the low white building that is the Meteorological Station, staffed by South African met. officers for a year at a time – true isolation indeed! Radio contact was made between the RMS Captain, Rodney Young, and the met. station, and an interesting two-way conversation followed about life on this lonely outpost where ships rarely venture. The shore-to-ship discussion also included comment on plants, mammals and birds to be found on and around the island, for Gough is a major habitat for the endangered wandering albatross and also has World Heritage Site status.

Another interesting point along the Gough coastline was at Quest Bay, where there was a fine view into The Glen – a deep green valley dominated

Simon on RMS leaving Tristan – 6,760 feet summit of The Peak visible beyond

Sailing away from Gough Island after circumnavigation on course for Cape Town

Chapter 4 ~ *Tristan da Cunha* ~ Potato Patch Pedal Power ~ 115

by a huge volcanic plug known as the Hag's Tooth. With that, and a few more strangely-shaped rocks such as Penguin Island and Church Rock (the latter with a 'steeple tower' at one end!), the circumnavigation of Gough Island was complete.

At length the RMS made course for a five day passage to Cape Town, and I was able to reflect on a remarkable week. Another month or so and I would be collecting my bike off the ship at Portland. Cycling on Tristan da Cunha had indeed constituted 'Potato Patch Pedal Power' on several occasions, but it had been a great deal more (not forgetting all the wonderful experiences and incredible hospitality of the Tristanians when I *wasn't* cycling!)…I had come to appreciate the incredible variety of scenery to be found within the few square miles forming Tristan's settlement plain, and so came to understand this part of the island more intimately. I may not have ridden my bike on Nightingale…I certainly cycled less than 100 miles on Tristan over the course of the week…*but* my bicycle travelled for a total of over four months up, down and across the Atlantic – almost 32,000 miles – just to make it possible: Now *that* has to be some kind of record!

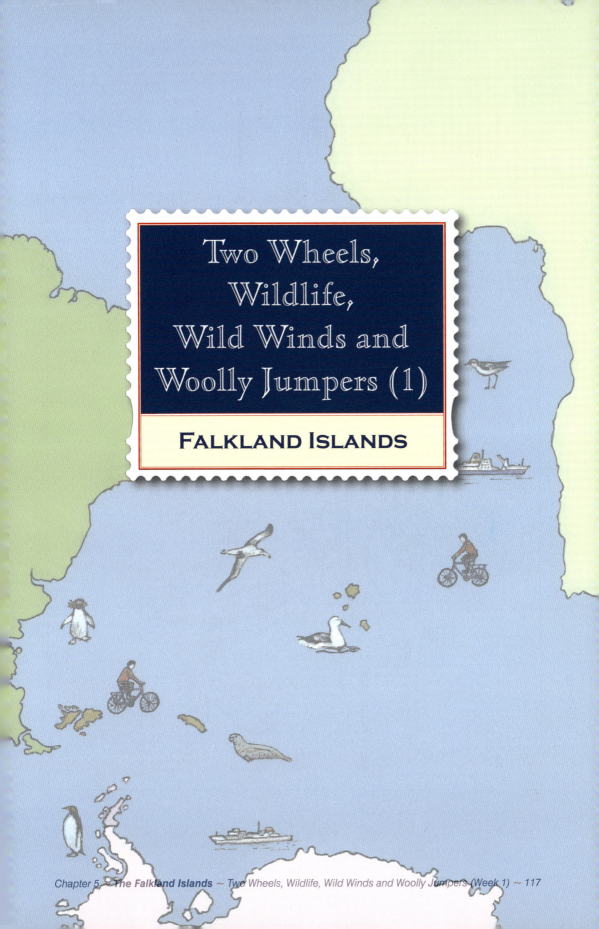

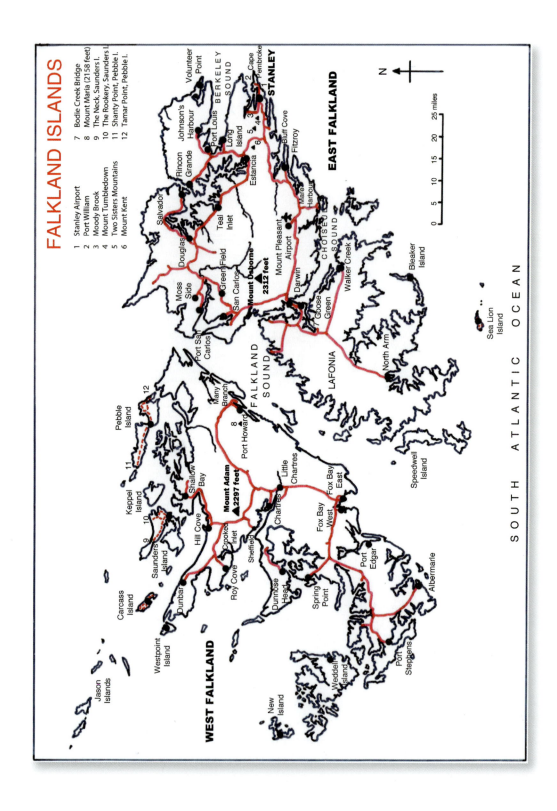

118 ~ Chapter 5 ~ **The Falkland Islands** ~ Two Wheels, Wildlife, Wild Winds and Woolly Jumpers (Week 1)

Chapter 5
Flying Around the Falkland Islands with a Bike (Week One)

Two wheels, wind & woolly jumpers – Simon & Falklands wildlife, Saunders Island

I never originally intended cycling on the Falkland Islands….In fact I hadn't in truth planned to even *visit* the Falklands!...The circumstances which led to me continuing my cycling progress across the South Atlantic to include this group of islands represented more of those 'unintended consequences', albeit that it was arguably the logical 'next step' after my two-wheeled travels around Ascension, St Helena and Tristan da Cunha.

As a result of my initial journeys to those three islands onboard the RMS *St Helena*, and the ongoing interest fostered in their respective communities, I had met and come to know several fellow passengers including Guy and Liz Marriott: Guy had become greatly interested in my cycling exploits to the South Atlantic islands served by the ship, but felt there was definitely some 'unfinished business'.

In conversation with Guy one day, he suggested that "As you've started cycling across the South Atlantic, perhaps you should think about visiting the Falkland Islands?"...although when I *did* start thinking about it, I very soon realised that cycling on the Falklands would be a *very* different proposition compared to the three South Atlantic islands where I had already done so. In fact had I appreciated at the time *just* how challenging it would be, on a number of fronts, I would probably have abandoned the idea there and then. However, I have always relished a challenge, and Guy's gentle persuasion spurred me on to plan and ultimately complete a two-wheeled exploration of yet another fascinating British Overseas Territory.

As ever with cycling in the South Atlantic, challenge number one was the matter of a bicycle – I had utilised the RMS to convey my own bike by sea to and from both St Helena and Tristan da Cunha, whereas for Ascension it had made more sense to have one sourced locally. As for the Falklands, given that – as with Ascension – travel for me would be by air, courtesy of the Royal Air Force via RAF Brize Norton, I reasoned transporting my own bike by this mode wasn't going to be an option.

Interestingly though, I never formally investigated it, and ironically at the initial planning stage I had no idea what would unfold once I reached the Falklands. Fortunately, Guy Marriott was – via an intermediate contact by the name of George Mann – able to put me in touch with an islander on the Falklands – one Robin Goodwin – who provided me with a bicycle, and without whose encouragement, resourcefulness and support the expedition would have been pretty disastrous.

Having made initial contact with Robin Goodwin and introduced myself, I discovered that he was as enthusiastic about my plans – as an islander, as I was – as a prospective visitor. It transpired that, as something of a local entrepreneur, he was considering the idea of setting-up a cycle hire business in Stanley – the Falklands' capital – principally for the benefit of short-stay day tourists arriving on expedition or cruise ships. For the more adventurous visitor (with more time) this concept could perhaps, he believed, be extended to include cycle hire for longer exploration of the wider Falklands countryside over several days:

Enter stage left one keen cyclist who also happened to be an 'island nut', and – we quickly concluded – there were all the ingredients for a very successful partnership, at least in terms of 'trial running' the concept, not forgetting suitability of the type of cycle he was hoping to use (or that which he had available for *my* use at any rate!) The only minor snag was that although he had a mountain bike available, he was unable to easily source a carrier for it (which I would need to convey my belongings as I toured the islands). Fortunately, with some research, I was able to buy a suitable one in England that I hoped would be compatible with the make and model of bike that was waiting for me in the Falklands.

So far so good then, as far as my intended island transport was concerned, that just left (apart from the rather fundamental matter of booking my RAF flights to and from the Falklands!) the question of island accommodation based around an optimum touring itinerary: It was at this point that my problems *really* started. My first mistake was trying to plan a cycling route round the islands as if they were an archipelago of Scotland such as the Outer Hebrides, Orkney or Shetland, all of which I had previous experience of. At this stage, I should have paid a little more attention to the geographical realities of where I was intending to visit, so for the record – and to put this remark in context – here are a few key facts:

The Falkland Islands, located in the South Atlantic Ocean between 300 and 400 miles east of the southernmost part of South America, are an extensive group of over 700 islands spread over an expanse of ocean the size of Wales and which combine to create a total land area of 4,700 square miles, which is about the size of Northern Ireland. Or – to put this in a South Atlantic context – the Falklands are *one hundred* times the size of St Helena! The civilian population of approximately 2,500 (plus 1,000 or so military personnel) is spread across the two main islands – East Falkland and West Falkland – and about a dozen smaller islands. Apart from a concentration of population based at the military establishment around Mount Pleasant Airport on East Falkland, three-quarters of Falklanders live in Stanley; the remaining quarter are spread over a number of widely-scattered sheep farming settlements throughout the rest of East Falkland, West Falkland and several smaller islands.

It very quickly became apparent that if I was to travel 8,000 miles all the way down to the Falklands, *and* attempt to do them justice, I would not only need to allow enough time to explore (I settled for just over two weeks), I would also need to approach the matter – from a cycling perspective – quite differently from the three previous South Atlantic destinations, where everything was contained on single, compact islands. This would inevitably mean a degree of compromise, as I was torn between trying to cycle round as much of the Falklands as possible and / or visiting most of the 'highlight sights' – many of them wildlife-based – which are spread far and wide across the smaller islands…and that was without factoring in inter-island transport practicalities!

I initially concluded that the best course of action would be to concentrate on cycling across as much of East and West Falkland as I could using the fairly extensive road network which I knew to exist on both the main islands – with a ferry to hopefully convey me and my borrowed bicycle between them. However, that left out the opportunity of visiting any of the smaller islands which – as I subsequently discovered – are not to be missed. Just looking at a map of the Falklands was somewhat unfathomable – the easiest way I can think of describing them in outline is as a shark chasing a sea horse (or maybe a dolphin chasing a dog!) representing West and East Falkland respectively, surrounded on nearly all sides by a shower of sea spray (made up of widely varying shapes and sizes) representing all the other smaller islands and islets.

At this stage, I resorted to the Falkland Islands Tourist Board for assistance, and was in turn directed to two companies which both claimed to specialise in assembling bespoke itineraries for intending Falklands visitors. There seemed to be little to choose between them so, almost at the toss of a coin, I opted to engage the services of one of them. It was at this point that I made mistake number two – I chose the wrong one! When I say "wrong one" I mean that their idea of bespoke – and my idea of bespoke (i.e. that which included a bicycle) – were clearly incompatible. It seemed that a 'normal' bespoke Falklands itinerary would start (or finish) in Stanley, followed (or preceded) by two nights each at a range of tourist lodges, mostly on the smaller 'wildlife oriented' islands – and generally in a defined sequence.

The idea of scheduling other overnight stops – notably almost anywhere else on the two main islands or on less frequented smaller islands, never mind with a bike *and* in an order that made logical, sequential sense from a cycling point of view – was obviously unprecedented and not what 'fitted the mould'. I could go on at length about how utterly frustrating and draining the business of trying to arrange my Falklands touring itinerary was, such that I nearly abandoned it altogether, but that would become tedious – as indeed it was!

Enter stage right Robin Goodwin, who – as a proud Falklander (or Kelper as they are known) – wanted to ensure that my experience of his homeland was a positive one. I was immensely grateful for the assistance given by him during the lengthy telephone calls we had in the run-up to my visit, and his offer to 'fill in the gaps' that the standard itinerary could not – or would not – provide. In the end, the final confirmed plan was something of a hybrid 'best of both worlds' solution: I managed to persuade the company arranging my itinerary to organise my accommodation in an order such that – following an initial night in Stanley staying with Robin and his family – the sequence would then be elsewhere on East Falkland, visits to three of the smaller islands, some time at two locations on West Falkland, a further small island, and finally two nights back in Stanley, one of them again with Robin and family.

This would offer some decent cycling opportunities on both East and West Falkland, experiencing some of the finest wildlife sights and other attractions of the smaller islands, and yet still give me time to explore Stanley properly. So…bike sorted, flights booked, accommodation arranged and itinerary confirmed – all seemed to augur well for my expedition to the Falkland Islands – what could possibly go wrong….That was to be mistake number three, although I didn't know it at the time.

The epic trip began for real one day in late January 2008 when, as I had done before when flying to Ascension, I arrived at RAF Brize Norton and presented myself at the entrance office to collect a security pass before proceeding to the passenger terminal building to check-in for my flight. As this was to be a very long journey (just how long would soon become apparent) I took advantage of a filling complimentary dinner and availed myself of a comfortable lounge bar on the military base, before undergoing a final passport check and other formalities prior to boarding the plane in the late evening.

The flight left right on time and was uneventful; during the next eight hours or so I variously ate, slept and ate again as the plane flew over the North Atlantic to the west of Europe and West Africa, crossed the Equator and reached the South Atlantic, before finally landing at Wideawake Airfield on the mid-ocean 'pinprick' of Ascension Island. Here I expected – instead of exiting through the small terminal as previously – to remain in the small courtyard with picnic tables that serves as a transit area for an hour or so enjoying the tropical heat, sipping a cold drink from the NAAFI café and stretching *my* legs while the aircraft was refuelled in readiness for *its* second leg down to the Falklands.

Shortly after re-boarding the plane there came the sort of announcement one always dreads at railway stations when a train is severely delayed or – worse still – cancelled: "Due to high cross winds affecting the runway in the Falklands, there will be a delay of 'some hours' before departure, subject to the meteorological situation 'down there' improving". Everyone returned to the airport transit area, and after another wait came another announcement: "The meteorological situation is not improving therefore the flight will be delayed until tomorrow morning". Arrangements were then made to convey all transiting Falklands passengers – myself included – to bunk-bed dormitory accommodation at RAF Travellers Hill military base on the island. A series of buses conveyed us to our temporary new home, before lunch in the mess room on site, and a whole host of instructions about where to be and at what time – it was starting to feel as if I had suddenly joined the armed forces by accident!

Knowing I would be 'detained' on Ascension for some time, rather than join the island bus tour that the RAF had organised to fill people's time (I knew all about those already!), I decided to telephone my Ascensionite friends Sylvia and Cedric (Cedi) Henry. Pleased at my sudden surprise visit, they met me at Travellers Hill, and a pleasant afternoon was spent in the coolness of Green Mountain as well as 'catching up' on news over a drink at Two Boats Club. I also spent some time with them at their home – South West Lodge – and "Turtle Nest" shop in Georgetown that evening, having first partaken of another mess room meal courtesy of the RAF.

It was an early start the following morning – a Saturday – and after my RAF breakfast I joined a military bus to return to Wideawake Airfield, the terminal building and the (still) waiting plane: I hadn't even reached the Falklands, but was running 24 hours late already, and – given the knock-on effect on 'that' tight itinerary – I had telephoned Robin Goodwin from Ascension so he could activate a contingency plan at his end of things. Needless to say, it was with some anxiety and a doom-laden sense of 'everything going wrong' preoccupying me that I re-boarded the plane that morning, feelings which continued as the much-delayed plane took-off and climbed away above Ascension's volcanic peaks, out over the deep blue waters of the South Atlantic, and turned south-west on course for the Falklands.

The journey continued over the ocean for almost another eight hours, the plane flying well to the east of the South American countries of Brazil, Uruguay and Argentina, the turquoise-blue water far below interspersed with a myriad of different cloud formations. Meanwhile, the time zone changed three times, adjusting from GMT (as observed in Ascension and the UK) to GMT minus three hours in readiness for local time on the Falklands – at least I was gaining back *some* of the lost time and lengthening the day! Finally – when it seemed the ocean would go on for ever – the aircraft began its descent, which was quite dramatic, dropping through thick cloud and mist – quite a contrast after a flight characterised by bright sunshine.

As the plane emerged from the clouds, I had my first view of the Falkland Islands – a vast, empty, grey-green landscape of rough, peaty grassland, devoid of trees and rising to stone-topped hills and crags, punctuated by small lakes and penetrated by large sea inlets defining a much-indented coastline: It could almost have been Scotland's Shetland Islands. This however was East Falkland – the largest and most 'populous' island of the group, yet the slate-grey and pale-green buildings of the military base (the first man-made structures to be seen on the final approach) were seemingly 'lost' in this wilderness. The plane landed on the runway at Mount Pleasant Airport at around 3.30pm local time after a flight of around 4,000 miles from Ascension, and twice that from the UK.

Unfortunately, the late arrival of the RAF flight meant a clash with the once-weekly plane connecting the Falklands with Chile, which had recently arrived, so it was not possible to exit through the main terminal building owing to it already being fully utilised. Instead, passengers were led down the steps from the aircraft into what was now driving rain, onto (yet another) military bus, and conveyed to a huge green hangar which had been hurriedly pressed into service for arrivals purposes. Inside the hangar, immigration took place (I acquired another sought after handstamp in my passport), luggage was reclaimed (which I hadn't been able to access for two days), and a final security check was carried out before I 'stood down' after what seemed like 48 hours as a member of the armed forces – the only thing missing was the uniform!

Once outside, I was duly met as arranged by my host for the first night – Robin Goodwin – along with his son Kenton. After greeting each other, we proceeded to Robin's four-wheel drive vehicle (though not a land rover as many are in these parts) which contained – as also arranged – the mountain bike for my use whilst on the Falklands. We then drove out of Mount Pleasant Airport (locally abbreviated to MPA) and its associated military base, and immediately began to explore. Turning right out of the base, the tarmac was left behind as we headed west along the South Camp Road (or Darwin Road) – my first experience of a typical Falklands gravel road, which in the first couple of miles offered good views back towards the MPA area, emphasising its isolated location effectively in 'the middle of nowhere'…well, the middle of East Falkland anyway!

As outlined earlier, the 'hybrid solution' itinerary that had eventually been confirmed for my 16 day visit to the Falklands included a mixture of cycling on East and West Falkland, visits to several of the smaller islands, and some time in Stanley. However, even with just over a fortnight, this would still preclude a complete coverage of the road networks on the two main islands given the distances and practicalities involved: This is where Robin came in, as he had offered to drive me and the bike in his four-wheel drive over large parts of the road system on East Falkland to enable me to appreciate as much of the scenery as possible, with opportunities for cycling at and between various key sites. This approach was now more crucial than ever since the RAF flight delay meant I had already lost a day, reducing my stay to 15 days, and therefore a contingency plan *had* to be brought into play immediately:

Plan A had been to spend one night with Robin and family at their home in Stanley (the Friday I should have arrived), with the Saturday spent exploring the 'southern half' of East Falkland along the Mount Pleasant Highway / South Camp Road axis extending from Stanley in the east, past MPA, right through to the communities of Darwin, Goose Green and San Carlos in the west. Meanwhile, the 'northern half' – along the North Camp Road corridor from Stanley towards the small settlements of Estancia, Port Louis, Teal Inlet and Port San Carlos (from where I would leave for the smaller islands) would be saved for the Sunday. The delayed arrival meant this was no longer an option, at least not totally, however Robin – as a resourceful Falklander determined to ensure I didn't miss anything – had a Plan B, which he wasted no time in putting into action in the remaining hours of daylight and by now dry weather available to us.

The consequence of all the above explains why rather than heading east towards Stanley that afternoon, Robin instead drove west on leaving MPA, which I really appreciated as there would otherwise not be another opportunity to return to that part of East Falkland over the following fortnight, and I would thus have missed out on seeing some key attractions and notable sites. The gravel road towards Darwin proceeded for some

Mount Pleasant Airport after arrival on Falklands in 2008 via RAF flight from UK

Simon & bicycle at Darwin settlement – first Falkland Islands cycling experience

*Chapter 5 ~ **The Falkland Islands** ~ Two Wheels, Wildlife, Wild Winds and Woolly Jumpers (Week 1) ~ 127*

20 lonely miles, barely passing any sign of habitation (apart from a sheep farming settlement named Swan Inlet) as it rose and fell, meandering through a bare, treeless landscape of peat bog and rough grass moorland with frequent ponds and larger lakes.

At length, we took a track to the left and I was immediately confronted with the first of many reminders of the Falklands Conflict, fought during three months of 1982 over sovereignty of the islands: The track led to the immaculately well-kept Argentine Cemetery, containing the graves of a number of Argentinean military victims of the events of 1982 – a sombre reminder of what had happened here a little over 25 years previously. A nearby hillside marked where some of the fiercest fighting took place in the Battle of Goose Green.

On returning to the road, Robin unloaded the brand-new bicycle from his vehicle, and from this unlikely yet poignant spot I began cycling on the Falklands for the first time, following the gravel road until a turning to the 'camp' settlement of Darwin – 'camp' being a term used to describe anywhere in the Falklands countryside outside Stanley. The small farming community – typical of many such settlements on these islands – consists of just a handful of buildings, including the visitor accommodation at Darwin House where I had originally hoped to stay: This would have been ideal as a first staging post for exploring this part of East Falkland, but it hadn't been possible to arrange that 'officially' (hence Robin's intervention as 'tourist courier' at this point!) As well as a meat salting shed, Darwin also boasts a round stone corral used to contain livestock and dating from the days when South American gauchos engaged in cattle ranching on the islands.

From Darwin, I cycled past another memorial to the 1982 conflict, and continued along the road another mile or so to the village of Goose Green, announced by an attractive sign picturing two geese. Goose Green has a colourful mix of buildings and is the largest settlement in 'camp', attractively situated close to a sea inlet (Choiseul Sound) which, but for the narrow isthmus of land I was now cycling on, would sever the very flat region to the south known as Lafonia from the 'main' part of East Falkland. Robin – who was accompanying me fairly close behind in the vehicle – pointed out the largest sheep shearing shed in the Falklands (I would be learning a lot about the sheep business in the days ahead), as well as the local store, school and community hall. It was in the latter building that over 100 people were for a time held captive by Argentinean forces in 1982.

Simon & bike next to attractive "Welcome to Goose Green" sign, East Falkland

End of day's cycle at Bodie Creek Bridge, World's southernmost suspension bridge

*Chapter 5 ~ **The Falkland Islands** ~ Two Wheels, Wildlife, Wild Winds and Woolly Jumpers (Week 1)*

From this modest farming settlement (though Goose Green is large by Falklands standards) I cycled on south, beginning on the road which leads towards the remote community of North Arm many miles further on across the flat, empty and windswept wilderness of Lafonia. However, I very soon turned off left onto a road which became a track and finally just vehicle ruts in the peaty grassland, passing another unfortunate legacy of the former conflict – an area of fenced-off land marked with warning notices as a known minefield.

More positively, after two miles or so, I reached the truly magnificent sight of Bodie Creek Bridge – the southernmost suspension bridge in the World – which was built to shorten the overland route across Bodie Creek (a wide channel leading into the even wider Choiseul Sound) and formerly provided a 'short cut' to the Lafonia settlement of Walker Creek, but now sadly deteriorating and rusting away. We then returned to the gravel road, requiring some driving skill on Robin's part to avoid getting "bogged" – Falklands-speak for getting a vehicle stuck in the soft peat bog that is so prevalent in these parts.

With my first day's 'introductory' cycling completed, the bike was loaded back into Robin's four-wheel drive and we drove back to Goose Green where we visited some friends of Robin – Liz and John Lee, who were welcoming hosts with tea and cake: Actually, it was a thoughtful gesture on Robin's part to introduce me to them, as another contingency plan (Plan C!) for ensuring I had sufficient time for this corner of East Falkland (given nearby Darwin House was full) had been to spend my first night with Liz and John, but the full day's delay had unfortunately precluded that too!

As dusk fell, we said farewell and began the long journey back east, first the 20 miles to MPA, then a further 35 miles into Stanley which was reached well after dark. I eventually arrived at Robin's home where I met his wife Mandy and two daughters Rachel and Joanne. A welcome supper followed, and – with tiredness now well-advanced – an even more welcome bed.

I awoke on the Sunday morning after my first night on the Falklands staying with Robin and his family at their house in Stanley, and following breakfast there was time for a brief exploration of the town – capital of the Falkland Islands – which I had not yet seen in daylight. I wandered downhill through the town streets to Stanley's waterfront – a long promenade which faces north and enjoys the natural shelter of Stanley

Harbour. Along the waterfront – called Ross Road after a famous Antarctic explorer (a theme giving rise to several names on the Falklands) – I noted in particular Christ Church Cathedral, the nearby Whalebone Arch, post office and tourist board office as well as a few shops, largest among them being the supermarket and hardware store called simply the West Store. However, my itinerary still allowed for two nights in Stanley at the end of my travels, and there was a very full day ahead.

The plan was to explore as many features and places in the remainder of East Falkland as possible before my booked itinerary required me to leave for the smaller islands: Accordingly, I joined Robin – along with daughter Rachel and 'my' bike – in the Goodwin family four-wheel drive, initially heading in the direction of MPA. This included two stops quite early on – the first was to photograph me (for the record!) by the "Welcome to Stanley – Twinned with Whitby" sign (the Yorkshire connection, also for the record, being links to the former whaling industry and interestingly both towns have a whalebone arch). The second stop was to view the quirky sight of Boot Hill – numerous discarded (mostly army) boots on poles by the roadside…my earlier experience on Ascension had taught me that wherever the armed forces are present in an area, one comes to expect roadside 'art' in this genre!

A little further on, we left the MPA road and turned right onto the North Camp Road, which headed first uphill through a mountain pass around the flanks of mist-shrouded Mount Kent, before dropping gradually and crossing some spectacular stone runs – or 'rivers of rocks' – snaking down from the hills and a particularly notable geological feature of the Falklands landscape. As we descended, the visibility improved as the mist lifted, offering views across the camp settlement of Estancia and far to the west. At this point though, we took a road branching off to the north-east which in turn gave a panoramic vista taking in the sea inlet of Berkeley Sound, Long Island, on towards Johnson's Harbour and – far to the north – further camp settlements by the names of Rincon Grande and Salvador. The recurrence of place names on the Falklands of Spanish origin is testimony to the Spanish settlers of earlier times who had – in common with other nations – claimed rights over the islands…a complex history, more of which I would quickly discover.

Our route lay straight ahead however, coming at length to the community of Port Louis, famous in Falklands history as the place where the French set-up their 'capital' when explorer Louis-Antoine de Bourgainville landed nearby in 1764, a garrison was built there and France claimed sovereignty of the islands. Meanwhile, in 1765 Captain John Byron landed at Saunders Island elsewhere on the archipelago, where a settlement was later established at Port Egmont, the islands claimed for Britain and named the Falkland Islands. Then in 1766 the French sold their colonial interest on to the Spanish, and in 1767 Port Louis was renamed Puerto de la Soledad and the islands Islas Malvinas by the Spanish. The Spanish and British retained their respective positions until 1774 when the British decided to leave, and the Spanish likewise abandoned in 1811.

In the early 1820s the Spanish colony in South America that was later to become Argentina asserted a claim as successor to Spain, and by 1828 had established settlements on the islands. The British returned in 1833, and by 1845 had established a new capital on East Falkland at Stanley, where it remains to this day. Today, Port Louis consists of a small fort dating from after the original garrison (the modern-day occupant of which I met) along with an old cannon, stone corral and several houses attractively situated around a quiet sea inlet – in effect, another typical camp farming settlement.

From Port Louis, I did the first stretch of cycling for the day, taking me across camp grassland from the settlement, along the rough track which serves it, and then back along the road towards Estancia, alongside a couple of beaches, to reach the turning to a small settlement called Green Patch. I was by now discovering that cycling on the gravel – supposedly 'all weather' – roads of the Falklands was surprisingly hard work given the friction on the tyres and need to concentrate on steering through the more compacted areas away from loose stones, not to mention the unremitting wind. Robin, Rachel, me and of course the bike then continued in the vehicle to Estancia, where we rejoined the North Camp Road to proceed further west.

This spectacular road rose and fell for miles, crossing ridges of land and sea inlets in succession, and also incredibly isolated Riverbank Farm with fine views of the mountain range known as the Wickham Heights to the south. Along this stretch we stopped for a picnic lunch before continuing on to the next camp settlement, called Teal Inlet, where we stopped to talk to the owners of one house with an amazing collection of ancient land rovers – the almost ubiquitous vehicles of choice on the Falklands – lined up outside! As the road continued westwards, the scenery became ever more beautiful, and by the time the Hope Cottage and Douglas areas had been passed, it was possible to see Mount Usborne – at 2,312 feet the highest

Simon about to cycle away from Port Louis, site of original French 1764 settlement

Simon about to freewheel down to San Carlos on typical Falklands gravel road

*Chapter 5 ~ **The Falkland Islands** ~ Two Wheels, Wildlife, Wild Winds and Woolly Jumpers (Week 1) ~ 133*

point in the Falklands – and several other mountains forming a backdrop to the expansive, undulating moorland.

We then took a left turn and forded the San Carlos River – famous as the best fishing river on East Falkland – and took a steep and winding road across hill country, through many gates which interrupted progress every so often, to a ridge known as the Verde Mountains. From this lofty vantage point there was a magnificent view down the sea inlet called San Carlos Water, which – in the Falklands Conflict of 1982 – became known as 'Bomb Alley' due to the aerial bombardment of the British naval fleet by Argentinean forces. Here – and at nearby Port San Carlos – the British troops made their first landings on the beaches before moving across East Falkland towards Goose Green and Stanley. In stark contrast, some 25 years or so later, all was peaceful in the afternoon sunshine.

From this viewpoint, I resumed cycling, and enjoyed a wonderful freewheel downhill, again taking care on the loose gravel road, especially for enforced stops to open and close a couple of gates along the way. At the bottom of this lengthy hill the road reached a junction, the route left (south) leading over the Sussex Mountains to the Darwin and Goose Green area visited the day before, and along which I would probably have come with Robin and son Kenton to reach San Carlos as part of that excursion had there not been the RAF flight delay. Robin had of course thought of that, and managed to 'squeeze in' a visit to San Carlos as part of day two, albeit approaching from the other direction! I however turned right at the junction and a mile or so more cycling brought me to San Carlos settlement and – just beyond – the British War Cemetery, beautifully situated next to the coast and sensitively constructed in the style of an old stone corral, evoking yet more memories of 1982.

After talking to two men whose naval ship was anchored out in the bay – a reminder of the ongoing military presence in these parts – we returned to the four-wheel drive and resumed our tour by retracing the route back over the ridge past Green Field Farm – Robin's family sheep farm in a stunning location – and on to nearby Corriedale Farm which was gradually being developed by Robin as a new rural venture but at the time a basic set of outbuildings. Shortly afterwards, we again forded the San Carlos River to regain the North Camp Road, and a further turning brought us to Moss Side, a farm which was home to Robin's sister-in-law who we visited for the obligatory chat and cup of tea.

Whilst here, the pannier bike carrier which I had brought from the UK was fixed to the mountain bike, and a fortuitous combination of good pre-planning (i.e. bringing appropriate fixings and tools) and teamwork meant Robin and I were able to successfully unite bike and carrier, an important consideration as the next day I would be leaving East Falkland and therefore need to be able to carry everything with me. I then commenced the third and final period of cycling of the day: After leaving Moss Side (meeting Robin's brother-in-law returning to the farm on the way) I pedalled still further west along the North Camp Road, a ride of just a few miles but the most testing so far owing to much of it being uphill and against the wind on an unforgiving gravel surface, from which I nearly slid off sideways once or twice.

At last, a panorama of Port San Carlos and the San Carlos River estuary opened out below me, and a final freewheeling descent brought me into Port San Carlos itself. I arrived at Race Point Farm – my home for the night – and was welcomed by my hosts John and Michelle Jones. After a chat over yet another cuppa I said "goodbye" to Robin and Rachel who then returned to Stanley.

Meanwhile, just before Michelle served me a filling supper, I was subjected to a very strange 'initiation ceremony' as John brought out the bathroom scales to weigh me, my luggage and the bicycle! I was getting quite used to 'going with the flow' by now, although my puzzled expression doubtless ensured the full explanation which followed: This was my introduction to the quaint delights of the Falkland Islands Government Air Service (FIGAS) which I would be using to reach my next destination, and John explained that he needed to telephone through some 'vital statistics' to the pilot of my flight!

On waking Monday morning, I was soon aware of a noise in the background – that of a power generator engine: Such is the remoteness of camp farms that maintaining an electricity supply in this way is quite common, and whilst still – just – on East Falkland, I was nevertheless now around 70 miles from Stanley. Meanwhile, my breakfast at Race Point Farm was interrupted by a phone call from the FIGAS pilot asking whether I might be ready to leave two hours earlier than scheduled as an opportunity had arisen to 'fit me in' on an earlier flight. A few moments of sheer panic ensued, as that left me only half-an-hour to finish breakfast, finish packing and get out to the airfield! I needn't have worried though, as John was due to load about 200 sheep into a truck that morning and was still waiting for the stockman to arrive, so wouldn't be available to man the airfield, hence the plan quickly reverted to the later time.

This did however give me a chance to cycle briefly around Port San Carlos settlement before it was time to leave for the airfield – actually a sloping grass airstrip on which horses were grazing until a short while before the flight time! I was now about to experience the delightful idiosyncrasies of the Falkland Islands Government Air Service for real: I cycled up to the nearby airfield, while John, Michelle and their daughter arrived in a land rover. After raising a windsock, they radioed the FIGAS pilot with the wind speed and direction. They then backed the land rover into a little shed and connected-up to a trailer on which was mounted a miniature fire tender...and then we all waited for the flight to arrive.

In a matter of minutes, a small plane appeared on the eastern horizon and very soon afterwards landed on the grass airstrip. The pilot emerged and it was decided that – owing to weight restrictions on this particular flight – my bike would be sent on to the right destination the following day. In the event that wasn't a problem as I hadn't intended using it at my next 'port of call' anyway...I however *did* get on the plane – a small, twin-propeller bright red-and-blue Britten-Norman Islander with just eight seats – and after I had clambered aboard, we set off across the bumpy grass field, quickly took-off into the air and left East Falkland behind.

The FIGAS planes fly only a few hundred feet above sea level, so I was able to enjoy intimate aerial views of the Falklands on the 35 minute flight west to Carcass Island. The plane first crossed Falkland Sound – the wide stretch of water separating East Falkland from its similarly-sized neighbour West Falkland – before flying over many tiny islands or islets lying between the north coast of West Falkland and the outlying islands of Pebble, Keppel and Saunders. Just as everyone was getting used to the aerial tour, the plane descended and landed swiftly on the grass airfield serving Carcass Island (the name actually deriving from a ship – HMS *Carcass* – dating from the 1760s when the British first settled the islands). I and five other passengers were met by two land rovers, a fire tender and our host – Rob McGill. After backing into a little shed and detaching the regulation fire appliance, Rob drove us slowly along rough tyre tracks in the grass, up and over a ridge and then down into the tiny settlement, where home for the night was to be the attractive Carcass Island settlement house, a typical

Falkland Islands Government Air Service (FIGAS) plane, Port San Carlos airfield

The attractively situated Carcass Island settlement, home for night whilst on island

Chapter 5 ~ **The Falkland Islands** ~ Two Wheels, Wildlife, Wild Winds and Woolly Jumpers (Week 1) ~ 137

Falklands building with wooden weatherboarding walls and a bright red tin roof.

A filling lunch was served almost immediately, after which I joined three other newly-arrived residents on a visit to the south end of the island. Owing to an absence of predators such as cats, rats and mice, there is an abundance of wildlife on Carcass Island, particularly ground-nesting birds, and on reaching the extremity of the island I was immediately faced with a considerable number of shy Magellanic penguins running around the grass heathland, walking up and down the sand on nearby Leopard Beach or diving for cover in the tussock grass or their burrows, all of it very comical to watch! In addition to the groups of penguins, there were several examples of both Falklands upland geese and ruddy-headed geese, plus small birds such as wrens. Meanwhile, across a narrow isthmus on the beach at Dyke Bay there were some Falklands steamer ducks. After an hour of abundant birdlife, we returned to the Carcass settlement, eating penguins on the way (the chocolate biscuit variety that is!)

Back at the settlement house, Rob McGill showed me the daily printout from FIGAS showing the flight schedule for the next day, which was helpful as it enabled me to carefully plan the rest of my day: I then set off on foot towards the north end of the island, first taking a track along the west coast which offered views across to the Byron Heights on West Falkland and also nearby Westpoint Island. As I climbed over a ridge, I obtained further views far to the north-west towards the outlying and uninhabited Jason Islands. I then crossed the island close to the airstrip and climbed steeply onto the rough, stony flanks of Mount Byng (more a hill really) to reach a point high above the east coast with more wonderful views, this time towards Saunders Island.

I returned down a valley into the pretty settlement just in time for dinner which was – as lunch had been – well-presented and of good quality, thanks to the cheerful Chilean chef. An evening stroll round the shoreline and up through the tussock grass (with several squawking Magellanic penguins diving for cover) to witness the sunset beyond Westpoint Island ended an interesting and varied day.

I was greeted on Tuesday – as the day before – by another wonderful sunny morning, emphasising the vivid colours of the Falklands landscape and seascape. From the dining room at breakfast, I had good views over the bay (known as Port Pattison) and observed that an expedition ship had anchored there: The passengers – I was told – were due to 'drop in for tea' later that day, and soon afterwards a table laden down with cakes was set-up for the expected day visitors.

However, for me it was nearly time to leave Carcass Island, so after having my photo taken for posterity by a shed on the nearby beach declaring "Stop All Whaling", I went in the land rover with Rob back to the airfield, making pit stops along the way to hitch-up the obligatory fire appliance and check the windsock for the benefit of the pilot who was subsequently radioed. A little red-and-blue FIGAS plane soon arrived, signifying it was time to say farewell to Rob and board my flight to nearby Saunders Island, a journey which lasted just 10 minutes and offered distant views of Westpoint Island, the Jason Islands and West Falkland along the way.

Touchdown at Saunders Island (named after Admiral Sir Charles Saunders) was on a bare, dusty runway, following which the plane was met by Suzan Pole-Evans who took me in yet another land rover (the first *red* one I had been in!) to Saunders settlement and my accommodation. I had 'officially' been booked to stay at an isolated location called The Rookery some miles from the settlement, but as there was space in the nearby self-catering house known as the Old Military R & R Centre, on the spur of the moment Suzan agreed that I could stay there instead, which proved to be a wise move.

Once settled into my new surroundings – a typical 'wriggly tin' (corrugated iron) clad building – I went out for a short walk to explore the settlement, which turned out to be a 'textbook' Falklands camp farming community with a main farmhouse, a few other houses, various odd outbuildings, *two* wind generators and a small store for provisions. Being in self-catering accommodation, the latter was important for me, so when Suzan next returned I asked if she could open up the store to enable me to buy the necessary items of food. The store itself was basically a shed, and other than various items of tinned food, rice, chocolate, soups, cartons of drink and bread there appeared to be little else – a result, Suzan informed me, of the recent breakdown of the islands' cargo supply ship, the MV *Tamar*. This was a reminder of the difficulties facing the outlying islands of the Falklands archipelago when vital supply routes are disrupted...at least there was milk in the house...I was also relieved I hadn't relied on that ship to ferry the bike around!

I was also reminded of the other vital supply route in the Falklands, the FIGAS facility, something of relevance to me at the current time as I was still waiting to be reunited with the bicycle I had been parted from at Port San Carlos the previous morning: There was good news there however, as Suzan soon returned in the land rover and we made our way back down to the airstrip, during which time I discovered she was the aunt of an engineer working on the RMS *St Helena* whom I had met on the voyage to Tristan da Cunha two years previously; as I have said once already, the South Atlantic is a very small place! The FIGAS plane soon arrived, and so too did the bicycle, it actually having travelled via Stanley.

At this point, having been made aware again of the South Atlantic being 'a very small place', the supreme irony was not lost on me that whilst I had not even considered the possibility of transporting my own bicycle on a large RAF aircraft from the UK, here I was flying around the Falklands with a bike and on a very small plane! An unexpected bonus of my 'official' itinerary was that provision had been made to fly my borrowed bike not just between East and West Falkland and back, but also to two of the four smaller islands I was scheduled to visit – Saunders and Pebble – each of which I was booked to stay on for two nights.

I pedalled back to the settlement, and wasted no time in having an improvised lunch. With the bicycle now available, I decided to make the first of my Saunders Island explorations on two wheels. After fastening my haversack firmly (containing maps, cameras, drink and some wet-weather gear to be on the safe side), I left the settlement and soon branched off on a steep track that led north-east, up over a ridge on the flank of Mount Egmont (like Mount Byng on Carcass Island more properly a hill) and offering fine views across to West Falkland in one direction and across the island itself in the other. I enjoyed a fairly rapid freewheel down the other side, taking good care to ensure I didn't catch my pedals in the deep rutting caused by land rover tyre tracks. After running around the head of an inlet, the track continued over flatter, softer ground and passed behind a beautiful north-facing beach with a view of Keppel Island.

The main attraction here however was the birdlife, with several large groups of penguins standing on the sand – mostly Magellanic I think, as seen the previous day, although there may have been some gentoo penguins among them...whatever species though, they were incredibly difficult to photograph and kept running into the sea as I approached, only to rather sneakily reappear behind me further down the beach. Meanwhile, some albatrosses could be seen wheeling around the sky, whilst other birds wandered along the sand. I then returned to the bike and cycled up past numerous penguins just standing or disappearing into their burrows, and over the shoulder of Rookery Mountain to reach the isolated accommodation (where I had nearly stayed) known as The Rookery. Just beyond that was the fantastic sight of countless black-browed albatrosses filling the sky and resting on the cliffs.

It was, though, time to begin the five mile long slog back to the settlement, although on my return I varied my route: I opted (with the tide now out) to cross the exposed beach of the inlet I had earlier had to skirt round, and soon afterwards became lost in the spongy diddle-dee vegetation: On the Falklands, diddle-dee grows in profusion, and its red berries are used to make jam, but at this point I was myself well and truly in a jam as I very quickly became hopelessly lost in a green wilderness, the lack of any landmarks or reference points making navigation almost impossible. At least I had been on roads, of a sort, on East Falkland, but on the smaller islands tyre tracks in the grass are as good as it gets, or else there is nothing. Consequently, for the first time in my cycling history I resorted to using a compass in conjunction with a map to ensure I was heading in the right direction!

I soon ran into tyre tracks however, which I followed – seemingly for ages – and which brought me close by Port Egmont, the site of the original British garrison established on the Falklands from 1765 as referred to earlier: It seemed strange to think the British had once been here whilst – unbeknown to them – the French had already established themselves at Port Louis, testament in itself to the vast area which the Falklands archipelago covers. From Port Egmont, it was – fortunately – not far back to the settlement for dinner.

After a good night's sleep in the Old Military R & R Centre (appropriately R & R stands for Rest & Recuperation!) I was raring to go after breakfast, no doubt spurred on by another day of bright sunshine. My plan for Wednesday involved reaching the far north-west of Saunders Island and I would be away from habitation for most of the day, so made a point of checking over the bicycle and stocking up on food and water supplies. Once ready, I set out from the settlement along the same track as the day before, but on this occasion did not branch off but instead continued straight ahead. The track basically ran along the shoulder of the island's central range of hills, and offered good views across the sound known as Brett Harbour towards the hills of the south-west part of the island.

The track began as soft grass, but in the course of the next few miles the

Black-browed albatrosses nesting on cliffs at The Rookery, Saunders Island

Bike lost in diddle-dee vegetation & red berries near Port Egmont, Saunders Island

Simon standing with bike at Saunders settlement (Mount Egmont is beyond)

Approaching The Neck by bike – the 'penguin city' of Saunders Island

*Chapter 5 ~ **The Falkland Islands** ~ Two Wheels, Wildlife, Wild Winds and Woolly Jumpers (Week 1) ~ 143*

surface changed every few hundred yards – or so it seemed. Sometimes the track was across spongy diddle-dee, at other times sand or a form of sandstone, whilst hard camp grass would suddenly give way to soft camp bog (to use two Falklands-specific terms) thereby requiring a detour. As if coping with the surface on two wheels wasn't bad enough – and I thought I had it bad on the gravel roads of East Falkland – trying to navigate my way through the wilderness just added to the challenge of getting from A to B, or in this case from Saunders settlement to a location called The Neck: The track, such as it was, frequently split into two alternative routes – sometimes several more – and whilst all routes generally linked with each other, there was no way of telling which 'loop' would be shortest, have the least worst surface *and* minimise the amount of hill climbing.

There were occasional diversions (of my attention that is!) along the way, such as grazing cattle and timid sheep who all ran away as I approached, as well as the odd gate to negotiate and even a lonely portacabin used by the military. After around two-and-a-half hours and a distance approaching 10 miles, I at last reached The Neck – a narrow isthmus with beaches facing opposite directions connecting the 'body' of Saunders Island to the 'head', the most north-westerly part.

Abandoning the bike close to the green-painted portacabin that acts as accommodation in this lonely spot, I walked down onto the beach, only to discover it was anything but lonely, being occupied by hundreds – possibly thousands – of penguins who were variously swimming, rushing in and out of the water, jumping off rocks or standing, walking or running (as only penguins can!) on or across the sand. They were mostly gentoo penguins, characterised by an orange beak as well as black-and-white features. I tried looking for king penguins too, but they are much rarer here and maybe it was the wrong time of day...the gentoos provided much amusement though! Leaving the throngs of squawking birds who occupied 'penguin city', I walked on along the cliffs towards Elephant Point to enjoy a picnic lunch gazing out over a turquoise Atlantic.

Thus restored I started the long return journey back along the cliffs, across the mass of penguins at The Neck, then resumed my progress by bike. Whilst the return journey featured some familiar areas, I still ended up taking different routes to those on the outward trip. Two interesting stops were made on the way – one to view Falklands flightless steamer ducks in a pool, the other to try and photograph myself (another of those camera self-timer shots) against a backdrop of typical Falklands scenery, sitting on the bicycle, clad in a woolly jumper and hat, with 'woolly jumpers' (i.e. sheep!) and even a Magellanic penguin and chick outside a burrow to add interest. I finally reached the settlement in time for dinner, enjoying an amazing fiery red-and-purple sunset before retiring to bed – I had to be ready for the first FIGAS flight next day....

...Thursday dawned bright and sunny, but if the speed of the two wind generators and rattling of the corrugated tin cladding on the house was anything to go by, it was also a pretty windy day too. Shortly after breakfast I made preparations to leave, and it was not long before Anthony – a relative of Suzan Pole-Evans – arrived in the land rover not to take me to the airstrip as expected but to let me know the flight time had changed. There was some debate about whether FIGAS would be taking the bike on the same flight as me to my next destination – Pebble Island – or whether it would follow me there or *even* if it would be better to have it flown directly from Saunders to Hill Cove on West Falkland, my booked destination upon leaving my next destination! Whilst it would be a benefit to have the bike for use on Pebble Island, more important was ensuring that it arrived in time for my planned road-based cycling on West Falkland.

With time to spare, I rode the bike up to the airstrip and walked back to the settlement prior to 'being called' for my flight – basically, in FIGAS terms, meaning being collected in a local land rover and taken to the airstrip, stopping as ever to couple-up the fire appliance and radio through windsock information to the approaching pilot – I was getting the hang of it by now! After a wait of a few minutes, the red-and-blue FIGAS plane landed and I was greeted by the fourth local pilot I had met so far. Once the plane left Saunders, with me onboard, all eight seats (including the pilot's) would be taken, so there was further debate about how best to transport the bike: The pilot first removed the rear pair of seats (and their occupants!) to see if the bike could be stowed behind them, but that didn't work as the seats couldn't be replaced, so in the event I removed the front wheel and it all fitted-in satisfactorily.

Without further delay, I took my place aboard the plane and we took-off: I was in fact in the co-pilot's seat for this flight, which was quite a novel experience, especially when connected-up to the audio headset! The flight to Pebble Island lasted only 10 minutes, but offered another fascinating glimpse of the numerous islands of the north-western part of the Falklands archipelago laid out below as if on a map. Upon landing at Pebble Island airfield, I was met by Allan White – my host for the next two days – and another islander, and we carried my bags, the bike *and* a special carrier containing Falkland Islands Post Office mail (emphasising the important community role of the air service) the short distance to Pebble settlement.

I was very soon comfortably settled into the spacious Pebble Island Lodge, and asking Allan about the best options for cycling on the island. After the rigours of the 'roads' on Saunders Island I was looking for something a bit gentler on bike *and* body, so it was suggested I spent the day exploring the flatter, eastern end of the island.

So – armed with a map and packed lunch – I headed out of the settlement, past the inevitable wind generator and out across pasture land towards the north coast. My progress was affected though by a rather disturbing creaking sound every time I turned the pedals, so I decided to investigate only to discover that the left pedal was starting to work loose: Clearly the vibrations and frequent knocks whilst negotiating the rough terrain on Saunders Island were already taking their toll. Putting worrying thoughts to one side however, I continued onto the long sandy expanse of beach at Elephant Bay and cycled almost its complete length, noting birdlife such as Magellanic oystercatchers with their long red beaks – my ornithology recognition skills seemed to be improving!

I then crossed the sand dunes and continued over hard camp white grass, past numerous burrowing Magellanic penguins, to a 'parting of the ways' (tracks diverging in different directions): This low-lying landscape of heathland interspersed with small ponds and some larger lakes – such as Swan Pond – stretched on for miles, and bore a passing resemblance to a cross between the Outer Hebrides and the Norfolk Broads. Consequently, despite a map, it was quite difficult to navigate, and I was again glad of the use of a small compass for direction finding. On both Saunders and Pebble Islands I was reminded just how difficult travelling around camp must have been in days gone by, when fairly routine journeys would have taken most of the day – or longer – particularly before the roads developed on East and West Falkland.

After another beach covered in pebbles (Pebble Island takes its name from small translucent pebbles found on its beaches), my left pedal started to wobble more seriously: Clearly pebbles were not good for pedals, such

View of Pebble settlement, a typical 'camp' community – note the wind generator

Difficult cycling conditions through pebbles on Pebble Island north coast beach

that by the time I made a lunch stop above some fine cliffs, the pedal was virtually unusable. Fortunately my mood was lifted by the incredible birdlife seen in the next few miles towards Tamar Point, beginning with an amazing colony of both cormorants and my favourite penguin species – of Tristan da Cunha fame – the rockhoppers, comical creatures standing, flapping and squawking, just waiting to be photographed. These were followed a little further on by some rather tame gentoos who were keen to investigate me!

With photos taken, I started the long return journey to the settlement, cutting across beyond a sea inlet called Ship Harbour to regain the beach at Elephant Bay, where I followed my cycle tracks made in the sand on the outward trip to ensure I cut through the dunes at exactly the right point! Progress was slow, riding being interspersed with walking, as I was forced to frequently hand-tighten the pedal. After a pleasant dinner back at base, Allan – concerned at my plight – produced a spanner from a vast collection of tools and the pedal was soon fixed…I was quickly realising how self-reliant Falklanders have to be, and from my perspective a good job too!

On opening the curtains in my room at Pebble Island Lodge on Friday morning, the sun was out but the sky did look rather 'changeable'. After breakfast, and with a couple of hours to spare before I was due to be dropped-off towards the western end of the island for a day's exploring, I decided to walk out to the memorial to the naval vessel HMS *Coventry*, which was lost during the 1982 Falklands Conflict. I set off from the settlement under threatening skies and with a keen wind blowing, and once clear of the airfield the weather had reached such a pitch that I was glad of my waterproof coat and trousers, hat and gloves.

By the time I had climbed the lower slopes of First Mountain, and reached the HMS *Coventry* memorial, there was sleet and hail blowing in horizontally from the sea, and this on a day (1st February) that was supposed to be the equivalent of 1st August in the northern hemisphere – some summer! The simple memorial was adorned with several poppy wreaths and the exposed location only served to reinforce the reality of the sad and dramatic events of 1982, despite the passing of the years. In fact Pebble Island played a major role in the Falklands Conflict, one notable event being the SAS raid on grounded Argentinean aircraft on the airfield; a small cairn on the airfield's edge recalls the event.

I returned the same way back to Pebble settlement, and after a quick coffee, the bicycle was placed in the back of a land rover, and I – along with another visitor – was taken by co-host Jacqui on a very bumpy journey across camp which lasted about an hour until we reached a north-facing beach towards the island's western end. Here we were dropped-off at a stimulating location thronged by an almost exclusive colony of rockhopper penguins, and I spent some time transfixed by these 'loveable rogues with attitude' and enjoyed my picnic lunch watching their antics. Interestingly, there were two macaroni penguins amongst the colony – similar to the rockhoppers except macaronis have larger, more orange (as opposed to yellow) tufts and are generally taller; I may not have seen king penguins yet, but at least I had now managed to spot four distinct species.

I then continued my explorations by bike, heading further west past glistening Marble Mountain and a number of inquisitive horses (had they ever seen someone riding a bicycle before I wondered?) to reach the western limits of the island. My progress was slow owing to a strengthening and incessant headwind, but at length I reached a little shanty once used by shepherds, and walked down onto the beach near Shanty Point – with views across to Keppel and Saunders Islands – where I enjoyed the company of more gentoo penguins and a couple of striated caracaras, or "Johnny Rooks". The beach where Pebble Island's distinctive translucent pebbles are sometimes washed-up also lay nearby.

Once I started heading east back towards Pebble settlement, I had the wind at my back for most of the way, and the three peaks of Marble Mountain, Middle Peak and First Mountain passed reasonably quickly as I crossed mile after mile of wild camp, occasionally coming across a herd of timid sheep, and eased by a bike which no longer had a loose pedal. I finished the ride by cycling down the airstrip – another 'first' for me on a bike – and arrived back in the settlement just in time to see a huge number of those 'woolly jumpers', or sheep to be more precise, being herded back out to pasture after a day's shearing – needless to say they looked distinctly *less* woolly and *more* chilly! A convivial dinner followed, two other guests being a couple I had met on Carcass Island, and I ended the evening with a blustery walk around the settlement and immediate surroundings as the sun dipped over the horizon.

Saturday morning was heralded with sunshine streaming through the window, but accompanied by a keen wind, in fact a wind that had been

Simon on bike & rockhopper penguins along north coast of Pebble Island

Newly-shorn sheep in pens at back of shearing shed on Pebble Island

150 ~ Chapter 5 ~ **The Falkland Islands** ~ *Two Wheels, Wildlife, Wild Winds and Woolly Jumpers (Week 1)*

blowing almost incessantly for most of the night. Prior to breakfast however there was a chance to witness a very traditional Falkland Islands activity taking place – that of sheep shearing. I walked, along with another guest, the short distance to the shearing shed at the lower end of Pebble settlement, and upon entering was confronted with a frenetic scene of industry – several shearers (contractors who had arrived by air the day before) were mechanically shearing sheep to produce a single complete fleece, the operation per animal seeming to last little more than a minute or two: As each sheep had its wool removed, it was sent through a gate back into the enclosure behind the shed while a fresh, fully-fleeced sheep was allowed in, and so the process continued in a very methodical way. Whilst this was ongoing, other participants collected the shorn fleeces and placed them on a table to sort or grade them, before depositing them in various alcoves. The final stage involved placing the graded fleeces into a hydraulic wool press that compressed them into sacks (known as bales) for onward transfer.

Just before leaving though I noticed that the shearing shed clock was showing 7.50am when I was under the impression it was already 8.50am.... So came my first introduction to the strange concept of there actually being *two* time zones on the Falklands – what I had been used to up to now, GMT minus three hours or 'Stanley time' – and GMT minus four hours or 'camp time', the latter being the time zone traditionally adhered to in agricultural communities to give more daylight in the mornings.

For all that though, my impending flight from Pebble Island was at 10.00am (Stanley time) and it was not long before Allan White took me, my bags, the bike and another passenger in the land rover up to the airfield. With windsock raised, it was only a short wait until the red-and-blue FIGAS plane (I never saw any other colours!) landed, this time on the shorter cross runway owing to wind conditions. A few minutes later, after thanking Allan, I was airborne once again enjoying yet another birds-eye view of the Falklands. On this occasion there was a brief touchdown 10 minutes later at Saunders Island (to let off one person) and then a five minute 'hop' across the Byron Sound to land at Hill Cove, on the north-facing coast of West Falkland:

It was now my middle Saturday, and I was exactly half way through my fortnight's exploration of the Falklands. The first week had seen me cycling at several locations across the main island of East Falkland, as well as on two out of the three smaller islands I had subsequently visited. I had additionally experienced mile after mile of the Falklands landscape when I *wasn't* cycling – whether viewed from other land-based transport or appreciating the archipelago from the air during the various inter-island transfers...not forgetting several historic sites, wildlife havens and meeting some friendly Falklands folk along the way. The weather had also been (reasonably) kind to me, save for the seemingly ever-present wind, however there were still many more experiences...and much more weather...to come.

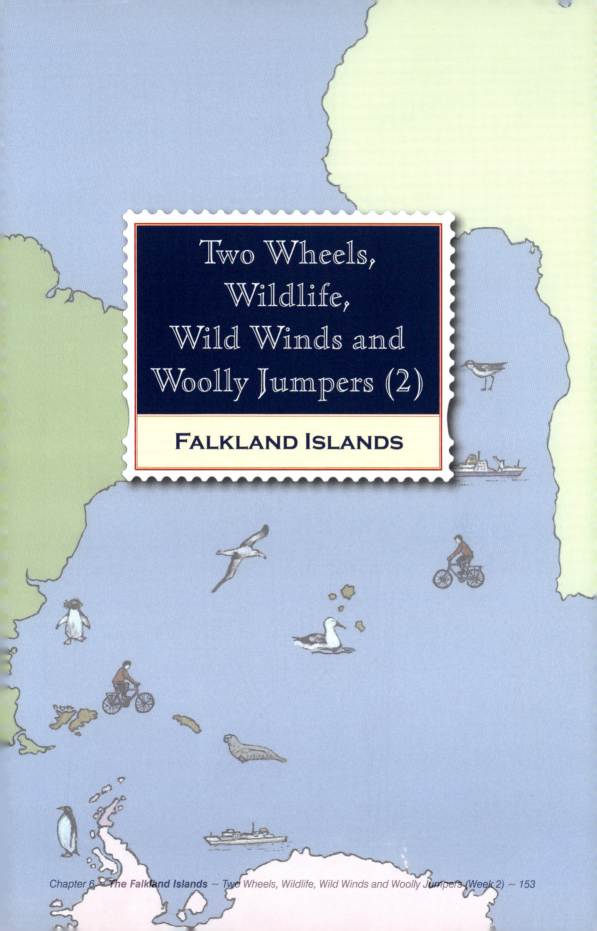

Chapter 6 ~ *The Falkland Islands* ~ Two Wheels, Wildlife, Wild Winds and Woolly Jumpers (Week 2) ~ 153

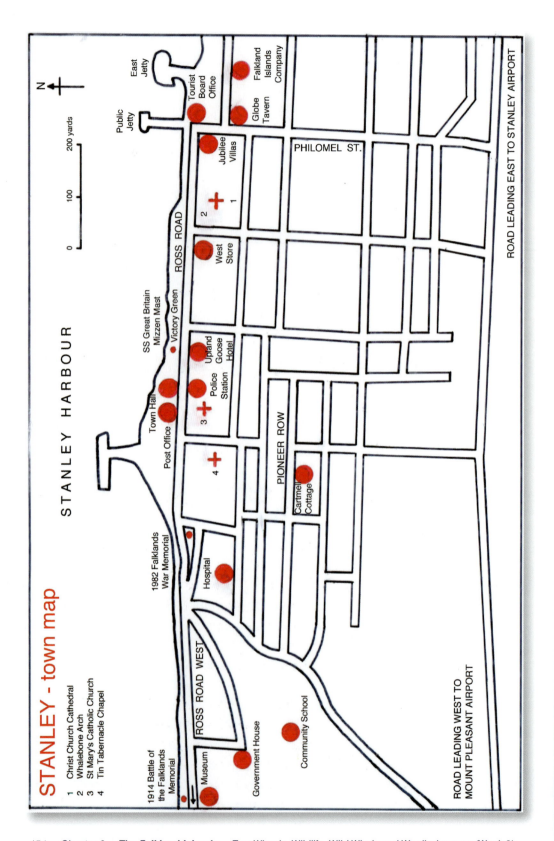

154 ~ Chapter 6 ~ **The Falkland Islands** ~ Two Wheels, Wildlife, Wild Winds and Woolly Jumpers (Week 2)

Chapter 6
Flying Around the Falkland Islands with a Bike
(Week Two)

Simon on Public Jetty in Stanley after two weeks of cycling around the Falklands

I had high expectations of my second week on the Falkland Islands – particularly from a cycling point of view – during which I hoped to tour the other main island of West Falkland fairly extensively, as well as visit a further small island, concluding with a return to East Falkland and further cycling – not forgetting sightseeing – in and around Stanley, the Falklands capital: Such was my anticipation as I left the FIGAS plane after landing on West Falkland's north coast at the Hill Cove airfield.

The plane was met by Peter and Shelley Nightingale, who were to be my next hosts. Soon afterwards I was taken in their four-wheel drive vehicle – via some houses near the airstrip to deliver (air)mail – to their house in another part of Hill Cove settlement about a mile away: West Lagoons Farm, which was to be my next temporary home, was another typical Falklands building with much 'wriggly tin' cladding.

I was welcomed in traditional Falklands fashion with mid-morning "smoko" – the term used for a restorative cup of tea or coffee with cakes – and was soon explaining to Peter and Shelley my plans for exploring West Falkland by bike. Given that I was due to be based four days on this other main island, it offered considerable scope in terms of cycling, and I was certainly keen to get in the saddle as soon as I could. What I *hadn't* considered, or perhaps *didn't want* to consider, was the extent to which the weather might play a factor in those cycling plans.

My initial intention was to cycle to Roy Cove settlement, situated several miles to the south-west, but given the increasing wind from the prevailing south-westerly direction, Shelley offered to take me and bike in the land rover uphill from the cove to the ridge of hills immediately south of the settlement by way of a 'head start'. Although in theory I ought to have been able to freewheel the first mile or so down the other side, the full-on headwind meant that was not possible, and riding (as in trying to turn the pedals) was interspersed with much bike pushing. Even after I took a right turn onto the Roy Cove road, the side wind still caused problems due to me and bike being blown across to the right-hand side of the road: It is as well, then, that traffic on West Falkland is light, I saw a grand total of just two vehicles going in the opposite direction! Meanwhile, I was having to get used to Falklands roads again – the rough, stony gravel surfaces which were either arresting progress on the uphill stretches or causing serious vibrations (to cycle *and* cyclist) on the downhill sections.

In spite of all this, and the loneliness, the scenery was wild and very atmospheric, dominated by the brooding presence of Mount Adam away to the east – at 2,297 feet the highest peak on West Falkland – and the curved sea inlet called Crooked Inlet to the south. After a worrying moment at an unsigned junction where taking the wrong turn would have been disastrous (I would have ended up in a place named Dunbar), and a final climb, a wonderful panoramic vista opened up of the west coast of West Falkland: In the far distance, beyond various islets a little way out to sea, was the outline of Weddell Island – third largest in the Falklands group (and therefore largest of the smaller islands) – while somewhere on the western horizon was New Island, both islands being noted for their wildlife.

I chose this viewpoint to eat my packed lunch, before descending into – and discovering suddenly – Roy Cove settlement, tucked away in a natural bowl. I found the farmhouse, but nobody appeared to be at home; however I spotted

West Falkland wilderness, a seemingly endless cycle along gravel road to Roy Cove

Panoramic view of Roy Cove settlement looking south-west towards Weddell Island

*Chapter 6 ~ **The Falkland Islands** ~ Two Wheels, Wildlife, Wild Winds and Woolly Jumpers (Week 2) ~ 157*

a land rover across in a nearby field, and quickly found farmers Dan and Joy Donnelly who were busy marking sheep. In the course of chatting to them I discovered they were originally from Northern Ireland – indeed so far I had come across English, Welsh, Scottish and Irish surnames amongst the islanders I had met, in many cases descendents of settlers who came out to start a new life in the Falklands during the 19th century along with thousands of sheep. As I was rather dehydrated by this point, I also filled my drinking water bottles from their tap ready for the return trip.

Cycling back towards Hill Cove was easier than the outward journey – which had taken a gruelling four hours – thanks to a following wind, and towards the end this was further aided by Peter who came out to meet me in his vehicle…the Donnellys had kindly telephoned to let him know I was on my way. I wasn't taken all the way back to base though, as before dinner I wanted to do the downhill run into Hill Cove from the ridge where I had been dropped-off that morning, which also offered a good vantage point above the largest forest in the Falklands, which is in truth a modest area of woodland, though notable in these parts.

Sunday morning dawned rather grey and there was more than a hint of rain in the air. Over the breakfast table I debated what my options were for the day, cycling-wise, given the weather conditions. I was keen to make a prompt start, and managed to leave Hill Cove settlement around 9.00am, although this being camp time (as I had discovered upon my arrival in West Falkland the previous day) it felt more like 10.00am. Whatever time it was, I was nevertheless glad to have warm clothing, suitable waterproofs and an ample food and water supply as I slowly made my way up the steep hill out of Hill Cove towards the ridge – actually a pass or 'saddle' between Mount Adam and Mount Fegan. The mist was down and forward visibility was not good as I rode on, past the turn to Roy Cove, and towards the green mountain interior of West Falkland – The West as it is termed, or (as it was increasingly starting to feel like it) the 'Wild West' on account of the rain and wind that seemed to get worse with each passing mile. The one consolation was that the wind was a north-westerly which was behind me for most of the way, although its main effect seemed to be to drive the rain ever more horizontally.

At a turning to a farm with the unlikely name of Sheffield, I started to wish I was in South Yorkshire during a British winter rather than battling the elements of a South Atlantic summer! The Falklands are actually located at an average latitude of 52 degrees south – the same distance from the Equator as London is north of it – yet the combination of a much greater proportion

Simon & bike at vantage point above Hill Cove & the Falklands' only 'forest'

Bike by road in Chartres settlement after a very wet & windy ride from Hill Cove

*Chapter 6 ~ **The Falkland Islands** ~ Two Wheels, Wildlife, Wild Winds and Woolly Jumpers (Week 2) ~ 159*

of ocean compared to the northern hemisphere and (relative) proximity to Antarctica means that direct comparison in meteorological terms can be misleading.

I briefly stopped here and met a lorry driver with a large culvert pipe secured to his vehicle: It turned out he was part of a 'road gang' working for the Falkland Islands Government, and said he would let others know I was out on the road – and to look out for me – due to it being such atrocious weather. I thanked him and went on my way, little realising that I was about to experience local hospitality and concern, West Falkland-style, something of importance to travellers in what is effectively a wilderness and where everyone looks out for everyone else. A few miles further on, I met an islander in a land rover who also stopped to check that I was alright. Although the wind was helping with my progress, the rain had by now turned the gravel road into a slippery, muddy track, and my bike and waterproofs were severely mud-splattered.

At length, I reached the point where the roads from Hill Cove, Port Howard and Fox Bay meet, and it was at this point that another Falkland Islands Government vehicle stopped – driven by two men who were also part of the road construction gang, based at nearby Little Chartres: They had been contacted by the lorry driver I met earlier and asked to take me on to my intended destination – the settlement of Chartres – so, with bike placed in the back of their pick-up, we went on our way. It turned out their names were Edgar and Martin – the latter being a brother of Ian Pole-Evans, engineer on the RMS *St Helena* whom I met in 2006, and whose aunt (Suzan) I had already met on Saunders Island a few days before…small world syndrome again!

We soon reached Chartres and my 'rescuers' unloaded the bike: I had been told by Shelley to call at the second house in the settlement where I would find two people by the names of Penni and Tex – on arrival I was made most welcome, and despite probably looking like some slimy brown creature from the deep, was able to dry-out in front of their traditional peat-fired range and eat my lunch in the warmth, having first had a hose-down in the garden, along with the bike! The rain started to ease off during the afternoon and the sun came out, so I took a short stroll and then cycled around the settlement which is attractively situated by the mouth of the Chartres River in West Falkland's 'mid-west'.

Returning to the house, I was soon joined by Peter who had driven over with one of two other guests also staying at West Lagoons Farm, and we spent a lazy Sunday afternoon discussing all manner of sheep-related business, where the size of a farm is denoted by how many sheep there are – generally in the thousands: I was by now realising that those engaged in the sheep and wool trade on West Falkland are an incredibly close-knit community! The journey back to Hill Cove in the land rover – with bike – enabled me to see the scenery in the sunshine and I certainly enjoyed dinner that evening after the rigours of the day.

I had begun to get rather used to the wind that seems to blow almost continuously in the Falkland Islands, although on certain occasions it seemed to be blowing just that bit more ferociously. The night I had slept through – well, only partly slept through to be more precise – was one such occasion, as I was aware for much of the night that the wind was rattling the windows of West Lagoons Farm. It was with a sense of unease that I went downstairs early that Monday morning, and observed the wind generator rotating at great speed and the 'white caps' out on the sea.

The reason for my unease was that I was due to transfer between Hill Cove and Port Howard, 50 miles away by rough gravel camp road, on the eastern side of West Falkland, and I would need to take all luggage with me on the bike. My experience of cycling on West Falkland thus far had not been easy, and I had come to the rather rapid conclusion that the best plan of action would be booking an extra FIGAS flight between Hill Cove and Port Howard. Whilst I was away at Chartres the day before, Shelley had made the booking on my behalf, and by the time I had returned it had been confirmed by FIGAS: There was, however, now the matter of the wind, and with it being strong to gale force it was soon apparent that all local flights were to be grounded for the morning at least.

The uncertainty created something of a problem, and so a back-up plan was devised: If Plan A (flying) didn't happen, Plan B was to involve me (plus bags and bike) being taken in the land rover as far as the junction I had cycled to the day before, me then cycling with all belongings attached to the carrier on the bike (courtesy of a following wind) for a number of miles towards Port Howard, and then somebody coming out from there to 'intercept' me. There was some further debate – and quite a bit of good-natured teasing at my expense – regarding what would happen if the contingency plan came to nothing (i.e. I would be on my own!) but it was generally agreed it was best to make constructive use of the morning as nothing was going to happen on the FIGAS front until at least noon.

Accordingly, after breakfast, Peter invited me and another of the guests to assist him with loading and carrying wool bales: We took a land rover and trailer, plus a pick-up, several miles along the road towards Shallow Bay, before taking a camp track across to the West Lagoons shearing shed, where I learnt the art of shifting, loading and securing 200 kilogramme wool bales. We then returned to Hill Cove shearing shed and unloaded the bales ready to be shipped-out from the adjacent boat jetty; this would be via the much-delayed MV *Tamar* cargo vessel that I had heard about from Suzan Pole-Evans when explaining the lack of provisions on Saunders Island.

After my modest contribution to the local wool-based economy, I returned with the others to the house for some lunch…then it was decision time: Just in the nick of time a message came through that FIGAS were flying again, so Peter took the decision to go sheep chasing with the other two guests and we said our goodbyes. I meanwhile waited for the flight with Shelley, although still managed a quick cycle round the settlement – actually it was a slow cycle, as the wind was still of such strength that I was blown off, albeit with a soft landing, but it convinced me trying to cycle to Port Howard in such conditions would have been dangerous.

In due course, I went up to the airfield with Shelley, said farewell, and took a flight, via Saunders Island again, and back across West Falkland, to land at Port Howard – total flying time 20 minutes. I was met by co-hosts Sue and Wayne who took me the short distance to Port Howard Lodge, where I found Phil and Jill (the couple I had met on both Carcass and Pebble Islands) were already staying, plus another couple from England.

Once settled in, I wasted no time in exploring the settlement, starting with the store where everyone from the area seemed to be gathering as witnessed by the concentration of land rovers! My explorations continued by bicycle, and included a brief ride back up to the airfield to enjoy the view one way across the stretch of water known as Port Howard Narrows and the other across the pretty green-and-white painted settlement towards Mount Maria. Actually, calling the landing strip at this location an airfield is to do it an injustice, as the words "Port Howard Airport" bear witness to on a modest shed which acts as the airport 'lounge!'

I then continued by bike through the heart of the settlement, over a rustic bridge and ford across a stream, and down past the ever-so-predictable shearing shed to the jetty, which at Port Howard includes fencing and gates presumably to direct sheep down to the waiting cargo vessel. I continued

Port Howard Airport 'lounge' (plus bike) with settlement & Mount Maria beyond

Simon outside Port Howard Lodge about to explore more of West Falkland by bike

uphill, through a gate bearing the legend "Welcome to Port Howard", and out onto open sheep pasture where there were numerous 'woolly jumpers' spread across the hillside in all directions. I then cycled along a bypass road behind the settlement as far as a shed proclaiming that I was passing Chippy Hill Golf Course, before completing my circuit back at Port Howard Lodge, which I found to be a substantially built and homely establishment with wood panelling, a very antiquated telephone on the wall and wildlife pictures around the rooms: In fact, if I hadn't known otherwise, I could have suddenly been transported to a dated fishing hotel or shooting lodge in the Scottish Highlands! A very good dinner with the other four guests followed and a chance to relax and exchange news of our experiences.

I had set my alarm clock for a rather unsociable hour on Tuesday morning, principally owing to my arrival in Port Howard the previous day somewhat later than originally envisaged, and the intention I had of climbing Mount Maria (which rises up directly behind the settlement) during the time I had available in this part of West Falkland. I was therefore up and out of Port Howard Lodge by 5.30am, making my way on foot up the valley of the nearby stream and then onto sheep pasture rising all the time towards a jagged outcrop known as Freezer Rocks. During this time I witnessed the sunrise, illuminating in fiery red the eastern slopes of Mount Maria which were above me to the west and still a stiff climb over rough ground and stone runs. After nearly two hours, I reached the 2,158 feet summit – one of the highest peaks on West Falkland and offering a fantastic all-round panorama.

From the summit there were views of a number of smaller islands to the north, the mountain wilderness of West Falkland to the west, the flat lands of Lafonia on East Falkland to the south, and finally out over the sheltered waters of Port Howard and Bold Cove towards Falkland Sound to the east: It is generally believed that the islands were first discovered by English mariner John Davis in 1592, although the first landing is credited to fellow countryman Captain John Strong in 1690 who landed at Bold Cove and named the nearby sound after Viscount Falkland, the name eventually used for the island group. Given its strategic elevated location Mount Maria is also home to a fair number of telecommunications masts serving the entire islands. Having enjoyed the excellent view, I made the descent in about an hour, arriving back just in time for breakfast.

However, there was still the main part of the day to be filled, and in this respect I had arranged to go out with two other guests in a four-wheel drive vehicle on a day's tour to Fox Bay, another of the main West Falkland settlements some 50 miles away and somewhere I would have liked to stay had the itinerary permitted it. So – with bicycle aboard – we left Port Howard, past the Purvis Pond airstrip used as an alternative airfield in certain weather conditions, and out onto a long and lonely gravel highway called simply the West Falkland Road. There were distant views of mountains to north and south for mile after mile, with occasional distractions such as some roadworks, the crossing of the Warrah River and the sight of farmers occupied in sheep gathering: In many ways, the Falklands are a microcosm of the way of life that exists across the vast sheep stations of Australia and New Zealand, and every day I spent on West Falkland I became more aware how much of life revolves around these animals.

Back on more familiar territory, the junctions of roads to Hill Cove and Chartres were passed, then a river crossing at Little Chartres, immediately followed by the 'road gang' base where I recognised the vehicles instrumental in 'rescuing' me two days before: The base, I had earlier been told, was to service the building of a new road link to isolated Dunnose Head, located on the west coast of the island, and an example of the ongoing process of gradually improving communications across the Falklands.

Another landscape of numerous small lakes ultimately brought the West Falkland Road to Fox Bay, facing south into the cold blue waters of the South Atlantic and framed by headlands on either side. Here the road split into two; our route to the left brought us through Fox Bay Village (or Fox Bay East) and on to an off-road section leading to a small gentoo penguin colony. I opted to start cycling from here, back over camp tracks to Fox Bay East, a camp community big enough to have a few streets as well as the inevitable boat jetty and shearing shed that are the hallmarks of such settlements and – significantly – a former woollen mill.

I then cycled round the large arc of the bay on a gravel road, moving gradually into a headwind as I went, and passing a turning to Spring Point and Port Stephens – both areas in the extreme south-west of West Falkland – however seeing their names on a white signpost was the closest I could hope to get to them! The curving bay brought me to Fox Bay West, the smaller of the twin settlements, a collection of a few houses where I had my picnic lunch on yet another jetty in the shadow of yet another shearing shed.

The return trip in the four-wheel drive included a stop at Little Chartres Farm for tea with the owners Jim and Lesley Woodward – and a walk around its

Fox Bay East, a large 'camp' settlement featuring an old wool mill & shearing shed

Cycling round bay into Fox Bay West, like its 'twin' facing the cold South Atlantic

pretty riverside environs – before 'hitting the gravel' again. I was dropped-off on the approach to Port Howard however so as to give me an opportunity for some more cycling: I took a winding road leading to Many Branch Farm, where I enjoyed *more* tea and cakes, courtesy of owners Bill and Shirley Pole-Evans – parents of Ian the RMS *St Helena* engineer and Martin my 'road gang rescuer'…and for the record, it was Bill who had been asked by Shelley Nightingale to be on standby to rescue me had I risked cycling from Hill Cove to Port Howard in the gale force winds of the day before, hence I owed it to him and Shirley to pay a visit! I finally pedalled back to Port Howard Lodge for a long-anticipated dinner, tired but fulfilled after a long but rewarding day.

After the intense activity of the previous day, it was a later start and more leisurely breakfast for me on Wednesday morning, including porridge – the sustenance-rich qualities of which were to become more important as the day ran its course….Whilst there was definitely a hint of sunshine, right from the start it was fairly obvious that the succession of bright intervals and intense hail or rain showers brought on by strong winds would be the order of the day. It had been confirmed that the FIGAS flight on which I would be leaving Port Howard was not scheduled until the afternoon, so I had planned two short excursions out of the settlement: The first of these would be my only cycling of the day, and involved taking the road above the jetty out of Port Howard and generally in a south-westerly direction for about a mile until I reached a small inlet called Second Creek, where the original settlement once stood. I soon returned to the settlement though, grateful of the following wind which had almost brought me to a standstill on the outward trip.

    My second short excursion – on foot – took me across the airstrip and along the shore of Bold Cove to reach a little cemetery which contains a mixture of graves, both local islanders and military, the latter yet another reminder of the Falklands Conflict. The events of 1982 are a recurring theme in and around Port Howard which witnessed some of the action (around 1,000 Argentinean troops occupied the area) and a number of relics are on display in the small war museum next to the lodge which I had already made a point of visiting. The walk back to the settlement was against a strengthening wind and hailstones, so I was glad to return to the warmth of the lodge for a filling lunch.

Whilst I waited in the lodge to be called for my flight, I took refuge in the lounge, passing the time browsing some Falklands-related books, although there was one worrying moment when host Sue told me that FIGAS had called to say they could only fly the front wheel on the forthcoming flight, not the whole bike: It turned out she was joking, though evidently news of my unorthodox cycling progress across the Falklands by air – generally with the front wheel removed so as to fit the bike in – was quickly progressing across the island airwaves!

At length, co-host Wayne took me up to the airstrip, and we awaited the plane after first chasing some recalcitrant cattle out of the way. I thanked Sue and Wayne and moments later the plane took-off into rather stormy weather and made its turbulent progress down Falkland Sound, with views away to the east of the empty, flat land forming the Lafonia region of East Falkland. A 25 minute flight brought the plane to a touchdown on the bare, windswept Speedwell Island to let off one passenger and deliver some mail, before another flight of about 15 minutes across a very stormy looking sea to land at the small Sea Lion Island in yet another squally shower.

As the plane continued to Stanley (with the bicycle still aboard as I didn't require it for the small island I had just landed on) I was taken from the airstrip to nearby Sea Lion Lodge, described as "the World's remotest southerly lodge hotel" and with rooms named after different penguin species. After a welcome cup of tea, I set out to explore the island, noted for the variety of wildlife in a comparatively small area. The weather wasn't getting any better, so I took the precaution of wrapping-up well (including woolly jumper of the knitted variety!) and then walked from the lodge initially in a southerly direction, then west along the southern coastline. It was immediately apparent that the island was fairly flat and, as a result, extremely windswept.

I came to a point on the coastline where I was able to look down from cliffs at sea lions on the rocks below – given the island's name I would have been disappointed if I hadn't seen any! However, I decided not to attempt any photographs at this point but instead crossed a fence by a sign bearing the warning "DANGER (LIONS)"...I was hoping the prefix "SEA" before the second word was implied in the circumstances! This gave me access to a precipitous clifftop path backed by dense tussock and with views down to a rocky beach called East Loafers. The strong wind and frequent shiver-inducing showers of hail and rain made walking difficult, and in the absence of any sea lions on this section, I decided to retrace my steps to the more open clifftop where I had first seen them to obtain a record on film: This was not an easy feat given the weather conditions which could, due to wind and slippery cliff edge, have resulted in me being 'fed to the lions!'

Exploring Sea Lion Island – "DANGER (LIONS)" warning sign & an angry sea

Several huge elephant seals hauled up on Elephant Corner beach, Sea Lion Island

Chapter 6 ~ **The Falkland Islands** ~ Two Wheels, Wildlife, Wild Winds and Woolly Jumpers (Week 2) ~ 169

Having seen sea lions on Sea Lion Island, I continued along the coast behind the fringe of tussock and eventually reached a rocky and dramatic headland called Rockhopper Point, home to a colony of rockhopper penguins and king cormorants. On this wild promontory facing due south towards the far-distant outlying island of Beauchene, and lashed by heavy seas, stood the simple cross and pile of stones that is the memorial to the loss of HMS *Sheffield*, which – like sister naval ship the *Coventry* – also succumbed during the 1982 conflict. The memorial may have been modest, but all the more moving and powerful in its impact given the backdrop of the raging South Atlantic.

Thinking on this – and the fact I was now further south than I had ever been in my life – I moved inland, with views towards the western extremity of the island, past a shed serving the island's alternative airstrip and a lake by the name of Long Pond, noting various ground nesting birds on the way. A succession of rainbows, resulting from the continually changing weather, livened the return trip to the lodge, where I was glad to warm-up with a hot dinner to round off the day.

As I was only scheduled to stay one night on Sea Lion Island, I was particularly keen to maximise the opportunities for observing wildlife there, and accordingly Thursday meant yet another early start. I set out from the lodge in an easterly direction just before sunrise, and made my way carefully past a nearby gentoo penguin colony to reach the south-facing beach at Elephant Corner – no sign informing me to "beware of the elephants" although one would have been appropriate, for I was fortunate enough to see a number of huge, lumbering elephant seals hauled up on the beach, occasionally rearing up or snorting noisily; these beasts can weigh several tons, and it doesn't do to get in their way! From here, I crossed to the north side of the island to observe a noisy group of seabirds on rocks below the cliffs, before continuing as far as a slight elevation towards the west known as Bull Hill before returning for breakfast.

The FIGAS flight on which I was due to leave Sea Lion Island was not scheduled until late morning, which still gave me over an hour to do some final wildlife spotting. This time I walked a little further east than before and – in amongst a large gathering of gentoos – I at last saw them, the species that had eluded me for nearly two weeks: Two tall, stately-looking king penguins, the first I had ever seen in the wild. This was a great result, and not surprisingly I spent time taking some quality photographs of these beautiful birds with their distinctive yellow markings. From the king penguins, I moved on to see more elephant seals on the beach, before exploring the sand dunes towards the eastern end of the island.

However, little time remained, so I returned to the lodge to await the plane. I was accompanied on the aircraft by English visitors Phil and Jill – with whom I had coincided at several points already – and another visitor first encountered on Pebble Island. The flight was in two stages, the first of about 10 minutes taking us past long and thin Bleaker Island to land at the remote North Arm settlement. The second stage, taking a further 30 minutes, saw us flying over the flat, empty vastness of East Falkland's Lafonia region, then the Choiseul Sound, the garrison at Mount Pleasant Airport and associated naval port of Mare Harbour, and finally the small communities of Fitzroy and Bluff Cove to reach Stanley Airport.

The terminal building at Stanley is a fairly modest affair, but equipped appropriately for its function, by which I mean a public weighing machine for baggage *and* passengers...*and* of course bicycles!...I was quite relieved to find the bike waiting for me, so without further delay I cycled off to explore some of the attractions in the immediate locality.

The first of these attractions involved a ride along a sandy track to reach black-and-white striped Cape Pembroke Lighthouse, marking the most easterly point of the Falklands. From here there were extensive views back west towards the range of mountains behind Stanley, as well as north towards Berkeley Sound and another coastal extremity at Volunteer Point. There was also a helpful information panel – of the circular type often placed on mountain summits indicating distances to key places in a 360 degree sweep – informing me the Antarctic Peninsula was barely 700 miles away, and South Georgia a similar distance, no wonder the wind felt cold!

I returned from Cape Pembroke and then cycled along the Airport Road, past Surf Bay, on the first tarmac road I had experienced in nearly two weeks – a novel experience to say the least, although despite the smoother surface the wind still proved to be the controlling factor on speed. I soon came to a tall 'totem pole' post by the roadside on which scores of direction signs with distances to places all across the World had been fixed – quite a colourful display, and another of those military-inspired pieces of artwork!

I next took a road to the right which led over a box bridge crossing a sea inlet known as The Canache and past several wrecks of old sailing ships in Whalebone Cove (notably the *Lady Elizabeth*): During the mid-19th century, Stanley became important as a centre for repairing ships that had been damaged in the storm-lashed waters around South America's Cape Horn, however some vessels were deemed beyond economic repair and were consequently abandoned. (This trade declined in due course, brought on

Stanley Airport terminal & control tower after FIGAS flight back to East Falkland

The colourful Direction Sign Totem Pole along tarmac road from Stanley Airport

172 ~ Chapter 6 ~ **The Falkland Islands** ~ Two Wheels, Wildlife, Wild Winds and Woolly Jumpers (Week 2)

by the development of reliable steamships and ultimately by the opening of the Panama Canal in 1914 which provided a short-cut link with the Pacific Ocean. This gradual decline was accompanied by the rise of the Falklands sheep-based economy). Finally, I reached a point overlooking a beach at Gypsy Cove and the large sea inlet of Port William which in turn – via a channel called The Narrows – allows ships to access the sheltered haven of Stanley Harbour.

From here, it was a short ride in a loop back to Stanley Airport, where I had a late 'vending machine lunch', retrieved my panniers and attached them to the bike carrier. I then rode a fully-laden cycle – another novel experience as well as tiring against the wind – the few miles into Stanley itself, proceeding from FIGAS territory past FIPASS territory (the acronym means Floating Interim Port and Storage System, a floating dock used by cargo ships). I entered the town proper past an industrial area and descended the very steep Philomel Street during the afternoon 'land rover rush hour' to reach Ross Road, marking Stanley's waterfront. I then undertook a 'familiarisation tour' of the key streets and points of interest in the town:

Stanley is built on a north-facing slope, and generally on a grid system in the older part of town such that east / west roads running parallel to the shore are fairly level, whereas north / south roads running up from the waterfront are quite steep and have right-of-way. Amongst this grid of streets, I variously encountered a large number of public buildings, private businesses and shops: These included (in no particular order) the post office, town hall, tourist board office, shops, pubs, schools, hospital, Government House, power station and Cable & Wireless (telecommunications provider) – and all this in a settlement the size of a large English village!

Eventually I reached Callaghan Road – a residential street and home to the Goodwin family, where I had stayed on my first night on the Falklands; I was again greeted by Robin, wife Mandy and daughter Rachel who were keen to hear about my experiences of the islands since I was last in Stanley. After some tea, we went in the four-wheel drive to visit their intended new house at Ross Road West and also out of town to the west to view Stanley from the reservoir above Moody Brook…oh, and I saw two more king penguins – all that travelling and I could have seen them on Stanley's 'doorstep!' We returned home for supper, and for me a very welcome night's sleep as almost a fortnight's intense touring was by now starting to take its toll physically.

Despite my tiredness, I was still up and awake fairly promptly on Friday morning, as I had decided to spend my final remaining full day on the Falkland Islands exploring Stanley – the 'capital city' – but generally known as 'town' by most islanders, particularly those living in 'camp': I therefore didn't linger after breakfast and began what was to be a very full and busy day. I left the Goodwin family residence in Callaghan Road and cycled into town, mixing with the morning equivalent of 'land rover rush hour', still something of a shock to the system and difficult to get accustomed to after the scarcity of vehicles out in camp. I began by descending the steep Philomel Street to reach the waterfront at Ross Road, with the aim of making a photographic record of as many of the key landmarks and points of interest in Stanley as I could.

I began with the Falkland Islands Company (FIC) building near the East Jetty, the FIC being the latter-day trading organisation whose origins date back to the establishment of large agricultural land holdings on the islands in the mid-19th century. Within the yard of the FIC I spotted quirky sight number three (after Boot Hill and the Direction Sign Totem Pole) – an old red London Routemaster bus, used to transport day visitors from cruise and expedition ships on local sightseeing tours. I then moved on, past the Public Jetty where boats take people from and to those same ships which generally anchor in Stanley Harbour or further out in Port William beyond The Narrows. Nearby I noted the incongruous sight of Jubilee Villas, a row of Victorian brick terraced houses literally 'shipped out' from Britain, before moving on to the grassed area between Ross Road and Stanley Harbour called Victory Green which includes some old cannons and – most notably – the wooden mizzen mast from the SS *Great Britain*, the famous steamship that once lay shipwrecked in Stanley for years before being returned to its namesake country and restored.

My comprehensive tour on foot and cycle continued by way of the police station and St Mary's Catholic Church, then the only bank on the Falklands, to reach the town hall and my ultimate destination – for the time being at least – Stanley post office. Although I had been on the Falklands almost a fortnight, I had still not sent any postcards to relatives and friends, and time was rapidly running out. Postcards had been scarce out in camp, and – as I had observed during my FIGAS flights – mail was all sent to Stanley for handling anyway, so it made sense to wait. In fact, it was a very straightforward exercise once I had arrived at the post office to buy an assortment of penguin and Stanley themed postcards, then stamp, address, write and post them. By

Falkland Islands Post Office in Stanley, plus philatelic bureau, pillar box & phones

Cycling towards Mount Tumbledown & Two Sisters Mountains, near Stanley

way of some souvenirs for myself, I also visited the adjacent philatelic bureau where I was able to obtain a wider selection of Falkland Islands stamps and related items, noting that it also stocked the stamps of both South Georgia and British Antarctic Territory.

From the post office I proceeded towards the western edge of town and came at length to the Falkland Islands Museum, where I spent almost two hours, made all the more interesting after my time touring the islands. The well arranged museum includes galleries devoted to a number of relevant subjects such as history of the islands' discovery and settlement; maritime history; the 1982 Falklands Conflict; geology; natural history; communications; camp life and finally trades and businesses. There were also a few exhibits outside, however to view the largest 'outside exhibit' I had to ride back towards the centre of town in order to visit the museum's additional site: Cartmell Cottage, in Pioneer Row, is a 'kit form' house which was brought out to the Falklands some time in the 19th century and later added to; it is suitably furnished in period style, and very much the forerunner of the typical island dwellings which grew up in Stanley and across the Falklands.

I then, almost on the spur of the moment, decided to venture out into camp once more – well, just about anyway – as I was keen to maximise my opportunities before I had to hand back the bike. I rode out along Ross Road West until the edge of town, where the tarmac road suddenly reverted to the type of gravel surface with which I had become so familiar. I battled against the wind (no change there!) for about a mile until the crossing of Moody Brook, where the two king penguins were still there from the day before. This fairly short ride gave me good views west towards the craggy outlines of Mount Tumbledown and the Two Sisters Mountains which – together with other peaks in the area – were significant in the final stages of the Falklands Conflict immediately prior to the re-taking of Stanley by British forces. By this stage though, despite its great significance, I was starting to feel hungry for a bit more than history, so I returned along the road into Stanley where sustenance was sought at Michelle's Café just up from the waterfront.

During the post-lunch period I started doing the inevitable 'touristy' things as apart from Falklands stamps I was hoping to obtain a few memorable souvenirs of my two week visit, although unlike my earlier visit to the post office this was not quite such a straightforward exercise as it might appear, not least owing to there being a visiting tourist ship, hence large numbers of passengers were thronging the few gift-related shops in Stanley and many items were consequently in short supply. I had fortunately already obtained a copy of the latest edition of "Penguin News" – the Falklands newspaper – so that was one off the list.

Over the next hour or two I visited several retail outlets, and in so doing managed to obtain a Falklands mug, tea towel, penguin drinks coasters, an interesting book about the islands, a detailed island map and woollen goods... naturally...including a jumper and a hat; I even found time to pay the tourist information centre a visit during this frenzied period of souvenir hunting! After taking my purchases back to the Goodwin household to 'lighten the load', I made my way to my final place of residence on the Falklands – Bennett House bed & breakfast – where I was greeted by host Celia Stewart.

I was soon out around town yet again though, as I still wished to record on film the remaining points of interest in Stanley that hadn't yet been 'snapped for posterity' due to various worthy diversions earlier in the day. I therefore spent a further hour or two on what I can only describe as an 'urban cycle tour' of Stanley taking in several more sites, starting with Government House, official residence of the Falkland Islands Governor and set in attractive grounds. This was followed by the impressive yet moving 1982 Falklands War Memorial (commemorating the islands' liberation) located in front of the Government administration building. I noted – within a long list recording the ships which played a part in 1982 – mention of the first RMS *St Helena* which was requisitioned at the time to serve as a support vessel.

In random order, I then proceeded via the 1914 Battle of the Falklands Memorial; the wreck of another old ship called the *Jhelum*; the King Edward VII Memorial Hospital; both the community and junior / infant schools; the radio station; Cable & Wireless sites; power station; two pubs (one of them the photogenic Globe Tavern with red telephone kiosk outside) and the Tin Tabernacle Chapel (clad in corrugated iron). Most impressive of all though was Christ Church Cathedral – southernmost Anglican cathedral in the World – the peaceful interior of which I managed to visit.

Time was now pressing on, and my stomach was rumbling again, so I made my way to Kay McCallum's B & B, where I had earlier arranged to have dinner. Kay turned out to be yet another Falklands character (I had certainly met some interesting people on my travels) and I enjoyed a filling meal with Falklands lamb on the menu and in the company of several other guests whom I had already met during my progress across the islands. There was also the bonus of viewing – just outside her traditional Falklands house – Kay's

Stanley sightseeing - Christ Church Cathedral & Whalebone Arch on Ross Road

Bennett House, Stanley – where I spent last night on Falklands during 2008 visit

amazing 'garden of gnomes', and another attraction in its own right! I finished the day with a drink at the Upland Goose Hotel on Stanley's waterfront, before finally returning to Celia Stewart's Bennett House.

Before turning in for the night though, I made one final short ride back to Robin Goodwin's house, to return the loaned bicycle, as well as the spanner which had been an essential tool since Allan White lent it to me on Pebble Island, and without which the bike's left pedal would probably have fallen off completely failing regular tightening. It was a case of un-tightening at this stage though, as Robin and I together removed the UK-purchased pannier carrier from the bike, and which had likewise been crucial to the success of my travels.

It was also a time for reflection for both of us in terms of the success of 'trial running' Robin's concept of a cycle hire business venture on the islands. We concluded that it may well work in and around Stanley, where distances were comparatively short, roads reasonable to good, and gradients not too taxing, and where day visitor numbers were sizeable owing to the numerous tourist ships visiting in season: Therefore, the type of bike he had loaned to me would probably suffice in that respect. The idea might also have some merit at certain of the other key visitor locations for modest local excursions, such as Darwin and Goose Green elsewhere on East Falkland, and maybe Port Howard or Fox Bay on West Falkland, provided that bikes were locally available at those places.

By contrast though, extending the concept to the rest of the Falklands camp countryside and smaller islands would be a very different matter altogether, owing to the vast distances, difficult road surfaces and off-road terrain, not to mention the inter-island transport challenges and of course the even more challenging weather: For that, by his own admission, Robin concluded a more robust and reliable mountain bike than the one he had supplied me would be essential, and by my own admission, an even more robust 'cycling nut' than the 'island nut' whose proverbial wheels had just about fallen off! Pondering such thoughts, I thanked Robin and his family for all their help and hospitality, and said my goodbyes before retiring for the night.

I awoke around 6.00am on the final Saturday morning to cram in one final wander around Stanley before I had to leave the Falkland Islands. My route took me out of Bennett House up the hill to an unusual display of artefacts in a residential front garden forming an anti-whaling display – not as cheerful as the gnomes of the previous evening, but nevertheless conveying an important message. From here it was all downhill to Ross Road for one final view of Stanley's waterfront before returning to Bennett House, where Celia had a tasty breakfast ready for me before I had to begin my long journey home. I then waited in an attractive rose-filled conservatory attached to the front of her traditional timber-clad house for the pre-arranged transport to arrive which would take me to Mount Pleasant Airport. It was not long before a bus – and accompanying luggage van – arrived, so I bid farewell to Celia – who had been yet another charming Falklands host – and boarded the bus.

The journey from Stanley, of about an hour, was along the Mount Pleasant Highway – part tarmac surface, part gravel road – over which I had last travelled in the opposite direction with Robin Goodwin and son Kenton on my first evening in the Falklands. On that occasion it had been dark, so it was a bonus to be able to appreciate the typical East Falkland scenery on this stretch as the bus made its way west past the small settlements of Bluff Cove and Fitzroy to reach MPA. Upon arriving at the military base, security was immediately apparent and all things suddenly became quite regimental – a reminder of when I had travelled down to the islands a fortnight before. Unlike the previous time however, on this occasion it was possible to use the airport terminal building as opposed to the hangar as had been the case on arrival.

I wasted no time in checking-in for my forthcoming Royal Air Force flight which was scheduled to take me from MPA, via the regulation 'pit stop' at Ascension, to RAF Brize Norton. With the inevitable passport and security checks complete, I entered the modest departure lounge, took advantage of a cup of tea from the NAAFI café and waited to board the plane for the long flight back north to the UK. After a modest wait, passengers were called for the flight, and I walked across Falklands soil – or rather airport tarmac – for the last time before boarding an identical grey-coloured Douglas DC10 aircraft to that on which I had flown down to the Falkland Islands…it may even have been the same plane.

At 11.00am local time (GMT minus three hours) the RAF flight took-off. My last view of the Falkland Islands was the same as my first – bare, peaty moorland and lakes – before the plane ascended into the clouds and the Falklands were gone…apart from one final flourish to enliven the early part of the journey: Shortly after the departure from Mount Pleasant there was a sudden appearance of two RAF Tornado jets, one on either side of the DC10 and flying at the same level, so close in fact it was possible to see the pilots, who were effectively 'escorting' us on our way.

The plane set its course in a generally north-easterly direction, well to the east of South America, and for much of this first stage of the journey the view was of the deep blue South Atlantic and various dispersed cloud formations just as it had been on the outward flight. Similarly, during the following seven hours the time zone also changed three times, although this time reverting to GMT thereby losing the three hours gained two weeks before. Travelling in this direction, the consequential effect was that bright sunshine quickly gave way to darkness at least an hour before reaching Ascension, and when the plane touched down at Wideawake Airfield for the refuelling stop it was already after 9.00pm GMT.

The stopover at Ascension lasted an hour or so, and was a welcome chance to stretch my legs, have a coffee from the NAAFI café and simply enjoy the still warmth of a tropical evening whilst waiting in the little courtyard transit area. Fortunately, on the return journey there was to be no enforced overnight at 'the crossroads of the South Atlantic' which had so delayed the outward trip, and by 11.00pm GMT the plane was thundering down the Wideawake runway and Ascension was also left behind. The plane continued north through the night, crossing the Equator and on into the North Atlantic, to the west of West Africa and Europe, finally landing just under nine hours later at RAF Brize Norton where a fresh winter morning was my introduction back to the United Kingdom: Total flight time (including stopover) 18 hours; total flight distance 8,000 miles; total exhaustion on the part of one cyclist!

Looking back, my experience of the Falkland Islands was – from a cycling perspective – quite different from my earlier two-wheeled travelling around other South Atlantic islands. I had of course known that would be the case even at the initial planning stage – merely the statistic concerning the Falklands covering one hundred times the land area of St Helena convinced me of that, not to mention there being more inhabited islands in the group than there are months in the year, or the domestic travel challenges – whether on-island or inter-island – or the weather!

A lengthy and costly journey of 8,000 miles each way demanded an approach which, within the two week time 'window' I had available, needed to give me opportunities to complete a worthwhile and *respectable* amount of cycling, yet at the same time *respect* the wider attractions of the Falklands – be they the history, the wildlife, the way of life and of course the Falklanders themselves. The challenges and frustrations in preparing for this ambitious journey were undoubtedly immense…yet an accidental, fortuitous interweaving of an 'approximately' bespoke tourist itinerary with the invaluable intervention of an islander determined to present his land in the best possible light meant my memories of the Falklands are a rich tapestry of experiences on many levels over and above those that a visitor concentrating on one or two aspects could hope to have....

...I estimate that, taken together, I probably cycled and walked around 200 miles in total on the Falkland Islands, 175 miles being by bike. I may not have cycled every road on every island, yet I cycled in four different areas of both East and West Falkland, and saw much of the country in between. I even managed to cycle on two of the smaller islands – thanks to the assistance of FIGAS and their planes – and visited two more, whilst also viewing most of the others from the air or across the sea. I was enthralled by some incredible wildlife, engaged by a powerful sense of history – much of it within living memory – and enlightened by the distinctive way of life across the camp sheep farming settlements as well as in Stanley. However, above all, I was enriched by the friendliness, hospitality, thoughtfulness and resourcefulness of the Falkland Islanders, justly proud of their diverse South Atlantic home. Yes, I had flown around the Falklands with a bike, and I had experienced them on two wheels, along with the wildlife and the wild winds...not forgetting the 'woolly jumpers'...but I had also experienced a great deal more.

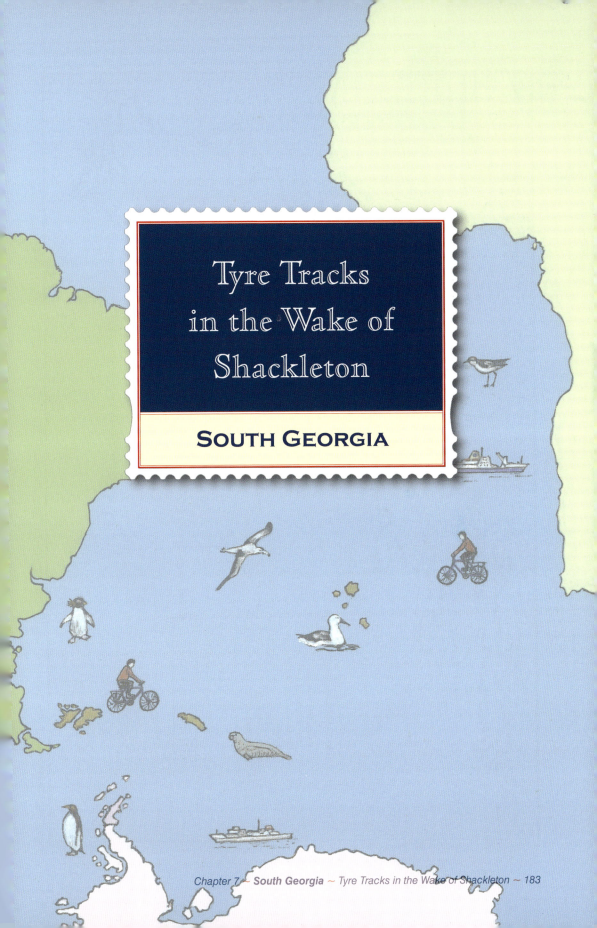

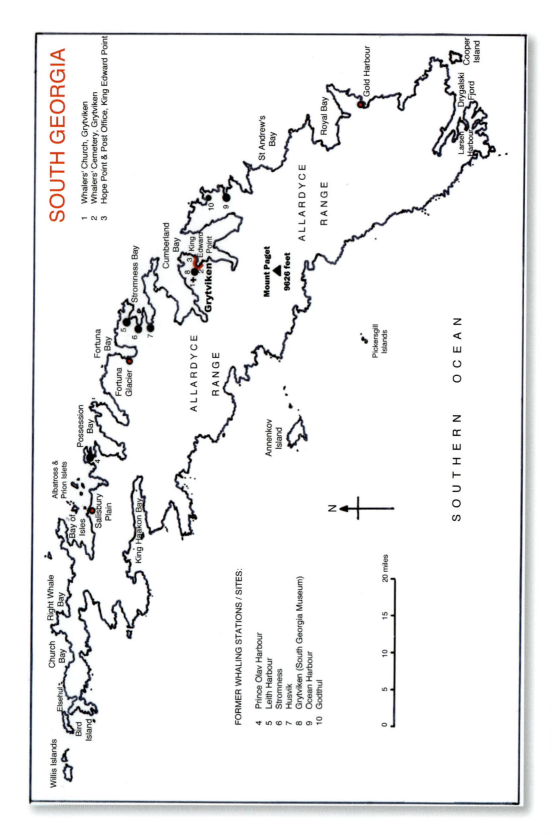

Chapter 7
An Unexpected Cycle on South Georgia

Simon cycling past South Georgia Post Office at King Edward Point near Grytviken

I would imagine that "cycling" and "South Georgia" are rarely – if ever – mentioned in the same sentence: I certainly would never have thought of considering the idea, at least not in a practical sense, were it not for a set of circumstances coming together which, quite unexpectedly, gave me an opportunity to do just that. However, unlike the Falkland Islands – which I had never originally planned to visit *or* cycle on – in the case of South Georgia I definitely made a conscious decision to go there. As for the cycling part…that basically evolved whilst I was travelling to the island. Having said that, South Georgia – and cycling thereon – well, I couldn't *really* see much of a connection there!…

…My reasons for travelling to South Georgia are probably threefold, and – given my 'island nut' credentials – probably not all that surprising: My first reason concerns the Falklands, as whilst I had explored those islands fairly extensively during that frenzied fortnight in 2008, there were still some areas of the archipelago I was keen to see, and more particularly *by sea*....Incredibly, despite having visited a group of islands that are numbered in the hundreds, I never once travelled on – or even stepped into – a boat, since (as has already been portrayed in the previous two chapters) the 2008 visit was dominated by air transfers and land-based travel.

My second reason concerns South Georgia itself – and, I have to confess, a certain degree of inevitability along the lines of "where should I go next?"...and South Georgia – in terms of my South Atlantic 'agenda' – was the obvious next oceanic stepping-stone. Perhaps I was influenced during my earlier Falklands visit, where South Georgia is a place often talked about – and with which there are definite links being a 'neighbouring' island in relative terms. In fact my inspiration was arguably not that different from being motivated to visit St Helena and Ascension after meeting St Helenians on my first RMS voyage to Tristan da Cunha.

The third reason concerns Antarctica – the 'great white continent' – and the fact that if I was going to South Georgia, I would be tantalisingly close to reaching 'the bottom of the World'...in a loose sense of the expression....It was, therefore, very much a case of now or never!

Nevertheless, as with all previous journeys to the isolated territories of the South Atlantic, there was an appreciable amount of pre-planning required and transport issues to overcome – after all, South Georgia isn't exactly an everyday destination and is a seriously long way from the UK! During my time on the Falklands, I had been very aware of the various expedition (as opposed to cruise) ships that regularly call at Stanley and certain of the smaller islands as part of a wider voyage usually originating from South America; indeed, a far greater proportion of tourists to the Falklands visit this way as opposed to the land-based type of tour (with local air transfers) that I had enjoyed. A fair number of these voyages are bound for Antarctica, and some of them also include South Georgia in their itinerary.

Fairly predictably then, it was this latter version of an expedition voyage that attracted me, since a chance to visit the Falklands (this time by sea), South Georgia *and* Antarctica all in the one trip – plus a 'taster' of South America for good measure – seemed like too good an opportunity to miss...and I didn't even need to worry about a bicycle! That said, given there is still a fair degree of choice in such matters, I was anxious to ensure that I secured a passage on a ship that offered a suitable itinerary, plenty of opportunities to go ashore at the various destinations, and of course was affordable...admittedly the latter criteria was never likely to be achieved, therefore value-for-money assumed an even greater criticality: I figured it unlikely there would be another 'bite at the cherry' so to speak…or perhaps more appropriately 'crack at the ice'…thus I needed to get it right.

I was fortunate in terms of 'getting it right' (although realistically I only fully appreciated it after my expedition) in that – as a result of painstaking research – I eventually settled on booking with an expedition company by the name of Peregrine, who in turn had been recommended by a specialist overseas travel company based in the UK called Audley Travel. The recommendation from the travel consultant came with the benefit of personal experience of the Antarctic and sub-Antarctic regions, and as a consequence of the attentive service I received, I secured a berth on a ship scheduled to leave the Argentinean port of Ushuaia in mid-February 2009, and booked to sail for 18 days via the Falklands, South Georgia and Antarctica, before returning to South America in early March.

Many of the ships used for Antarctic (as well as Arctic) expedition voyages are Russian polar research vessels, with ice-strengthened hulls suitable for sailing in the often treacherous waters of the polar regions, and the two ships regularly used by Peregrine were no exception: Research Vessel (RV) *Akademik Ioffe* and its sister ship RV *Akademik Sergey Vavilov*. My voyage was to be undertaken onboard the latter ship.

Before that however, there was the not inconsiderable matter of reaching the ship in the first place, and so it was that I found myself leaving home one cold February morning in 2009 – with snow lying on the ground as if to put me in a frame of mind for the southern latitudes I was bound for – at the start of a very long journey indeed: This in turn involved a two hour flight from London Heathrow to Madrid; an early morning transfer to a long-haul trans-Atlantic flight lasting over 12 hours between the Spanish capital and Buenos Aires; then – after a night in a hotel – a third flight from the Argentinean capital taking a further three hours or so to reach Ushuaia on the island of Tierra del Fuego (Land of Fire) in the extreme south of South America. The outward and return journeys provided chances to briefly explore both Buenos Aires and Ushuaia:

Buenos Aires is an extensive metropolis, and – being at similar latitude to Cape Town in South Africa (for me a more familiar 'gateway' to the South Atlantic) – enjoys a not dissimilar warm climate to that city. Having visited Cape Town on a number of occasions before when travelling to or from Tristan da Cunha, St Helena and Ascension, it was interesting to make comparisons with the Argentinean capital: Cape Town has a legacy of Dutch – as well as British – influences, which are manifested in its buildings and way of life, along with those of Africa and the Far East. In contrast, Buenos Aires has an undeniable Spanish atmosphere, both architecturally and culturally, the inevitable result of much earlier settlers from Spain, but with evidence of influences from other European nations, as well as South America.

However, Ushuaia – almost 2,000 miles further south than Buenos Aires – has a very different atmosphere altogether. For a start, I noticed – even in the austral summer – just how much colder it felt, an effect reinforced (at least in visual terms) by the dramatic backdrop of the Andes Mountains: This huge mountain chain, running the length of South America, makes a final flourish here, its snow-capped, glacier-threaded peaks rising loftily above 'the southernmost town in the World', as Ushuaia is generally described.

As for the town itself, it reminded me in some ways of Stanley on the Falklands, only on a larger scale, being likewise located on a sloping site overlooking a sea channel – in this case the Beagle Channel – and laid out in a grid pattern of streets. Even the buildings have some similarities with those in Stanley – an assorted jumble of styles, many of them clad or roofed in timber or corrugated tin, and often painted in a variety of bright colours. There is a naval base nearby, and the town has a very 'end of the World' feel which is emphasised to the visitor in no uncertain terms: There is even El Tren del Fin del Mundo (The Train at the End of the World) – a narrow-gauge steam railway which runs from a point near Ushuaia up a steeply-graded line into the mountains of Tierra del Fuego National Park....Fairly predictably this is also promoted as 'the World's southernmost railway'. It was in these spectacular surroundings that I spent a night in a hotel on Ushuaia's seafront before departure day of the voyage to the Falklands, South Georgia and Antarctica.

On waking in my hotel room the next morning, and looking out of the window, I noted – as I had the afternoon of my arrival – that there were several expedition ships berthed along the pier in Ushuaia's nearby port area, although not the same 'line up' that had been there when I closed the curtains. The previous day, the *Akademik Ioffe* – sister ship of the vessel I would be travelling on – had set sail for the Antarctic, while reassuringly the *Akademik Sergey Vavilov* had arrived overnight to take its place.

After some sightseeing in the morning (which principally involved El Tren del Fin del Mundo *and* obligatory photographs of the "Ushuaia – Fin del Mundo" sign) I arrived at the entrance to the Port of Ushuaia: After a remarkably swift and straightforward security and passport check, I walked along the pier to the *Akademik Sergey Vavilov* – generally referred to simply as the *Vavilov* – then climbed the gangway and was welcomed onboard ship. I was soon afterwards being shown to my cabin – no. 327 on the starboard side – where I was relieved to see my two large bags had already been deposited, having been brought separately from the hotel by agents.

After settling into my new 'home', I quickly set about some initial exploration of the ship: I discovered that the *Vavilov* was registered in the Russian port of Kaliningrad, as well as having Russian officers and crew. However – like its sibling the *Ioffe* – it was actually built in Finland. From an interior perspective, I further noted that it was well-appointed in terms of facilities in keeping with its function. The tonnage and size were not dissimilar to the RMS *St Helena* and the ship similarly incorporated ample open deck space on several levels – of importance for fully appreciating the incredible seascapes and landscapes that would unfold over the next 18 days.

The other 'staff' on the ship were the expedition leaders – overwhelmingly Australian – who would be responsible for organising activities both onboard and, more importantly, the numerous shore excursions which are the principal feature and attraction of such expedition voyages. The passenger base seemed to be dominated by those from Australia as well – but that shouldn't have surprised me, as the antipodean nation is renowned for producing some of the World's most intrepid travellers!

At around 6.00pm on what – for the record – was Tuesday 17th February 2009, the Research Vessel (RV) *Akademik Sergey Vavilov* set sail from Ushuaia in beautiful late afternoon sunshine and made its way eastwards down the Beagle Channel, separating Argentina's Tierra del Fuego to the north from several islands – principally Isla Navarino – forming the southern extremity of Chile. The scenery was green, mountainous and magnificent, continuing until night fell a few hours later and the *Vavilov* headed out into the open waters of the South Atlantic. The ship was set on a north-easterly course of 350 nautical miles bound for the Falkland Islands, and fortunately the two nights and one day spent at sea on this initial sector of the voyage were blessed with blue skies and calm seas.

There wasn't *too* much time to relax though, as I quickly became conscious of the routine onboard. Although I had become used to a certain amount of daily routine onboard the RMS *St Helena*, things on the RV *Vavilov* were somewhat different: Fair chunks of the day – during those days wholly at sea – were given over to presentations and briefings by the expedition staff on various issues of relevance, and on the first day alone I attended four talks on Falklands geology, birds of the Falklands, 'protocol' when in Antarctica, and – last but not least – safety briefing in relation to going ashore during the voyage which would be via small inflatable powered boats (called zodiacs), a number of which I had already spotted secured on the aft deck of the ship. The time between was punctuated by periods spent out on the open deck watching as various ocean birds made their presence felt, or in the bar / observation lounge getting to know the expedition staff – led by an enthusiastic Aussie called David Wood (or "Woody" as he preferred to be known) – as well as the other passengers, notably a couple by the name of Dave and Pam Tindall who hailed from Queensland.

I was awake around 5.00am and some time before sunrise on the Thursday morning, and from my starboard cabin porthole I was just able to discern – in the moonlight – an undulating black line between sea and sky: It did of course signify that the ship was now approaching the western outlying islands of the Falklands, and one of the reasons for choosing this particular voyage was to see appreciable parts of the Falklands by sea, especially the extreme western coast and islands which my 2008 itinerary had precluded me from visiting. I quickly went up on deck to enjoy the sunrise and was rewarded on this particular morning with a fantastic fiery red light which progressively illuminated the landforms, the colours of which gradually became more intense and vivid as the light improved and the *Vavilov* sailed closer.

To the east of the ship I had a fine view of Weddell Island – dominated by its peak Mount Weddell, as well as New Island – one of the most westerly in the Falklands archipelago, plus several lesser islands and islets, not forgetting the much-indented and wild western coastline of West Falkland. Meanwhile, along the horizon to the north-west were the Jason Islands, rich in marine birdlife. The ship then sailed through a narrow channel between Westpoint Island and the Byron Heights peninsula of West Falkland, which was followed by a good view of the tiny settlement on Westpoint Island, a typical 'camp' community along similar lines to those with which I had become very familiar during my two weeks on the Falklands the year before.

Shortly afterwards, the ship arrived in surroundings that were more familiar to me and came to rest at an anchorage off Carcass Island. A number of the aforementioned zodiacs were then craned-off the ship into the water, the

Sailing away from Ushuaia in 2009 on Research Vessel Akademik Sergey Vavilov

Magellanic & gentoo penguins on Leopard Beach (Carcass Island, Falklands)

gangway was lowered and the first of what would turn out to be an appreciable number of shore excursions during the voyage swung into action. Having donned waterproofs, wellington boots and lifejacket, I joined other passengers on one of the zodiacs for the short ride ashore, landing on the beach at Dyke Bay. It seemed strange to be arriving on the Falklands this time in an open boat at a wildlife-populated beach of a small island rather than on an RAF plane at a military base – but this was the 'alternative' sea-based experience of the islands that I had been looking for. Suddenly, it all seemed as if I had never been away – *déjà vu* in the best possible sense – the upland geese and penguins on nearby Leopard Beach, the walk round the bay of Port Pattison to the Carcass Island settlement house, and there I was back in the familiar surroundings where I had spent a memorable 24 hours the previous year, only *this* time I was there as a day visitor 'calling in for tea':

The owner, Rob McGill, remembered me, and this time I was also able to meet his wife Lorraine who had been away from the island when I stayed there. The catering staff had meanwhile prepared a fine spread of tea, coffee and cakes. All too quickly though it was time to say "goodbye", and I was soon speeding back across the water to the waiting ship. An efficient re-boarding of passengers and lifting of zodiacs back onboard meant that by lunchtime the *Vavilov* was steaming away on a short trip eastwards lasting an hour or so bringing us to another anchorage, this time in the shadow of Saunders Island – another of the smaller islands I had stayed on in 2008 and where the day's second shore excursion was planned to take place.

Another swift zodiac ride brought me and fellow passengers to the south-facing beach of The Neck – the narrow sandy isthmus also boasting a north-facing beach and connecting two parts of the island together. The island's owners had travelled in a land rover from the Saunders settlement to meet the 'new arrivals', yet the principal point of interest here was of course the wildlife spectacular of 'penguin city', just as I experienced it when I cycled there in 2008: The shy Magellanics running for their burrows; the friendly gentoos keen to investigate the 'human penguins' who had just landed; the squawking, squabbling and ever-entertaining rockhoppers; and the KINGS!...Yes, unlike when I was last on Saunders Island, I found the king penguins – some 20 of them – standing in a stately huddle and seemingly aloof from their 'commoner' cousins.

Yet there was more, as a walk conducted by one of the expedition leaders along cliffs north-east of The Neck brought rewards in terms of rock shags, Magellanic oystercatchers and black-browed albatrosses on their nests.

Penguins at The Neck landing beach & view of ship (Saunders Island, Falklands)

"Welcome to the Falkland Islands" sign seen when landing at Stanley Public Jetty

*Chapter 7 ~ **South Georgia** ~ Tyre Tracks in the Wake of Shackleton ~ 193*

Even a few Falklands steamer ducks turned up on the beach to bid us farewell as we re-boarded the zodiacs and returned to the ship. With the day's second excursion over, the ship weighed anchor and set off eastwards again, passing north of the island and neighbouring Keppel and Pebble Islands, offering an ever-changing panorama of spectacular Falklands scenery reflecting the rays of the lowering sun.

I was again awake at around 5.00am on the Friday morning while it was still almost dark, and observed from my porthole that there was land to starboard: In fact, there had been throughout the night, as the ship had steadily cruised along the north and east coastline of East Falkland. Not long after I arrived on deck, the ship turned to the west to enter Port William – the channel leading into Stanley Harbour – after a passage of well over 100 nautical miles from the island stops the previous day. An opportunity was taken here to refuel the ship before the long voyage into the remoter regions of the South Atlantic which would follow.

After breakfast, and with the sun now bringing light and colour to the landscape, I boarded a zodiac for a short ride through The Narrows to enter the more sheltered inner harbour. This offered another new experience – viewing Stanley from the water – and I was able to appreciate the town's brightly painted buildings in various hues of red, green, blue and white, spread across the sloping hillside. A few minutes later, the zodiac arrived at the Public Jetty on Stanley's waterfront, and I had the equally strange experience of arriving at the Falklands capital by sea. Bizarrely – considering that my 2008 visit had made so much use of inter-island air transfers – I noticed, alongside the adjacent East Jetty, a small blue-hulled ship bearing the name MV *Tamar* – the cargo vessel used to convey supplies and wool for export to and from the various islands, much heard about on my previous visit to the Falklands but never actually seen...until now!

Once ashore, I immediately set about reacquainting myself with Stanley (though this time without the benefit of a bicycle), initially walking past the familiar landmarks on or near the waterfront – the Globe Tavern; Jubilee Villas; Christ Church Cathedral; the Whalebone Arch; the West Store; the police station; and St Mary's Catholic Church – an eclectic mix of styles and functions, strung along the seafront like assorted beads on a randomly-threaded necklace. The building I dwelt at longest though was Stanley post office and its associated philatelic bureau: The year before, I had noted that it was possible to obtain not only Falkland Islands stamps but also those of

South Georgia and British Antarctic Territory, as well as postcards. Not wishing to waste valuable sightseeing time writing cards and licking stamps once I reached the latter two territories, I wisely stocked-up on these valuable 'tourist commodities' in advance!

Just outside the post office, from one of the very British-looking red telephone kiosks, I made a local call to my friend, host and bicycle supplier from 2008 – Robin Goodwin – as I planned to try and pay him and his family a surprise visit whilst in 'town'. It so happened they were only a short distance away at the time I called, and about to go home for lunch, so within minutes I joined Robin and family in their four-wheel drive vehicle (erstwhile East Falkland bike conveyor!) and returned to their new home in Ross Road West, attractively located with views over Stanley Harbour. Needless to say they were all pleasantly surprised to see me, and kindly gave me lunch – appropriately Falklands lamb and mutton – and a convivial hour was spent 'catching up' on a year's worth of news. Unlike 2008 however, I was on this occasion only a day visitor, so after my fleeting visit I wished them well and returned eastwards along the waterfront into town, paying a return visit to the excellent Falkland Islands Museum as I did so.

After a pleasant meander through the streets of Stanley, I arrived back at the Public Jetty just in time for the last zodiac back to the ship, which had meanwhile relocated to an anchorage within Stanley Harbour itself. At length, the *Vavilov* set sail, out through The Narrows into Port William, then eastwards past Cape Pembroke Lighthouse – the 'east end' of the Falklands – and finally back into the open South Atlantic. The course was set east-south-east, this time for somewhere quite different – South Georgia.

The sea passage from the Falklands to South Georgia is around 750 nautical miles, and the *Vavilov* was scheduled to take three nights and two days to complete this sector of the voyage. There was therefore plenty of time to prepare for arrival at what is one of the most breathtaking, unforgettable and iconic places on Earth. Saying that, an hour was lost on the way on account of forwarding clocks from GMT minus three – which had been the time zone since leaving Ushuaia – to GMT minus two, so as to accord with South Georgia time; this was a sensible move in any case as the gradual progress eastwards meant sunrise was becoming earlier each day (and sunset was progressively occurring sooner) and using the available daylight to maximise viewing opportunities is an important factor on such voyages. The 'shipboard routine' on this stretch, not surprisingly, was very much focussed on South Georgia, and the various presentations and briefings given by the expedition team covered such subjects as the intended itinerary once there, wildlife themes including seals and sub-Antarctic seabirds, even photography tips, as well as the chilling matter of glaciers, ice and icebergs…the latter interesting if rather ominous!

There was also a – refreshingly different – talk given by David "Woody" Wood, the expedition leader, concerning the life and Antarctic expeditions of Sir Ernest Shackleton, made all the more interesting as I had brought along a book (to help pass the long days at sea) entitled "Shackleton's Boat Journey" relating to an amazing and inspirational story of human endurance and survival which – during 1916 – occurred in the very part of the World I would soon be travelling through. I may be an 'island nut', but it rapidly became obvious that Woody was in every sense a 'Shackleton nut'…such was his infectious enthusiasm for his hero that many of the places visited on this voyage had connections with the heroic events which took place nearly a century before, albeit that our progress was in the reverse direction to the sequence of events which unfolded in 1916: At this point, to put those events in context, a summary of the Shackleton story is worth recounting, for it is a story which I – like Woody – find more remarkable and uplifting than the more frequently recalled tales of polar exploration concerning the race to the South Pole by Amundsen and Scott in 1911/12.

Ernest Shackleton had set out to cross Antarctica, via the South Pole – heralded as "the first crossing of the last continent" – and sailed from Britain with a supporting ship's company onboard the *Endurance* in August 1914. By January 1915, *Endurance* had become stuck fast in Weddell Sea pack ice off the coast of Antarctica, ice which gradually crushed and destroyed the ship – on which Shackleton and the crew had been living – until it sank in the November. For the next five months all were forced to live on the shifting ice, over which they gradually advanced to reach its edge, before eventually sailing in three small lifeboats to uninhabited Elephant Island in the South Shetlands.

While 22 out of a total of 28 men were then left here under the command of Frank Wild to effectively camp under two inverted boats for four months of an Antarctic winter, the remaining six men – including Ernest Shackleton – set off on 24th April 1916 to seek help and raise the alarm. It is this part of the story that is arguably even more incredible, for it involved sailing *and rowing* in an open boat – the *James Caird* – across 800 miles of open ocean in appalling conditions, until they reached South Georgia 16 days later.

Yet there was still more endurance required, since their landfall – in King Haakon Bay on South Georgia's uninhabited south-west coast – meant a superhuman feat by three of the six (Shackleton, Tom Crean and Frank Worsley) was still required in order to summon help. This took the form of a 36 hour, overland 'hike' across inhospitable snow-covered mountains and crevassed glaciers to arrive on 20th May 1916 at the whaling station in Stromness Harbour on the north-east coast.

Needless to say, the arrival of three ragged-looking men with long beards initially caused shock to those working at this remote site, but the station manager quickly dispatched a whaling ship to collect the three crew members left at King Haakon Bay, and in the fullness of time a steamer named the *Yelcho*, lent by the Chilean Government, rescued the other 22 men left on Elephant Island at the end of August 1916: Thus not a single human life was lost on the otherwise ill-fated polar expedition. With sad irony, Shackleton sought to return again to the Antarctic region on the *Quest* expedition a few years later, but died upon reaching South Georgia in January 1922, and was buried on the island in the little whalers' cemetery at Grytviken.

In the course of talking to Woody about our shared interest in the Shackleton story, one thing led to another and very soon considerable interest was being shown in my own 'endurance' expedition or, to be more specific, my experience cycling across the South Atlantic. I described the diverse two-wheeled travels I had variously enjoyed on Ascension, St Helena, Tristan da Cunha and the Falkland Islands, but remarked that of course I never expected to cycle on South Georgia…."Would you like to cycle on South Georgia?" asked Woody, eager to ensure that I – along with other passengers – gained as much 'added value' from the expedition as possible, an enthusiasm that continued throughout the voyage. "I'd love to!" was the emphatic reply.

It turned out that the 'small world syndrome' and 'ocean grapevine' of the South Atlantic were again to my advantage, since the other expedition team member I had been talking with in turn knew a staff member at the South Georgia Museum in Grytviken, and also knew that they had a bicycle…*on South Georgia*…which – given my 'track record' – they might be persuaded to lend me. So it seemed I was now about to add a *fifth* South Atlantic territory to my list of cycling conquests, and out of them all this was probably the most unexpected!

As this sector of the voyage moved ever closer to South Georgia, the excitement mounted onboard ship, as meanwhile the weather became decidedly more excitable: The first full day on the South Atlantic after leaving the Falklands behind had been fairly warm and sunny, and the sea moderately calm. However, after a brilliant orange sunrise set against pink-hued clouds the following morning, the weather took a turn for the worse; it started to rain quite persistently, the wind increased markedly and the sea became considerably rougher. These sudden meteorological changes signified that the Antarctic Convergence (or Polar Front) had now been crossed, with the warmer waters of the South Atlantic Ocean exchanged for the colder waters of the Southern – or Antarctic – Ocean. Or, to put it another way, an invisible line of demarcation had been traversed, beyond which nothing could be predicted with any degree of certainty, and where time starts to become comparatively meaningless – a thought which must have preoccupied many a polar explorer over the years.

I pondered on this during lunch as meanwhile there was a brief sighting of Shag Rocks – a series of jagged protrusions rising straight out of the ocean, as smudgy and imperceptible as blunt pencil strokes viewed through the grey mist and murk of a Southern summer afternoon. For the benefit of the purists – and those who have been paying careful attention – it is perhaps also worth pondering on the fact that, despite its links to – and not being *significantly* far south of – the Falklands, South Georgia is *technically* not a South Atlantic island. Even so, much of this voyage *was* in the South Atlantic and I was hoping to cycle on South Georgia, so why let a mere point of detail spoil a good story?

~~~~~~

Monday 23rd February – the day of arrival at South Georgia – had at last come, the culmination of three days travelling from the Falklands, six from South America and nine from the UK. The 'island nut' didn't want to miss witnessing the approach to this spectacularly beautiful island, and I was consequently not just out of my bed by 5.00am, I was actually on deck by then in the semi-darkness. During the night, the temperature had been steadily dropping and the wind had been gradually increasing in force, such that it felt distinctly cold with an icy chill, whilst it was difficult to stand up as the *Vavilov* pitched in the heavy swell. Initially I was only able to discern the dark outlines of landforms to the starboard (south) side of the ship.

As the light slowly improved, I had my first view of South Georgia: A central mountain spine of spiky, serrated and forbidding-looking peaks and a rugged north-facing coastline. The mountains were of serious proportions, and mostly covered in snow and ice, with glaciers plunging down the slopes towards the dramatic coastal bays and headlands. At this distance and in the early dawn light, there appeared to be no vegetation – the overwhelming colours were white, silver-grey and black. South Georgia has been described as an alpine mountain range rising straight out of the ocean, and for once I cannot think of any other description – poetic, prosaic or otherwise fanciful – that would give a better impression. In short, it is utterly awe-inspiring. The island isn't just massive vertically, it is also of ample horizontal proportions, and forms a huge crescent-shape over 100 miles in length and upwards of 20 miles across at its widest points.

The coastline, particularly on the north-east side, is much-indented with fjord-like bays – indeed another comparison, if one was needed, could be in terms of a resemblance to Norway's North Sea coast. Whilst the south-west side of the island faces the full force of storms from the Antarctic, the more sheltered north-east side – with the added benefit of the frequent bays – 'enjoys' (...and that is very much a *relative* term...) a somewhat better climate: It is therefore no accident – and oddly 'appropriate' – that the Norwegians should have chosen to establish what was once a very industrious whaling trade based around the fjords of South Georgia.

During the early morning, the ship had sailed past a series of minor outlying isles (the Willis Islands and Bird Island) then bays – including Elsehul, Church Bay and Right Whale Bay – followed by the much larger Bay of Isles, before turning into the fjord-like Possession Bay to seek shelter from the increasingly wild weather. By this stage, the wailing wind had wound itself up into a 'full-on' Force 10 gale, gusting to Force 11, accompanied by a heaving, battleship-grey sea, and inevitably a number of passengers had succumbed to the dreaded *mal de mer*. I had previously experienced the "Roaring Forties", but located between 54 and 55 degrees south latitude, South Georgia is well and truly in the "Furious Fifties".

The enforced period of refuge in the bay only offered partial protection from the worst the elements were conspiring to deliver, but did give an opportunity to appreciate classic South Georgia scenery, with snow-capped and glacier-strewn mountains ascending directly from the sea, as well as a glimpse of a former whaling station at Prince Olav Harbour. Interestingly, this site could have been the target for Shackleton's 1916 trek across the island – being the nearest whaling station to King Haakon Bay on the opposite coast – but it is thought Shackleton chose the much longer route to Stromness station as he believed the Prince Olav station would have already closed for the winter.

Possession Bay is so-named in recognition of it being the point where famous explorer Captain James Cook first landed in 1775 and took possession of the island for the Crown, naming it Georgia after the then-monarch King George III. Ironically, it is believed that his published description of the wildlife – notably fur seals – gave rise to a mad rush to capitalise on the abundant supply of fur seal skins and elephant seal oil, and sealing in turn led to whaling which – on South Georgia – became big business.

Although Captain Cook is credited with claiming the island for Britain, South Georgia is generally recognised as having been discovered a century earlier in 1675 by London-based merchant Antoine de la Roche, whose ship sailing from Lima to England was blown off course after rounding Cape Horn. Meanwhile, returning to 2009, the wind was still doing its worst as the *Vavilov* received more of the 'washing machine treatment' and breakfast was served…honestly!

The ship eventually emerged from Possession Bay and attempted to enter the Bay of Isles a little to the west, but sea and weather conditions were still too difficult, so instead the vessel held steady into the wind to ride out the storm. There was, it seemed, not going to be an opportunity to land on South Georgia this particular day, so a film about Shackleton's *Endurance* expedition was shown, possibly to quell any mutinous thoughts on the part of the passengers who – having travelled so far – were desperate to step ashore! Upon emerging from the film screening, I noted the ship had moved a little further west back along the north coast, and spotted my first-ever iceberg floating past some distance north of the island. Another attempt was made to enter Bay of Isles after lunch, and *this* time it was successful.

The bay takes its name from the series of small, low-lying (and consequentially green) islands which are contained within it, including Albatross and Prion Islets where mighty wandering albatrosses nest. Bay of Isles is a huge, sweeping inlet several miles across, and when viewed from the sea offers an exciting and superb panorama of glaciated mountain peaks and impressive, wide glaciers sweeping down into the sea. At the head of the bay lies Salisbury Plain – a large expanse of relatively flat land, in part cloaked in green vegetation including tussock grass. The wind had by now dropped dramatically – such are the sudden and extreme changes of weather on South Georgia – and once the ship had come to rest in a more

Arrival at South Georgia – Possession Bay & Prince Olav Harbour old whaling site

First South Georgia landing – king penguin colony on Salisbury Plain, Bay of Isles

*Chapter 7 ~ **South Georgia** ~ Tyre Tracks in the Wake of Shackleton ~ 201*

sheltered location, the zodiac boats were lowered and the 'weather window' was taken full advantage of to travel ashore.

I landed for the first time on South Georgia at around 4.00pm that afternoon, on a beach fronting Salisbury Plain, and was immediately faced with a 'welcome party' made up of scores of fur seals and hundreds of king penguins spread along the sand. However, the best was yet to come, for behind the beach – spread right across the plateau of Salisbury Plain – were not hundreds, nor thousands, but literally *tens of thousands* of king penguins, by far the largest such colony I had ever seen! There were – I was told – an estimated 20,000 to 30,000 birds. In king penguin terms, the Falklands – impressive as they were – had been a warm-up act, but without a shadow of doubt South Georgia was – indeed *is* – the main event, or 'penguin metropolis' if you prefer! These beautiful birds were variously standing huddled together (there was still an icy wind funnelling down from the mountains), waddling in a peculiarly penguin way between beach and breeding site, moulting, preening themselves, incubating eggs, caring for chicks or whatever else penguins do!

Climbing a slight elevation through tussock grass, I was rewarded with an aerial view of the vast colony which had begun to climb the slope behind the plain. This amazing sight was matched only by the incredible chorus of sound that resounded across the air. Yet all good things come to an end – at least they did for the human interlopers – as it was soon time to return to the ship. I reluctantly left the massed choirs of penguins behind, jumped into a zodiac and was swiftly conveyed back to the *Vavilov*. Dinner was served as the ship sailed out of Bay of Isles under a cold but atmospheric evening sky...a spectacular introduction to South Georgia.

Tuesday – expedition leader Woody had declared – was to be a 'full-on' day, with three 'main events' so as to take maximum advantage of the weather whilst it was in an accommodating mood. It was also – provided everything went to plan – due to be the day when I had the opportunity to at last cycle on South Georgia. With such a busy programme, an early start was essential, and on emerging from my cabin onto the open deck as dawn broke I was just in time to see that the ship was starting to turn into Fortuna Bay, another fjord-like incursion into South Georgia's virtually impregnable mountain interior. It was a beautiful sunny morning, complemented by still conditions – in fact the very opposite of the previous morning – and by 6.00am the zodiacs had been launched and I had made my second landing

King penguins & fur seals at Fortuna Bay – second South Georgia beach landing

Stromness former whaling station – Shackleton found help here to rescue his crew

*Chapter 7 ~ **South Georgia** ~ Tyre Tracks in the Wake of Shackleton ~ 203*

on the island at a lovely beach inhabited by king penguins and fur seals.

There were quite large concentrations of the latter, both adults and young pups, and it was mesmerising simply watching their particular behaviour patterns. The fairly sizeable king penguin colony (though not of Salisbury Plain proportions) was also a joy to behold, spreading across a green plateau at the head of the bay, with a backdrop of soaring mountains and snaking glaciers. I even spotted some reindeer, though clearly these are an introduced species! Fortuna Bay also featured in Shackleton's trek across South Georgia, as he and his two companions descended from the Fortuna Glacier into this bay which they then skirted round before a stiff climb over the ridge to finally reach the next bay to the east – Stromness Bay – which was also to be our ship's destination for the second excursion of the day.

As breakfast was served, the *Vavilov* steamed a few miles down the coast before entering Stromness Bay – actually three smaller bays within a larger sea inlet, each of the three sub-bays containing a derelict old whaling station at its head: Whilst there was only a brief view of the former whaling site at Leith Harbour, and an even more fleeting glimpse of that at Husvik, the ship did sail right into the middle bay of the three, providing a chance to view the rusting red buildings, workshops and associated apparatus of Stromness whaling station. There was something quite surreal about the place – a ghost town frozen in time – for whaling here finished in the early 1960s.

It was from the ridge behind Stromness whaling station – forming a dramatic backdrop to the scene as if part of a film set – that Ernest Shackleton, Tom Crean and Frank Worsley descended after their 36 hour walk of endurance, and ultimately survival, across the icy island from King Haakon Bay. Shackleton famously arrived at the station manager's house on 20th May 1916, and this therefore marks the point in the story where the rescue of other members of the *Endurance* crew – whether on the other side of South Georgia or stranded hundreds of miles away on Elephant Island – could at last be assured. Almost 100 years on as I gazed across at the deserted manager's house – still standing just to the left of the rusting relics of a bygone era – I had a palpable sense of living history in the face of such decay and dereliction.

It was, however, whaling that initially put South Georgia 'on the map' as it were, and the next 'port of call' for the ship – as well as the third and

Arrival at Grytviken, South Georgia's 'capital' – Whalers' Church visible in centre

Simon on Grytviken landing beach – King Edward Point & RV Vavilov are beyond

*Chapter 7 ~ **South Georgia** ~ Tyre Tracks in the Wake of Shackleton ~ 205*

longest excursion of the day – was to be to Grytviken, the nearest thing to a 'capital' on South Georgia in the loosest possible sense of the expression! Upon leaving Stromness Bay, the ship again proceeded along the coast with fine views of the highest peaks of the island – giving full credence to the snowy alpine mountain range analogy – including Mount Paget, rising to well over 9,000 feet and South Georgia's highest point. As a light lunch was served, the *Vavilov* turned towards the twin incursions of Cumberland Bay West and Cumberland Bay East, although it was the latter that was pursued until the ship turned suddenly around a headland at King Edward Point and entered the sheltered natural harbour at Grytviken, where it came to rest at the anchorage.

From the deck, I had fine views of the 'settlement' – primarily another old whaling station – as well as the Government administrative and various research buildings at King Edward Point. I was particularly keen to try and maximise my time at this interesting location, and went ashore on the first zodiac, landing on a stony beach on the south side of the bay at Grytviken. There was much to see and do…*including some cycling*…and I had been assured before leaving the ship that "arrangements have been made".

The first stop was at the little whalers' cemetery, a square enclosure surrounded by a white timber fence, and situated on a slight grassy elevation above the beach. As well as the graves of former whalers there is a simple granite stone pillar – the grave of Sir Ernest Shackleton – who, as previously mentioned, died in 1922 on arrival at South Georgia whilst pursuing a subsequent polar expedition onboard the *Quest*. From here, I made my way slowly round the bay – known as King Edward Cove – and past some elephant seals resting on the beach, to begin exploring the other main points of interest in Grytviken. I initially noted the tiny turbine house and generators – driven by a small hydro-electric system – and a reminder of the power needs of the present-day Governmental and research community based on South Georgia who number around 20 in summer and nearer 10 in winter.

The whaling industry on the island began in 1904 when a Norwegian company (based in Argentina) established the first whaling station at Grytviken. As the best harbour along the island's coast, it was chosen by Norwegian Captain Carl Anton Larsen as the site of a venture which grew considerably over the ensuing decades – indeed, it was whaling which marked the beginning of South Georgia's permanent occupation. Grytviken

– which means "Pot Cove" after the sealers' trypots which were discovered there – was not only the first whaling station to open, it was also the last to close in 1965.

Whilst the industrial remains at the Grytviken site are not as extensive as those at Stromness, they nevertheless give an informative insight into the 'procedures' of this once-prevalent trade. Wandering around the red-orange, rust-encrusted relics was a strange – and in some ways nauseating – experience, which included such areas as the "flensing plan" where – having been hauled up the slipway by a winch – the unfortunate whales were cut-up. The blubber was then processed into whale oil (stored in large drum-shaped tanks) while meat and bones were reprocessed for various uses. Four rusting old ships hauled up on the beach in front of the former station were further visible testimony to the support vessels needed for the industry, including a whale catcher boat – the *Petrel* – and a coaling hulk – the *Louise*.

During my tour of the site, I suddenly heard the bizarre sound of two church bells chiming mournfully across the scene of dereliction: The sound came from the nearby Whalers' Church, again of Norwegian origin, which I visited next – a simple timber building with a fairly plain interior and a squat steeple containing the two bells that I had just heard and which visitors are invited to chime – and of course I just had to have a go myself!

Another 'must see' attraction in Grytviken is the superb South Georgia Museum (housed in the former station manager's villa) which I made a point of visiting: This includes exhibits covering polar and ocean exploration, whaling, life on South Georgia and natural history – including a preserved wandering albatross suspended from the ceiling. There is also a small souvenir shop. Yet arguably the most poignant exhibit, located in its own gallery, is a replica of the *James Caird* – the open boat in which Shackleton and five other crew members from the *Endurance* sailed – and rowed – the 800 miles from Elephant Island to seek rescue in South Georgia.

However, it was – at last – time for me to cycle on South Georgia, an unexpected opportunity that I was determined *not* to miss in the limited time available. I therefore collected, as arranged, a remarkably smart-looking mountain bike from a member of the museum staff and began my two-wheeled exploration of the island. Actually, that is something of an exaggeration in the extreme, as it will have been gathered by now that South Georgia offers very little scope indeed from a cycling perspective!

View from whalers' cemetery towards Grytviken (Shackleton's grave in foreground)

A stop on cycle ride by South Georgia Museum & Grytviken former whaling station

Borrowed bicycle outside South Georgia Post Office at King Edward Point

View from Shackleton memorial cairn & cross at Hope Point over Cumberland Bay

*Chapter 7 ~ **South Georgia** ~ Tyre Tracks in the Wake of Shackleton ~ 209*

Nevertheless, there is *one* 'real' road – more of a gravel track really – which begins in the vicinity of the whalers' cemetery and turbine house, closely following the Grytviken shoreline between the four abandoned ships and whaling station, before proceeding past the museum and continuing for another half-a-mile or so to – and just beyond – King Edward Point. The surface may have been rough, but at least it was flat, and afforded me one of the strangest – but admittedly easiest – cycling experiences I can ever recall having! In fact, the novelty value of it was such that I deliberately pedalled as *slowly* as possible in order to savour the moment!

My 'herculean efforts' quickly brought me along the north side of the bay to King Edward Point, where I found the South Georgia Post Office, another obligatory visit of course, and where I was able to post a selection of postcards to family and friends. I was indeed grateful to have bought the cards and stamps back in Stanley, and of course pre-written them, as business was brisk and time was very precious – even so, I did still buy a few philatelic mementos such as first day covers that I could at least genuinely say came from South Georgia!

Beyond the post office, I cycled past the modern chalet-like buildings housing the administrative offices and research facilities run by the British Antarctic Survey – and where most of the tiny population 'lives' – to reach a small raised promontory of land called Hope Point: There I found a simple stone cairn and memorial cross, erected in commemoration of Shackleton, and offering a remarkably rewarding view of the Allardyce Range of ice-strewn mountains forming the island's 'backbone', Cumberland Bay and also out to sea.

Alas, time was pressing, despite which I *still* cycled leisurely back through the King Edward Point 'community', past the post office and then the half-a-mile along South Georgia's 'main road' to arrive back in the heart of Grytviken outside the museum. I returned the borrowed bicycle with grateful thanks, having of course ensured photographs had been taken of me...and the bike...for the record. With my two-wheeled exploration finished, I boarded the last zodiac back to the ship, which promptly set sail, and I enjoyed dinner that evening reflecting on a very fulfilling day indeed.

Wednesday was to be the last day in and around South Georgian waters, and overnight the *Vavilov* had been slowly making its way along the east coast past the former whaling sites at Godthul and Ocean Harbour, plus the wildlife-abundant St Andrew's Bay and Royal Bay. As I emerged on deck, I discovered that the weather had obviously changed for the worse again and was overcast with squally rain and gusty winds. I was however just in time to see the ship turn in towards Gold Harbour, where the anchor was dropped. The location had a typical South Georgian backdrop – an amphitheatre of dark, menacing peaks and cliffs, cloaked in snow and ice. After an early breakfast, as I waited at the top of the gangway, I noticed a brilliant, vividly-coloured rainbow appearing to rise straight out of the sea before curving in a perfect arc back down into the water, thereby arching over and beautifully framing the view of Gold Harbour.

A bumpy, spray-filled zodiac ride brought me ashore at what was to be the fourth and final landing site on South Georgia – but what a landing! The boat surged onto the beach at what proved to be a treasure-trove of wildlife: Immediately apparent were at least a dozen huge elephant seals wallowing, sleeping and occasionally stirring. Most were females, but a couple were males – having a much more pronounced nose (or proboscis) and emitting loud snorting noises at intervals. They were remarkably docile and accepting of us humans despite their immense size, and quite unlike the much more diminutive fur seals slithering energetically around the beach which were quite willing to chase after any 'invader' with two legs! Moving further along Gold Harbour, I was presented with yet another of South Georgia's king penguin colonies, and it was entertaining to watch them in their courtship routines, attending to their young, swimming in – or rushing out of – the water, and also interacting with other wildlife such as skuas and petrels (both predatory birds), the seals and even the odd gentoo penguin.

With the rain persisting and time moving on, the hour had come to leave South Georgia for the last time. Once back on the *Vavilov* I again noted a distinct – but on this occasion shallower – rainbow, at the end of which I had indeed found a proverbial 'crock of gold' in terms of the wildlife present within the aptly-named bay. Lunch was served as the ship left Gold Harbour and continued south: As it rounded the south-eastern extremity of the island in the vicinity of Cooper Bay and the small offshore Cooper Island, it headed straight into fierce Force 10 gale conditions again, with seas to match, accompanied by a not very steady procession of 'smallish' icebergs 'sailing' briskly in the other direction...by 'smallish' I mean at least the same size as the ship!

Suddenly the *Vavilov* made a sharp turn to starboard, causing it to roll

Fur & elephant seals at Gold Harbour landing beach – final South Georgia landing

Leaving South Georgia – sailing past heavily-glaciated mountains, Drygalski Fjord

alarmingly, before slipping quickly between two advancing lumps of ice (as if a small van crossing a gap in traffic between a convoy of thundering juggernauts). In consequence of this manoeuvre, the vessel entered the comparative calm of Drygalski Fjord, and its subsidiary fjord known as Larsen Harbour after the Norwegian originally responsible for establishing the whaling station at Grytviken. The stunning landscape of Drygalski Fjord – with massive, jagged and snow-capped peaks plus impressive glaciers forcing their way down steep valley sides to the sea – was both a worthy finale to South Georgia and a 'taster' of the wonders of Antarctica which were yet to come.

At the head of the fjord, the ship turned round and went out into the open sea, initially facing towards the south-east in which direction – several hundred miles further on – lay the South Sandwich Islands, a chain of volcanic isles incredibly forming part of a single UK Overseas Territory with South Georgia. However, another sharp turn was made towards the south-west and the ship set course for Antarctica. The voyage had been 1,300 nautical miles already since leaving Ushuaia, during which distance the Falklands and South Georgia had been visited. However, it would be approaching 800 nautical miles before the next landfall:

Looking north-west along South Georgia's southern coast towards King Haakon Bay, it was sobering to think that the ship's passage for the next three days would be over almost the same 800 miles of open ocean that Shackleton's party rowed the *James Caird* in the opposite direction back in 1916....As South Georgia receded into the distance, the waves grew mightier and soon the ship was pitching considerably as the Southern Ocean unleashed some violent weather over the bows. Dinner that evening was rather akin to a rollercoaster ride – no wonder tables *and chairs* in the dining room were chained to the floor....One can scarcely imagine what it must have been like for those six men back in 1916.

South Georgia, I had discovered, is an island which exceeds all expectations and one which can only be described in superlative terms: The landscapes are without doubt amongst the finest to be found anywhere in the World, while the wildlife is equally impressive and awe-inspiring. Superimposed on those attributes is the thought-provoking legacy of the whaling industry and its key part in the island's history. However, the most inspirational part of that history has to be the Shackleton story. As for me, I had not only experienced something of all those aspects whilst there, I had also managed – quite unexpectedly

– to cycle on South Georgia, thanks to the fortuitous provision of a borrowed bicycle, even if it was only for about two miles at most. In fact, considering I had travelled further from home to reach the island of South Georgia than I had to visit any of the other four South Atlantic territories – *and yet cycled far less* – it perhaps seems a little pointless, peculiar or even downright potty....Except there probably aren't many cyclists whose tyre tracks have been made in the wake of Shackleton – now that is something *really* special!

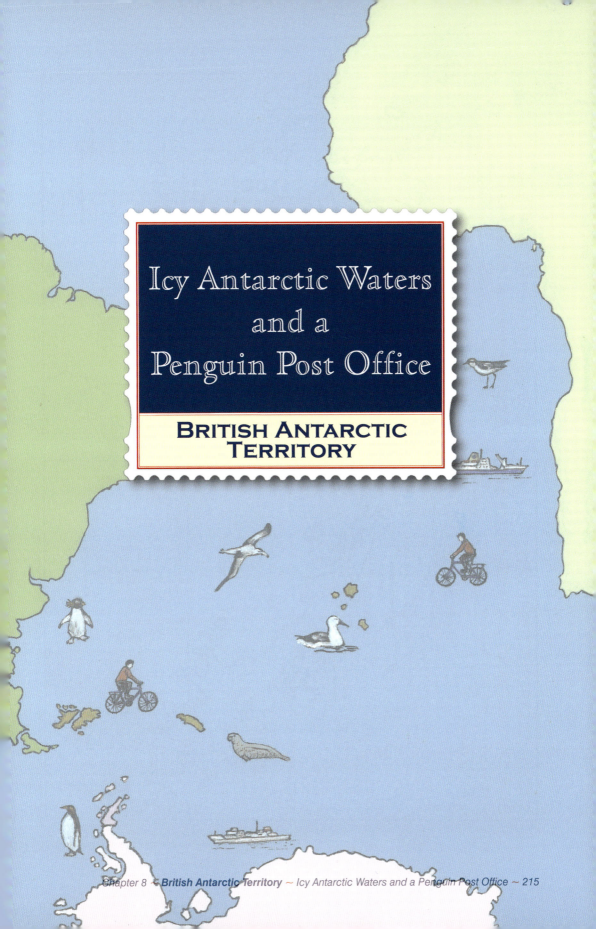

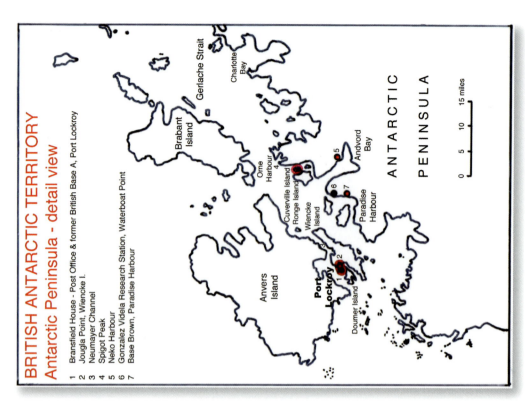

BRITISH ANTARCTIC TERRITORY
Antarctic Peninsula - detail view

1 Bransfield House - Post Office & former British Base A, Port Lockroy
2 Jougla Point, Wiencke I.
3 Neumayer Channel
4 Spigot Peak
5 Neko Harbour
6 Gonzalez Videla Research Station, Waterboat Point
7 Base Brown, Paradise Harbour

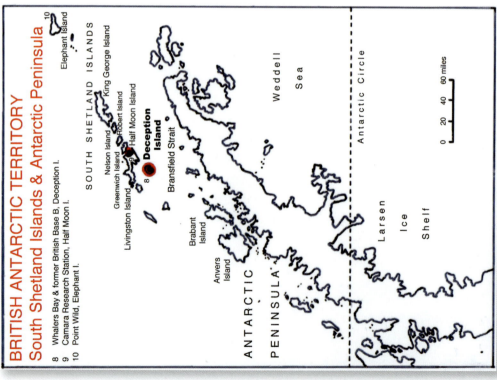

BRITISH ANTARCTIC TERRITORY
South Shetland Islands & Antarctic Peninsula

8 Whalers Bay & former British Base B, Deception I.
9 Camara Research Station, Half Moon I.
10 Point Wild, Elephant I.

216 ~ Chapter 8 ~ **British Antarctic Territory** ~ Icy Antarctic Waters and a Penguin Post Office

Chapter 8
British Antarctic Territory and a Bicycle

Simon & penguins at Bransfield House – Port Lockroy, British Antarctic Territory

I would imagine that a bicycle is not the first thing to spring to mind when talking about British Antarctic Territory, in fact any juxtaposition of cycling and the Antarctic would be most unlikely....Now if those words sound rather similar to the opening phrase of the previous chapter – and maybe a touch repetitive – then yes they are and yes it is...although the sentiment is arguably likewise relevant in the context of this chapter too. However, in contrast to South Georgia – where I *did* end up cycling – I didn't actually *bicycle*, so to speak, in the Antarctic...but I *did* nevertheless manage to have a bicycle....

...During the course of travelling across the South Atlantic – and beyond – I had become familiar with quite a few commonly-adopted acronyms describing certain sea and air modes of transport used in getting to, from and between the various islands: These included RMS (Royal Mail Ship); RAF (Royal Air Force); FIGAS (Falkland Islands Government Air Service); and RV

(Research Vessel)...then there was a BICYCLE....As I have already hinted, I *did* succeed in having one whilst in the Antarctic, or more specifically that part generally referred to as BAT (British Antarctic Territory).

At this point, I maybe should reiterate that I have perhaps already 'pushed the boundaries' a little by including South Georgia in a book which is primarily supposed to be about cycling across the South Atlantic, given *that* particular island territory lies south of the invisible ocean boundary defining the Antarctic Convergence so is *strictly speaking* in the Southern Ocean. Having said that, South Georgia is arguably close enough, and – even without the cycling element – I would have felt almost duty-bound to relate my 'extended' South Atlantic experience of such a memorable place.

As for Antarctica – or more precisely British Antarctic Territory – in the true spirit of adventure those 'boundaries' are going to have to be pushed quite a bit further still beyond even a 'greater' South Atlantic. Apart from that, having brought the reader from near the Equator so far south across the ocean towards 'the bottom of the World'...and doubtless heightened expectations of reaching the 'great white continent'...it would be almost unthinkable to 'abandon ship' so close to the grand finale that is Antarctica, never mind 'abandon bike' – or rather that bicycle which I happened to experience! Anyway, having got the poetic licence bit out of the way, on with the story...which of course must also include the conclusion – or rather earlier stages – of the Shackleton story...and the crucial matter of a penguin post office.

As far as abandoning ship was concerned, there wasn't any chance of that as the Research Vessel (RV) *Akademik Sergey Vavilov* sailed south-west from South Georgia across the icy waters of the Southern Ocean towards Antarctica in the closing days of February 2009, which were also the closing days of the austral summer....In any case, the only alternative was an involuntary and rather icy 'dip in the drink', as it were! After three very active days exploring in and around South Georgia, the opportunity to have a more restful day was welcome now that the RV *Vavilov* was out on the open sea again: The night had been rather 'rock and roll', with the thumping ocean 'music' against the ship's hull rhythmically beating out time, and on emerging onto the open deck a little after sunrise I noted that the vessel was still pitching through quite heavy seas accompanied by a fresh wind. Furthermore, the air temperature was definitely dropping again as the south-westerly progress towards Antarctica continued.

The days at sea were again filled with a programme of presentations, briefings and some films of relevance to the Antarctic part of the voyage, and covered a wide variety of subjects aiding both understanding of the ocean being crossed and the continent being approached: Whales of the Southern Ocean, Antarctic penguins, sea ice, the geology of Antarctica and the 'programme' of forthcoming shore excursions were all featured, as was a film about the photographic record of Shackleton's *Endurance* expedition taken by Frank Hurley, the expedition's photographer....It was obvious by now that *our* expedition leader – David "Woody" Wood – was determined for us to have the full 'Shackleton experience', albeit without the physical endurance part!

I meanwhile had reached the part in "Shackleton's Boat Journey" (my ocean reading matter for the voyage) where Ernest Shackleton and his five companions – Worsley, Crean, McNeish, McCarthy and Vincent – were in the final stages of their 800 mile, 16 day journey by open boat from Elephant Island to South Georgia to seek help, and ultimately rescue for all those from the *Endurance*. As I gazed out over the cruel, churning waters of the Southern Ocean, I tried to imagine a small boat with six men heading in the opposite direction across those same waters, and – not for the first time – the enormity of that feat of human survival back in 1916 was imprinted on my mind.

By the morning of the second full day at sea after South Georgia, around 400 nautical miles had been covered, and the ship was thus midway through the ocean passage to the next landfall. However, the nearest land actually lay due south – the archipelago known as the South Orkney Islands, named on account of being at a similar latitude south as the Scottish Orkney Islands are north. South Orkney Islands is the collective term for a group comprising four main constituent islands – Coronation, Signy, Powell and Laurie Islands – and the area includes both an Argentinean research base and a British Antarctic Territory post office:

Interestingly, when I had stocked-up on BAT stamps whilst at the post office in Stanley back on the Falklands, I had left some stamped self-addressed envelopes to be sent on to the post office at Signy Island. They eventually reached the UK many months later, albeit with postmarks from the South Orkney Islands as evidence of their journey! Actually, the delay factor is largely due to the fact that my 'novelty mail' would probably not have been sent from Stanley down to Signy until the post office at the latter reopened towards the end of 2009 after the Antarctic winter, only to have to wait for another ship to begin its long journey north to the UK. Together with the South Shetland Islands (predictably named due to their southern latitude reflecting the equivalent northern location of the Shetland Islands off Scotland), the South Orkneys form part of the UK territorial claim collectively known as British Antarctic Territory, which also includes the region of the Antarctic Peninsula (attached to the actual continental land mass).

One of the briefing sessions earlier in the voyage had been about Antarctic 'protocol' – or more specifically the matter of the Antarctic Treaty: Antarctica is unique among the World's land masses in that it has no indigenous people or permanent inhabitants, nor is it the sovereign territory of any nation. The Antarctic Treaty came about to deal with territorial claims that were originally made by seven nations during the first half of the 20th century, these being Argentina, Australia, Chile, France, New Zealand, Norway and the United Kingdom. The Treaty was signed in 1959 and came into force in 1961; it neither dissolves nor recognises any territorial claims, but instead ensures that the continent – and all land beyond 60 degrees south latitude – is 'governed' for exclusively peaceful purposes and in the interests of conserving its environment, wildlife and ecosystems. Over the ensuing years, several other nations have become co-signatories to this international agreement, which has been steadily increasing its membership, such that in the order of 50 parties are now represented. The 'population' of Antarctica is consequently largely made up of those who staff and operate the significant number of scientific research and meteorological stations established by several nations which are spread across the vast continent and its associated islands.

Thus, whilst I would be sailing around – and ultimately setting foot on – several parts of British Antarctic Territory, I would also be experiencing islands and a continent that is the sovereign possession of nowhere and nobody. In terms of 'protocol' which applied to those of us on the voyage, this was more concerned with protection than politics – protection of the environment and unique wildlife of Antarctica – which meant regular scrubbing and washing of wellington boots, waterproofs *and* rucksacks before and after each shore landing to prevent bio-contamination of sites or species….Fortunately, there had been plenty of practise during the Falklands and South Georgia parts of the expedition!

Day three after South Georgia dawned comparatively still and calm, although the temperature was now only slightly above freezing: Overnight, 60 degrees south latitude had been crossed, and therefore the Antarctic proper had been reached. In order to arrive in these southern latitudes, there is an inevitable 'rite of passage' over the often wild and swirling seas of the Southern Ocean, yet once closer to the Antarctic continent and its attendant islands, the wind can invariably drop in intensity and the waters also tend to become smoother. I was awake promptly as the 800 mile sea passage was nearly over, and just before 6.00am I went on deck in the early, grey light to witness the first truly Antarctic land of the voyage.

I did not have to wait long, as up ahead to starboard was a dark outline of land, signifying that the South Shetland Islands were at hand. The land was identified as Elephant Island, and – with the course of approach being almost due south – I was presented with the north-facing aspect of what, as the light improved, revealed itself as a barren, heavily-glaciated island of dark peaks and little evidence of landing beaches: There were just two colours – black and white. About a mile offshore, the *Vavilov* ceased its approach and came to rest in the shelter of the island. Immediately after this, the ship's crane started lifting several of the zodiac inflatable boats stored on the aft deck and lowered them into the water. Having descended the ship's gangway into one of the zodiacs, I was soon bouncing across the swell towards Elephant Island.

Elephant Island takes its name from the presence of elephant seals, although its shape from above does bear a superficial resemblance to the head and trunk of an elephant! On leaving the ship, the zodiac in which I was travelling had made straight for Point Wild on the north coast. Being such a small craft, it was possible for the zodiac to enter a slightly sheltered bay in the lee of the point itself, and sail very close to the low-lying rocky promontory. About half-an-hour or so was spent slowly cruising around amongst numerous small lumps of ice (called "brash" ice) floating on the water, and viewing a rookery of chinstrap penguins – another new species for me – crowded onto the rocks near the shoreline.

The significance of Point Wild, though, rests with its pivotal role in the Shackleton story: Named after Frank Wild – Shackleton's second-in-command – this bony finger of rock reaching out from Elephant Island is the place to which all 28 members of the doomed *Endurance* expedition came in three boats having escaped from the Weddell Sea ice, and from where Ernest Shackleton and five other men set off in the *James Caird* to South

Antarctic landfall – dawn approach to Elephant Island onboard RV Vavilov in 2009

Point Wild, Elephant Island – where 22 of Shackleton's men spent four months

Georgia to seek help. Meanwhile, as related in the previous chapter, Frank Wild and the remaining 21 men spent a miserable four months at this bleak spot until finally rescued. Rescue came in August 1916 in the form of the *Yelcho* – a steamer lent by the Chilean Government. In commemoration of this, a bronze bust of the captain of the *Yelcho* now stands at Point Wild, and is yet another visual reminder of the incredible survival story of all 28 men from *Endurance*, a story that for me had come alive through being so closely woven into the wider experience of the voyage.

A cold and bumpy ride back to the ship followed (with plenty of salt sea spray for good measure), whereupon the *Vavilov* began steaming away from Elephant Island, initially past its eastern extremity, before passing between a large rock called Cornwallis Island and outlying Clarence Island. The ship then turned towards the south-west once more, giving views of the south-facing coast of Elephant Island. A few more hours brought the ship past some minor islands and rocks, as it made for the stretch of water known as the Bransfield Strait which lies between the main group of South Shetland Islands and the Antarctic Peninsula. The largest of the South Shetlands is King George Island, which gradually appeared on the starboard side of the vessel: Sometimes termed "Antarctica's unofficial capital" owing to the large concentration of research bases representing no less than eight different nations, King George Island was – I noted – again typically glaciated, a study in black and white…well, more white than black to be truthful!

Throughout the afternoon the best views had been to starboard, but just before dark at around 9.00pm a new vista appeared – I spotted land on the port side which, if not outlying islands of the Antarctic Sound, could have been my first sight of the Antarctic Peninsula, beyond which lay the Weddell Sea – the ice of which crushed and destroyed the *Endurance* during 1915, thereby precipitating the Shackleton story: Now that our voyage had reached the true Antarctic, the ice-strengthened hull of the *Vavilov* was something to be thankful for, even if it was – just about – 'summer'.

The next morning I was – as per usual – up on deck at an early hour, although due to the ship steadily heading ever further south *and west*, whilst still being on time zone GMT minus two, both sunrise and sunset were becoming later each day and it was consequentially quite dark. Actually, time is pretty meaningless in the Antarctic anyway, as the lines of longitude gradually converge towards the South Pole meaning

Antarctica could claim to have no less than 24 time zones!...It is perhaps no accident then that I have stopped referring to days of the week. What *is* important is available daylight and how it is used, and being quite late in the austral summer a decision was made to keep the ship's clocks on GMT minus two throughout the Antarctic section to maximise useful late morning, afternoon and evening daylight for shore excursions as well as onboard sightseeing purposes.

Weather-wise, however, the day turned into one of almost unbroken sunshine and blue skies, which presented the stunning scenery in all its glorious, colourful brilliance...and I don't mean just black and white! As the sun rose, the *Vavilov* – having sailed overnight via (or at least past) King George, Nelson, Robert and Greenwich Islands – began to turn in front of the next island in the South Shetland chain – Livingston Island – and made for a sheltered anchorage in the bay formed by tiny (and appropriately enough) crescent-shaped Half Moon Island. Being low-lying, the latter island has hardly any snow cover during the Antarctic summer, unlike the much larger Livingston Island whose towering white peaks form a huge natural amphitheatre around it.

Once the zodiac boats had been launched, a landing was soon made on a sloping, rocky beach inhabited by more chinstrap penguins, whose faces are characterised by a black 'chinstrap' marking which gives the impression they are permanently smiling! An interesting walk right round the rocky ridge – or spine – of Half Moon Island yielded several features of note: These included the Argentinean "Camara" research station, various green mosses and lichens, and the phenomenon of pink snow – caused by algae which give the snow a reddish tinge – thereby proving that snow doesn't have to be white! There were also excellent panoramic views from the island's highest point.

On returning to the beach, there was the bonus of a Weddell seal – another new seal species to add to my list of sightings. A final look around the penguin colony and an old wooden boat on the shore – of unknown origin – concluded my first landing in icy Antarctic waters, before it was time to return to the ship. As the *Vavilov* steamed away from Half Moon Island, past Livingston Island, at least the sun managed to make it feel a little warmer on deck than had been the norm, and it was a pleasure to soak up the 'heat' of an Antarctic summer....The ship then set course for the last of the South Shetlands to be visited – the unusual Deception Island, where I was hoping to be able to experience *that* bicycle!

Crescent-shaped Half Moon Island & Livingston Island behind (South Shetlands)

Deception Island – about to pass between Neptune's Bellows into Port Foster

Chapter 8 ~ **British Antarctic Territory** ~ *Icy Antarctic Waters and a Penguin Post Office* ~ 225

Although typically white and black in appearance when viewed from the sea – and therefore like most other Antarctic islands – Deception Island is shaped like a horseshoe when seen from above, with a gap in the 'ring' called Neptune's Bellows providing access to a huge natural harbour within named Port Foster. The island is actually a circular volcano, and the body of water inside the outer rim is the flooded caldera of that volcano, formed following a massive eruption long ago which literally 'blew its top off'. The ship *very* carefully sailed through the 'gateway' formed by Neptune's Bellows – due to the presence of a shallow submerged rock – then proceeded to embark on a circular clockwise tour of Port Foster, offering fine views of the reds, browns, greys and blacks of the volcano rim.

Hold on a minute, this is starting to sound more like a description of the near-Equatorial island of Ascension rather than one in the Antarctic – but there *is* a good reason for that: The most recent volcanic eruptions were in 1967, 1969 and 1970, which destroyed a Chilean research base, and the site of these eruptions was clearly visible from the ship, as was the Argentinean "Decepcion" research base which – being located elsewhere around the volcano's rim – escaped destruction. I also noted a more recent Spanish base. Deception Island is in fact continually monitored, as it is classified as 'active'...a disconcerting thought. The last time I had a bicycle on a volcano's rim was in Tristan da Cunha, which similarly erupted in the 1960s and where heat from the inner earth could be felt decades later....I was starting to have second thoughts about having a bicycle here on Deception Island as well!

The ship came to rest at 'a bay within a bay' – known as Whalers Bay – where a shore visit was made by zodiac. The area around Whalers Bay is dominated by derelict reminders of whaling, such as red and rusting whale oil tanks and other apparatus, as well as old wooden water supply boats. There is also the eerie, tumbledown building of a former British base – "Base B" – and one-time post office, the first physical evidence (albeit derelict) I had so far spotted of a British presence in the Antarctic, and in small part a factor leading to Deception Island – and the other South Shetland Islands – being 'claimed' as part of British Antarctic Territory.

From Whalers Bay, I took a short walk up to a viewpoint on the caldera rim known as Neptune's Window, which afforded fine views across the Bransfield Strait towards the Antarctic Peninsula, and it is said that from this point the continent of Antarctica was first spotted. As for Deception Island, it takes its name from the fact that the presence of a natural

Deception Island – the derelict British base & whaling station at Whalers Bay

Simon at Whalers Bay, Deception Island – location of Antarctic 'bicycle' deception

*Chapter 8 ~ **British Antarctic Territory** ~ Icy Antarctic Waters and a Penguin Post Office ~ 227*

harbour 'within the ring' is deceptive from the outside: It certainly has a dangerously deceptive harbour entrance (on account of that rock lurking just below the surface), whilst the natural harbour within is not always sheltered due to winds funnelling downwards – yet more deception.

However, my favourite nomination for why Deception Island is so-called would be that the water in Whalers Bay is deceptively warm: Fresh water – which is subjected to geothermal heat from the volcano – runs off the land and beach, then mixes with the icy cold water of the sea, and if enough of the warmer water is present, the result – I had been told – is water that is often warm enough to bathe in...otherwise known as an Antarctic swimming pool....Or alternatively – from the perspective of a cyclist – a BICYCLE...that is to say a Bathe In Cold Yet Comparatively Lukewarm Environs! I decided to test out this 'deception', and – having brought the necessary swimwear with me – managed to swim for about a minute in a brief (but not brief enough) and barely comprehendible moment of madness, thereby discovering it to be briefly bearable!

To call it a "bathe in cold yet comparatively lukewarm environs" would be pushing it a bit – certainly from a physical wellbeing point of view – but as I said at the beginning of this chapter, I *did* manage to have a BICYCLE whilst in BAT....I suppose it could also be called a CYCLE – or Cold Yet Comfortable Lido Experience – but that would only serve to further increase the deception for both author and reader...and anyway that is quite enough acronym wordplay and contrivance! Needless to say, after my Antarctic 'bicycle' – I mean *swim* – I returned to the ship pretty well immediately to thaw-out and warm-up, but was still shivering somewhat as the *Vavilov* again carefully negotiated Neptune's Bellows and the voyage continued south towards *the* continent after an interesting day, not least from a 'cycle' angle!

It would never be possible, indeed futile, to attempt to do a whole continent justice in the closing stages of a story which is essentially about cycling across the islands of the South Atlantic, apart from which by this stage in my oceanic odyssey the cycling part was well and truly over, including of course the 'deception' of Deception Island. It is, however, cycling which brought me thus far and which – as I stressed in the introductory chapter – has for me always been an accessory to exploring the great outdoors in its own right. Nevertheless, I need to finish the story, and so a few geographical facts would be in order by way of setting the scene and putting in context my final few days of exploration:

Physically, Antarctica is the fifth largest continent on Earth – smaller than Asia, Africa or the Americas, but larger than either Europe or Australasia. It is very roughly 'circular' in shape, with two unequal 'halves' defined by the line of zero longitude – East Antarctica and West Antarctica, which are themselves divided by the Transantarctic Mountains. From the smaller 'half' – West Antarctica – a long tail of land snakes northwards generally towards South America's Tierra del Fuego – known as the Antarctic Peninsula. The continent could be described in plan as resembling a giant stingray, or perhaps the head and horn of a rhinoceros. Over 99% of the land mass is permanently covered with a huge glacial ice sheet, while there are two great coastal indentations – the Weddell and Ross Seas – each of which has its own ice shelf, effectively extensions of the Antarctic ice sheet literally floating out towards the surrounding waters of the Southern Ocean. The land beneath this white 'blanket' is extremely mountainous and elevated, yet much of the 'surface texture' is hidden beneath the huge depth of ice.

It was the second day of March 2009 and also the day of arrival at the Antarctic Peninsula – and therefore by definition the continent of Antarctica – after a circuitous journey lasting over two weeks since leaving home in the UK. It goes without saying that I was up and about early so as to witness the approach, and at first light the dark outline of the continent for real started to appear on the port side of the ship, gradually brightening as the sun began to rise, and so it continued until a great white land mass – in places thousands of feet high – made its presence felt. From initially seeing the landfall, it was well over an hour before the pure, brilliant white of the ice and snow cloaking the majestic mountains could be appreciated to the full, following a wonderful purple-tinged sunrise.

As the ship slowly made its way down the Gerlache Strait (separating the peninsula from the large Brabant and Anvers Islands) it arrived at the entrance to Charlotte Bay, extending around ten miles into the peninsula. Soon afterwards, I joined other passengers in a zodiac for a cruise deep into Charlotte Bay itself, during which time we were treated to quite close-up and impressive sightings of humpback whales in at least three separate locations around the bay, made all the more exciting by frequent displays of dorsal fins and tails as the whales dived down to feed, as well as tell-tale whale 'blows'. Apart from these magnificent creatures in their natural

Tail & dorsal fin of two humpback whales – Charlotte Bay (Antarctic Peninsula)

Approaching rock spire of Spigot Peak & Orne Harbour (Antarctic Peninsula)

environment, there were also sightings of Antarctic terns and penguins 'hitching lifts' on icebergs!

As for the icebergs, there were many to observe floating round the bay, large and small, some carved through the effects of wind and wave action into fantastic and incredible shapes. Many of them reflected not only pure white but also an intense blue – the true colour of ice, which can only be appreciated when it is present in such magnitude....First pink snow, now blue ice – surely this was a voyage of discovery, and in no way could it be termed a run-of-the-mill, black and white affair! All around was a brooding backdrop of high, rugged and ice-covered mountains, reflected in the still waters of the bay as if in a mirror.

After about two hours it was time to return to the ship, for despite sunshine and a lack of wind it was – at 64 degrees south latitude – needless to say quite chilly. Leaving Charlotte Bay, the ship slowly sailed further down the Gerlache Strait, giving ample time to enjoy the great views in all directions. There was yet more discovery (of another ship that is) when for a brief period the RV *Akademik Ioffe* – sister ship of the *Vavilov* and last seen in Ushuaia a fortnight before – was spotted sailing close by.

A little while later, the *Vavilov* turned to port and entered another spellbinding bay of the Antarctic Peninsula – Orne Harbour, overlooked by a dramatic arena of high, glaciated mountains and guarded at its southern flank by a soaring spire of rock almost 1,000 feet high called Spigot Peak. Once the ship had come to rest, the zodiacs were again lowered, and a wonderfully intimate exploration of Orne Harbour took place, during which there was more whale watching, some fur seals were seen, and chinstrap penguins were observed below Spigot Peak...*and* I even had the chance to 'touch' the Antarctic continent for the first time, admittedly by outstretched hand from the boat! More fabulous *blue* icebergs were enjoyed at close quarters, taking care not to get *too* close in case they suddenly toppled – the effect of their centre of gravity changing as a result of melting ice.

Of equal – if not greater – importance was keeping well clear of glacier fronts – or ice cliffs – around the bay in case they 'calved' without warning, referring to the process by which sections break off to form icebergs. As soon as everyone had returned to the ship, a memorable departure was made from Orne Harbour under blue skies, brilliant sunshine and flat-calm seas, with definite warmth in the air. This riot of colour and cheering weather continued into the evening as passage was again resumed down the Gerlache

Strait and a most impressive sunset turned the ice and snow pink (and that has nothing to do with algae), with daylight well beyond 10.00pm.

The next morning, on emerging from my cabin onboard the *Vavilov* for the regular open deck 'constitutional', I was able to verify that the ship had turned out of the Gerlache Strait and was now instead heading generally northwards. It was again following a channel between two land masses – Anvers Island on the port side and Doumer Island to starboard. The dawn was a little grey and overcast, with a few summer snowflakes falling, but it was otherwise fairly dry. As daylight improved, the – by now – familiar landscape of ice-covered mountains became more visible, with a third land mass – Wiencke Island – forming a breathtaking backdrop directly ahead. The ship soon came to an anchorage in a natural harbour by the name of Port Lockroy.

Meanwhile, as the light increased, it was possible to see a tiny island a short distance from the ship – known as Goudier Island – set in the waters of Port Lockroy, which had not earlier been possible to distinguish from its larger 'neighbour'. On the island I spotted a small building – 'the penguin post office' – and it was this site that the morning's shore excursion was scheduled to visit. A short trip by zodiac brought me to the diminutive, low-lying but nevertheless rocky Goudier Island, where a rock-strewn landing site and short uphill path (dominated by numerous gentoo penguins) led to a modest red-and-black timber building called Bransfield House.

Bransfield House was originally a British Antarctic Survey research station, known as "Base A", but in more recent years was restored and transferred to the UK-based Antarctic Heritage Trust, who have since operated the site as both a museum and shop / post office during the Antarctic summer. The post office was something I didn't want to miss, and is part of the British Antarctic Territory Post Office 'network' (with other sites at Signy in the South Orkneys, Rothera further south on the Antarctic Peninsula and Halley on the Weddell Sea ice shelf). As with South Georgia, I was glad to have 'done my homework' – or rather 'shipwork' – in terms of pre-writing, addressing and stamping several postcards, which were then posted in a very British-looking red post box using British Antarctic Territory stamps. I managed to buy a special stamp folder by way of a record of my visit to Port Lockroy, but unlike South Georgia I was unable to buy any first day covers as these had already been sent to Stanley post office on the Falklands to 'overwinter'.

This latter point was actually quite significant as this was the last day (Tuesday 3rd March) that the museum, shop and post office would be open for the 2008/2009 summer season, since the Port Lockroy staff – *all four of them and the only 'shore-based human population' I ever saw in Antarctica* – were due to leave onboard the *Vavilov* that afternoon. A consequence of this was that any mail posted at Port Lockroy would only have the penguins for company over the Antarctic winter, and not leave the island until November (the last ship to carry mail via the forwarding point of the Falklands having already left), with delivery – perhaps – by Christmas: I can however confirm that the postcards reached their destinations by December!

As well as philatelic items from one of the remotest – and strangest – post offices in the World, I also acquired a few Antarctic 'souvenirs' from the shop before progressing to the museum: The remainder of Bransfield House has been preserved in a 'time warp' to represent a typical small Antarctic research station of the mid-20th century, with period rooms (bathroom, kitchen, bunkrooms, work rooms, radio room, stores etc.) and was most interesting. I signed the visitors' book (as I had previously done at the museum on South Georgia) and naturally posed for some photographs, albeit fighting for space with the penguin custodians gathered outside. I then left 'the penguin post office' and 'a little piece of Britain in the Antarctic' – as evidenced by the Union Flag flying proudly outside – and re-boarded a zodiac.

A short ride of a few minutes brought me to Jougla Point, a small promontory of nearby Wiencke Island where – with more gentoos for company – I was able to examine some old whale bones strewn across the beach as well as a reassembled whale skeleton on the shore. During the afternoon – after all had returned to the ship *and* the four homeward-bound staff members from Port Lockroy had been brought onboard to add to our number – the *Vavilov* set sail and continued generally northwards into a truly spectacular fjord known as the Neumayer Channel, with icy mountains crowding in on both sides, and the sunshine – which was by now dominating the day's weather – reflecting their images in the crystal-clear and totally calm waters. After an enjoyable hour or so, the ship emerged from the Neumayer Channel and crossed the much wider Gerlache Strait, thereby intersecting the route taken the day before.

British Antarctic Territory Post Office, UK flag & penguins – Port Lockroy

View from Vavilov leaving Port Lockroy – Wiencke Island forms the backdrop

Sailing past icy mountains via crystal-clear & calm waters of Neumayer Channel

Dome-shaped Cuverville Island – noted for its vegetation & another landing site

*Chapter 8 ~ **British Antarctic Territory** ~ Icy Antarctic Waters and a Penguin Post Office ~ 235*

At length, the *Vavilov* made its approach to a modest, dome-shaped piece of land by the name of Cuverville Island, which was to be the subject of the afternoon visit ashore. Once the ship was in position, a zodiac journey delivered me to a pebbly beach landing site, and an island – or at least its coastline – which is home to one of the largest gentoo colonies in Antarctica. Although – as ever – entertaining to watch, the penguins are not the only feature of interest at this location: Cuverville Island is also noted for its vegetation, with a covering of green mosses and lichens growing on the cliffs behind the shore. The zodiac ride back to the ship was eventful, with leopard seal spotting, iceberg dodging, and even having to wait for the ship's gangway to be cleared of floating ice forms: These were smallish "growlers" or "bergy bits", which for the record are terms applied to chunks between a metre and five metres in height; any smaller is "brash" ice, and any bigger – sometimes to a colossal size – is an iceberg.

Whilst putting the record straight, I have not mentioned anything about meals during the Antarctic section of the voyage for the simple reason that food – excellent though it was – had to be fitted round excursions ashore…as I eluded to before, time is largely meaningless in Antarctica. I should however mention the barbecue dinner that was enjoyed out on deck at the aft end of the vessel this particular evening, with glorious Antarctic scenery in all directions. Finally – after our feasting on visual as well as edible food – the ship set off again under the setting sun, 'round the back' of Cuverville Island, resuming its passage south between nearby Rongé Island and the Antarctic Peninsula, through an ice-laden channel with water so still it reflected everything back to perfection….The effect was totally transfixing and timeless.

Wednesday 4th March 2009 is however a date worth recording, for not only was it to be the final full day in Antarctica, it was also to be the 'grand finale' – a particularly special day when I hoped to at last land on the actual Antarctic continent. The dawn was overcast but fairly bright, although as the day progressed the sun did shine through from time to time. On reaching the open deck, I observed the overnight passage had been comparatively short, taking the *Vavilov* slightly further south again. In cross-referencing the ship's displayed latitude and longitude with a nautical chart, I ascertained that the vessel was entering Andvord Bay – an inlet on the Antarctic Peninsula – which as the light strengthened revealed itself as another fabulous feast of scenery. The ship came in due course to an anchorage just off a subsidiary bay called Neko Harbour.

As this was to be my first continental landing, I arrived early at the ship's gangway, and so was able to board the first zodiac which went ashore at Neko Harbour. I finally set foot on the continent of Antarctica at around 9.00am, GMT minus two, almost exactly 18 days after leaving home, which did offer a certain feeling of accomplishment! Various celebratory photographs were taken – courtesy of my Australian friends Dave and Pam Tindall for whom I willingly reciprocated – after which I left the rocky beach, inhabited by a posse of penguins.

I walked on past the wooden debris from a former Argentinean refuge hut, probably destroyed in a recent storm – at least that is what expedition leader Woody surmised, who had been this way before – a reminder of how conditions can rapidly change and how fortunate we were weather-wise. I then began to climb steeply, trudging over ground covered in snow and ice up to the flank of a towering mountainside, where I came to a rocky viewpoint several hundred feet high overlooking both the nearby Neko Harbour and the more expansive spread of Andvord Bay. This location was worth the effort to reach, and offered an excellent vantage point to view the nearby glacier.

At intervals, there was a thunderous boom – like a major explosion – when an ice cliff (glacier front) calved, depositing tons upon tons of ice and snow into the calm waters below...thus I was initiated into the workings of the World's principal 'iceberg factory' in full production! After almost two hours ashore, I joined a zodiac down on the landing beach for an exploration of the deeper reaches of Andvord Bay, which was a remarkable experience offering lots of "pancake" sea ice to crunch through (the much denuded fragments of winter ice cover) and several icebergs fashioned into some unfathomable forms...not forgetting wildlife treats such as leopard seals and penguins resting on the floating ice.

A return to the ship was made about noon (although in reality the time is immaterial) which then sailed a short distance 'round the corner', past the Chilean "Gonzalez Videla" research station at Waterboat Point, and into the next bay to the south – Paradise Harbour – a fitting description for one of the most beautiful locations on the Antarctic Peninsula, where to describe things in superlative terms is simply insufficient! The ship came to an anchorage close by the wooden buildings of the Argentinean "Base Brown", where I landed at some steps after again boarding the first zodiac to go ashore.

Simon above ice cliffs of Neko Harbour – first landing on continent of Antarctica

View from ship sailing through floating ice out of Neko Harbour into Andvord Bay

238 ~ Chapter 8 ~ **British Antarctic Territory** ~ Icy Antarctic Waters and a Penguin Post Office

Steep & snowy ascent to Paradise Harbour viewpoint – second continent landing

Simon above Paradise Harbour – closest landing to Antarctic Circle & South Pole

*Chapter 8 ~ **British Antarctic Territory** ~ Icy Antarctic Waters and a Penguin Post Office ~ 239*

My second landing on the Antarctic continent lasted almost an hour-and-a-half, and similarly featured an uphill walk to a rocky headland, again with stunning views over the surrounding white landscape (perhaps snowscape would be more accurate), although the ascent was slightly steeper than the morning visit had been. More photographs were taken for the record before I returned down the icy slopes to the landing steps, with yet more penguins parading around as if emphasising that they are the true claimants of this territory, whatever the nations of the World may like to think. Poignantly though, these were the last penguins I would see, as the time in Antarctica was drawing to a close: The final flourish was a zodiac cruise round the inner reaches of Paradise Harbour, which included cormorants and shags on the cliffs, more intricate icebergs and mind-blowing blue-and-white ice cliffs fronting glaciers – but I have run out of superlative adjectives!

We had also run out of time....However, just prior to stepping into that zodiac which eventually returned me to the ship, I had noticed a wooden fingerpost sign near the Paradise Harbour landing steps pointing south (as if it could point anywhere else!) indicating that the South Pole was only a 'mere' 1,500 miles away: I was now around 65 degrees south, not far from the Antarctic Circle – a long way south and a *very* long way from home....It was finally time to begin the long journey back 'up north'.

That evening the ship sailed away, initially via the Gerlache Strait and between the large Anvers and Brabant Islands, before emerging into the open sea of the Southern Ocean. The time to finally bid farewell to Antarctica came at around 10.00pm, as the continent and its islands faded into the distance and were just a memory...but an incredible memory indelibly ingrained on the minds of everyone.

Three nights, two days and 700 nautical miles of the voyage remained, during which time there were plenty of Antarctic-themed organised talks and films, as well as visits to the ship's bridge and engine room to pass the time. The talks included a fascinating one by the outgoing staff from Port Lockroy about a season at 'the penguin post office', a season that can start with having to literally dig one's way into one's 'digs' owing to snow accumulation from an Antarctic winter...oh, and attending to mail left behind from the previous summer! The *Vavilov* meanwhile pursued a course resolutely northwards across the stretch of Southern Ocean known as the Drake Passage, which is amongst the most notoriously rough regions of ocean in the World.

During the first night, the wind and ocean swell increased, and there was much pitching and rolling. Whilst there was some respite from the weather later on, by the following day it was a case of more wind as well as rain to accompany the re-crossing of the Antarctic Convergence – signalling a return from the Southern Ocean to the 'true' South Atlantic – and it didn't happen quietly! With the swell increasing considerably and the ship heading straight into a strong north-westerly wind, I spent some time on the bridge watching the bows of the ship crashing through the waves, some of them creating spray that gave the bridge windows a good soaking, as well as anyone foolish enough to be on the open deck at the time....Meanwhile, trying to eat in the dining room that afternoon became an increasingly 'mobile' affair! The reason for all the increased motion was down to the fact that the last section of the Drake Passage was being traversed, and the ocean was exhibiting more of a "Drake Shake" than "Drake Lake" mood as yet another landmark loomed into view – the legendary Cape Horn (or Cabo de Hornos in Spanish).

Cape Horn – though a small rocky island rather than a continental promontory – marks the extreme southern limits of South America, and the point where the South Atlantic and South Pacific Oceans meet. Combined with the effects of the Southern Ocean, this coming together of currents creates sea conditions which are often turbulent and difficult. Almost as quickly as it had appeared, Cape Horn receded into the mist and was gone, while virtually immediately thereafter the wind dropped and the swell eased. A coastal passage through a number of small Chilean offshore islands followed, and overnight the *Vavilov* sailed slowly up the Beagle Channel, arriving back in Ushuaia, Tierra del Fuego, early the next morning.
 Having collected my passport (now with handstamps from South Georgia and British Antarctic Territory added to those which already adorned its pages), I walked down the ship's gangway onto the pier at Ushuaia after an epic 'circular' voyage covering a distance in excess of 3,000 nautical miles. Three flights and three more nights and I would be back home in the UK: Yet despite having left from the same place less than three weeks previously, as I walked round Ushuaia that morning – a town with streets full of people, traffic and crowded with buildings – everything seemed strangely alien and disconcerting after the solitude and 'other world' qualities of where I had travelled in the intervening time.

It was only then that I fully realised just what a special place the Antarctic is – a place where the wildlife, the wonderful landscapes and the weather rule supreme, and where humans are merely awe-struck bystanders. It had been an immense privilege to experience Antarctica's snow-capped mountains, its mighty glaciers, its icebergs, the whales, seals and penguins…even the weather, both when at its most serene and its most stormy: It's true, there really is nowhere quite like Antarctica – meaningful comparisons cannot be made, much of it defies description, and superlative adjectives seem inadequate. There is something else though…moving from the supremely sublime to the relatively ridiculous: I had travelled way beyond the South Atlantic into the icy waters of British Antarctic Territory to experience *that* 'bicycle' – the bathe in cold yet comparatively lukewarm environs – *and* managed to visit 'the penguin post office' into the bargain!

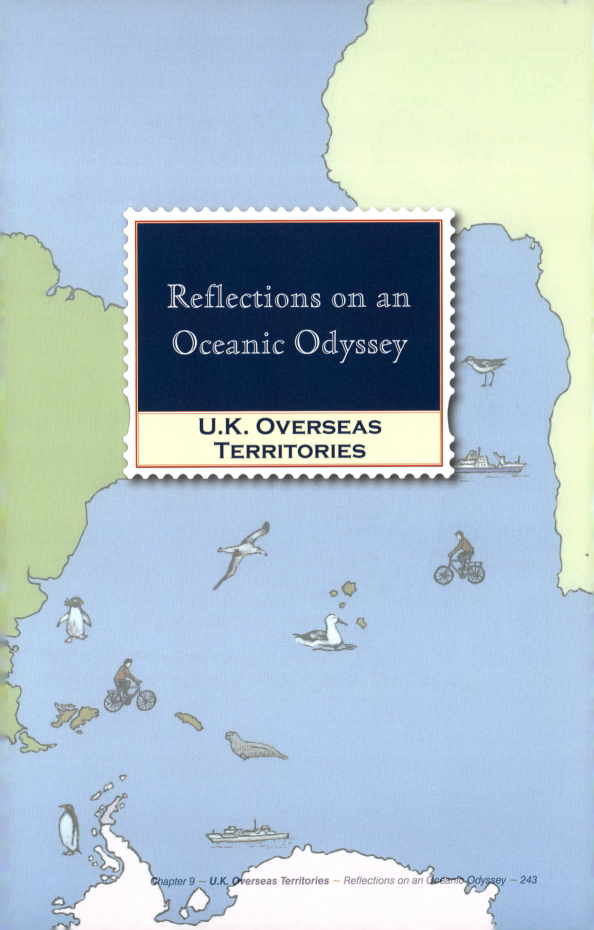
Chapter 9 ~ **U.K. Overseas Territories** ~ *Reflections on an Oceanic Odyssey* ~ 243

U.K. OVERSEAS TERRITORIES - SOUTH ATLANTIC

Chapter 9
A Cyclist Returns Home from the South Atlantic

Back home from the South Atlantic – Simon, his bike & the RMS at Portland, UK

Reflecting on the expedition to the Falklands, South Georgia and Antarctica, and the earlier explorations of Ascension, St Helena, Tristan da Cunha and the Falkland Islands, I realised that I had travelled to – or through – the South Atlantic region no less than ten times spread over a period of ten years. My oceanic odyssey had taken me from the blazing sun, heat and humidity of the tropics, through temperate – sometimes warm yet often wet and windy – climates, to the freezing cold of the Antarctic. For many of my island journeys, I had travelled in whole or part by bicycle, whether brought, borrowed or otherwise bargained for.

During the course of my progress across the scattered British Overseas Territories of the South Atlantic Ocean I had enjoyed – and quite often endured – some remarkably diverse and unique cycling experiences: The tropical heat and dryness of Ascension had been incredibly energy-sapping on a bike, but at least the roads were mostly well-surfaced and reasonably direct. St Helena had been almost as hot on occasion and quite humid, but the constant twists and turns, ups and downs, and huge changes in elevation – not to mention 'cycling bans' on certain key lengths of road – had tested my ingenuity and perseverance in simply cycling from A to B. Meanwhile, although Tristan da Cunha was limited in terms of length of conventional road to cycle on, by stretching the definition of 'road' and some imaginative off-road cycling I was rewarded – and the temperate climate was clearly a bonus.

Then there were the Falkland Islands – well, that was in every respect a most unusual cycling experience, whether in terms of its planning, how it materialised or the transport logistics once there…not forgetting of course the difficult road surfaces, draining distances and debilitating winds. Of course I must not forget South Georgia, where an unexpected opportunity arose enabling me to have the novelty of cycling briefly on a sub-Antarctic island that became iconic in the annals of polar exploration. Even the icy waters of British Antarctic Territory, whilst well beyond the South Atlantic and featuring no two-wheeled travel, nevertheless offered the surreal experience of an acronym-based 'bicycle' in the guise of a bathe in cold yet comparatively lukewarm environs…as well as 'the penguin post office'….

…I deliberately make reference again to 'the penguin post office' (a.k.a. Bransfield House at Port Lockroy), because there was something deeply significant about the fact that I should end up going there during the closing days of my quest to explore those half-a-dozen UK Overseas Territories: It was in essence representative of both a beginning and an end, the inception – and fulfilment – of an ambition.…Or – to express it another way – events had come full circle, the natural cycle (not to mention the cyclist!) had run its course.…A story that was originally inspired by postage stamps – and in turn a remote posting and a Royal Mail Ship – had finally brought me to 'the penguin post office':

A fledgling interest in philately back in the mid-1970s which resulted in me buying a stamp magazine at a London railway station bookstall began an enduring connection with Tristan da Cunha, which in turn – encouraged by my friend Bill Sandham and tales of his remote posting to the island – led to my first visit to Tristan in 2001 onboard the Royal Mail Ship *St Helena*. The experience of that ship inspired a desire to explore St Helena and Ascension in 2003, and it was the 'internal travel logistics challenge' of Ascension that first caused me to consider cycling in the South Atlantic. Consequentially I returned to St Helena in 2004 and Tristan da Cunha in 2006 – as well as Ascension some time later – to fully experience all three islands on two wheels.

Then, in 2008, came a change of direction – and approach – as I was persuaded to 'spread my wings' and cycle on the Falkland Islands by fellow 'island enthusiast' Guy Marriott, opening up for me a whole new dimension of the South Atlantic, and yet another series of islands. Finally, an awareness awakened on that journey of the possibilities for going that bit further than the Falklands resulted in the 2009 adventure onboard the Research Vessel *Vavilov* to South Georgia (where I unexpectedly cycled) and ultimately Antarctica, including British Antarctic Territory (where I had a 'bicycle'…of sorts…and at last visited *that* post office!)

During the course of my South Atlantic odyssey, spread as it was over several years of travelling, I increasingly came to appreciate what makes each of the various territories I visited so rewarding, unique and memorable. I also – inevitably – noticed changes over time, particularly in the case of those islands I was fortunate enough to visit on two or more occasions. I earlier mentioned the subtle changes which I noted on Ascension, given that I visited – or passed through – the island several times over the years. Yet there has been – or in due course will be – change on a number of the other islands, some modest, some much more significant:

On Tristan da Cunha, for example, the once-separate post office and museum / handicraft shop which I first experienced were later combined into a single facility, whilst a more recent and wonderful community project has seen the re-creation of a traditional Tristan home known as the Thatched House Museum. There have similarly been initiatives in relation to the museums on both St Helena and the Falkland Islands. On a larger and more far-reaching scale, there have been developments associated with transport provision to, from, within and between islands: These include infrastructure in connection with a long-planned airport for St Helena, whilst on the Falklands the road network has been further improved and a ferry was introduced between the two main islands of the archipelago. Even South Georgia and British Antarctic Territory, whilst only supporting tiny human 'populations', nevertheless support incredible wildlife which inevitably changes over time due to various external factors, climatic or otherwise.

However, the story of my oceanic odyssey is deliberately a 'snapshot' in time, a reflection of the islands, the landscapes, the wildlife and the people of the South Atlantic (and beyond) as I personally experienced them during the initial decade of the 21st century. Having said that, whilst time moves on there is – and one hopes there always will be – a timeless, unchanging and endearing quality about these remote and very special places spread far and wide across the vast, blue ocean that is the South Atlantic.

In cycling across the South Atlantic and beyond, I had explored six very different and – without exception – totally fascinating territories: So it was that I was also reminded again of that wall chart from the 1970s – the "World of Stamps" map – depicting stamps from over 200 places around the globe categorised by continent and ocean, and especially the little block in the bottom corner entitled "Atlantic Ocean Islands" and the even smaller "Antarctica" block alongside....The inspiration drawn from stamps – those miniature pieces of art – on my "World of Stamps" map grew, decades later, into something of a philatelic pilgrimage as, in turn, I visited the post offices of Ascension, St Helena, Tristan da Cunha, the Falkland Islands, South Georgia and finally 'the penguin post office' of British Antarctic Territory....What originally started as my remote posting of letters *to* the post office on Tristan had become remote posting in the opposite direction *from* Tristan and the other five territories of my postcards and other mail back to the UK.

Postage stamps may have been the initial catalyst for my association with the South Atlantic, and have remained a recurring theme throughout my travels in the region, but of course *cycling* has been the key thread woven through my exploration of those far-distant islands, and – like philately – my earlier cycling closer to home around island outposts of the British Isles expanded to include cycling on those half-a-dozen British Overseas Territories. Cycling, whilst enjoyable in its own right, was also a means to an end, a tool to engage in my passion for travel and the great outdoors, to discover the South Atlantic islands and beyond:

   Taken together, I discovered that the six territories – whilst they may initially appear from a map to be insignificant spots of paint on the vast canvas that is the South Atlantic – nevertheless include some of the most amazingly diverse and captivating landscapes to be found anywhere in the World; wildlife experiences that are World-class; and an incredible heritage and history which has both influenced, and been influenced by, almost every corner of the globe. Above all though I discovered the resilient, resourceful and welcoming people who are proud to call those islands in the South Atlantic their home, and who I am privileged to count as friends.

There is a quotation attributed to the 19th century Scottish author Robert Louis Stevenson who once famously said "To travel hopefully is a better thing than to arrive"....I believe that may be true, but only to a point: I eagerly anticipated my journeying over many years of waiting and dreaming, and I was indeed hopeful in my travelling...yet that hope was rewarded, indeed greatly rewarded, when I eventually arrived...but then I imagine – unlike a certain 'island nut' from the English Midlands – the famous Scottish writer, well-travelled though he undoubtedly was, never got around to cycling across the South Atlantic!

South Atlantic cycle transport – the RMS St Helena anchored off Tristan da Cunha